Frontiers of International Economic Law

Frontiers of International Economic Law

Legal Tools to Confront Interdisciplinary Challenges

Edited by

Freya Baetens and José Caiado

BRILL
NIJHOFF

LEIDEN | BOSTON

Library of Congress Cataloging-in-Publication Data

Frontiers of international economic law : legal tools to confront interdisciplinary challenges / Edited by Freya Baetens and Jose Caiado.
pages cm
Includes index.
ISBN 978-90-04-27017-6 (hardback : alk. paper) — ISBN 978-90-04-27019-0 (e-book)
1. Law and economic development. 2. International economic relations. 3. Foreign trade regulation. 4. Law reform. I. Baetens, Freya, editor of compilation. II. Caiado, José Guilherme Moreno, editor of compilation.

K3820.F76 2014
343.07—dc23

2014000266

This publication has been typeset in the multilingual 'Brill' typeface. With over 5,100 characters covering Latin, IPA, Greek, and Cyrillic, this typeface is especially suitable for use in the humanities.
For more information, please see brill.com/brill-typeface.

ISBN 978 90 04 27017 6 (hardback)
ISBN 978 90 04 27019 0 (e-book)

This book is printed on acid-free paper.

FSC www.fsc.org MIX Paper from responsible sources FSC® C109576

Printed by Printforce, the Netherlands

Contents

Acknowledgments

This book is the result of two years' work by several people. Its chapters draw on the scholarship of promising junior researchers presented at the 1st Conference of the Postgraduate and Early Professionals and Academics (PEPA) network of the Society of International Economic Law (SIEL).

At this Conference, all papers were commented upon by senior scholars including Jean d'Aspremont, Freya Baetens, Alexandra Diehl, Markus Gehring, Holger Hestermeyer, Alexander Lorz, Bruce Malashevich, Gabrielle Marceau, Simon Schropp, Yulia Selivanova, Christian Tietje, Anne Trebilcock, Isabelle Van Damme and Stefan Voigt. Their initial comments were crucial to the selection and further development of the papers that would eventually compose this edited volume.

In a later stage, we were fortunate to receive the additional input of reviewers such as Tomer Broude, Andrew Lang, Junji Nakagawa and Tania Voon. Many other members of the SIEL Executive Council have supported us during this project. By thanking the SIEL Executive Vice-Presidents, Meredith Kolsky Lewis and Colin Picker, we hope that they will all feel represented.

As the 1st SIEL/PEPA Conference was generously hosted by the University of Hamburg, we pay our respect to the 2011 Conference Committee consisting of Babette Ancery, Thomas Berghaus, José Caiado, Luis Montilla, Jessica Giovanelli, Beatriz Huarte and Daragh McGreal. Galina Zukova and Federico Ortino have spent a significant amount of time helping to rationalize the Conference budget.

A word of gratitude is due to our publisher, Brill, in the persons of Marie Sheldon and Lisa Hanson, as well as the anonymous reviewers of our book proposal and manuscript. Finally, we would like to especially thank the contributors for their restless enthusiasm, without which this book would still be no more than an idea.

Freya Baetens and José Caiado

Preface

Confronted with today's global interdisciplinary challenges, international economic law offers a myriad of legal tools to provide both procedural and substantive solutions. The contributions to this book pose clearly defined and provocative questions: why have States not disputed currency devaluation at the World Trade Organization (WTO)? Should an international investor who has violated human rights obligations nevertheless be compensated in case of an illegal expropriation? How could States use preferential trade agreements to promote climate change mitigation?

The book congregates various perspectives on international economic law: some chapters examine age-old continuing points of discussion within international law, while others explicitly address problems which have only recently emerged and are currently fiercely debated in the media as well as in legal practice and academic circles.

While this work mainly presents the results of legal research, a number of social scientists and economists conducting related projects were invited to share their views in a manner accessible to legal scholars. The focus lies on concrete problems and legal solutions that are international by definition. In those cases where a chapter zooms in on a domestic problem, it concerns a problem with an international appeal. The challenges analysed and the policy conclusions reached are intended to form the foundation of future research on similar and correlated topics.

This volume is based on the papers presented at the 1st Conference of the Postgraduate and Early Academics and Professionals (PEPA) of the Society of International Economic Law (SIEL) in Hamburg on 27 and 28 January 2012. Contributions were chosen based on reviews of senior SIEL members, so as to reflect the eclectic and multifaceted reality of international economic law, especially in its interface with current social, economic and political concerns. The authors are junior practitioners and academics from leading institutions in their respective fields, providing critical assessments on the most challenging topics facing the international community today. The selected papers called the attention of SIEL's experts because of the strength of their theoretical underpinnings and their particular capacity to operationalise this theory in order to offer pragmatic and coherent responses to legal and policy problems in the international and domestic arena.

This volume will appeal to those interested in the general theory of international economic law, but also readers looking for innovative solutions to practical challenges will be pleased to find a broad array of topics covered by the contributions. The book is structured along four frontier themes: first, facing economic crises and uncertainties; second, confronting environmental challenges; third, considering human rights and development objectives; and fourth, regulating energy transit and new technologies.

Part One—Facing Economic Crises and Uncertainties

Part One questions the legal and economic reasoning underlying rules aimed at regulating the behaviour of States and private agents in the area of monetary and financial law. The first chapter, by *An Hertogen*, discusses the relationship between monetary policy and trade commitments by looking at General Agreement on Tariffs and Trade (GATT) Articles XV:4 and XII:3(a), both of which deal with monetary issues but have not yet been applied in any disputes. The author explains why these Articles have received little attention in practice and examines how scholars could overcome empirical and legal uncertainty about the specific conditions under which they apply.

The second chapter in this section analyses the intent and effect of regulatory responses to economic crises. *Kuan-Chun Chang* focuses on Credit Rating Agencies to criticize regulatory measures put forward during the recent financial crisis. Chang investigates the US and the EU regulation reforms, arguing that due to the rating industry's issuer-pay business model and the regulators' lack of expertise, the proposed rules may negatively impact both the investors' and the issuers' reliance on Credit Rating Agencies' ratings. In his opinion, a combination of economic and legal theory could help us to understand the rationale followed by different participants on the international credit markets and provide the basis for the creation of an optimal regulatory system policy.

Part Two—Confronting Environmental Challenges

Part Two connects environmental concerns to the international economic law research agenda. *Matthäus Fink* opens this Part by discussing the establishment of Protected Areas as a tool to guard the environment. Taking up the debate about the fragmentation of international law, he addresses whether and how the law and policy of Protected Areas may conflict with investment law. General conflict rules aimed at a harmonized interpretation and application of legal norms, such as *lex specialis* and *lex posterior*, have had limited success in resolving conflicts between environmental and investment law. The author proposes that environmental impact assessments would be more suitable for the prevention of conflicts. Moreover, the concept of 'financial recourse', as applied by international investment tribunals, could play a relevant role in settling or at least tempering conflicts of norms.

Subsequently, *Daniela Gómez Altamirano* analyses the EU's emission-trading scheme to combat climate change. More in particular, she examines the Directive prescribing that all airlines, including those from third countries, have to acquire and surrender emissions allowances for their flights departing from and arriving at airports located in the EU. The author elaborates on the concept of extra-territoriality under international law and argues that the EU Directive is to be considered extraterritorial in its scope. This leads to a discussion whether extraterritorial unilateral trade measures are a legitimate means to combat environmental problems, and, if these measures are legitimate, under which conditions they should be applied in order to avoid a breach of WTO obligations.

The final chapter in this section deals with the complex relation between regional and multilateral rules on environmental protection. *Rafael Leal-Arcas* puts forward that Preferential Trade Agreements (PTAs) with strong climate change chapters could contribute to reducing greenhouse gas emissions. He defends the introduction of a regional model for promoting climate change mitigation as an alternative to the present structure of the United Nations Framework Convention on Climate Change and its Kyoto Protocol.

Part Three—Considering Human Rights and Development Objectives

Part Three discusses the relationship between human rights and development objectives in international investment law and related domestic rules. By means of a case study, *Lars Schönwald* examines whether and to what extent States can guarantee human rights through public-private partnerships. He shows how certain provisions of the International Covenant on Economic, Social and Cultural Rights and the African Charter on Human and Peoples' Rights promote the possibility of guaranteeing the right to housing through such partnerships. *Filip Balcerzak* then seeks to answer whether States' obligation to respect, protect and fulfill human rights may reduce the compensation due for a breach of investment treaty obligations. He investigates different rationales for States to invoke human rights clauses in international disputes and concludes that, regarding compensation for breaches of the fair and equitable treatment standard, Article 39 of the International Law Commission's Articles on State Responsibility (dealing with contribution to injury) provides a sound legal basis for claiming that such compensation may be reduced.

The section finishes with the work of *Jan-Christoph Kuntze* and *Tom Moerenhout*, who explain how WTO law applies to renewable energy feed-in tariffs (FITS) with local content requirements (LCRS) to promote domestic development. They argue that FITS with LCRS are inconsistent with specific GATT provisions, the Agreement on Trade-Related Investment Measures (TRIMS) and the Agreement on Subsidies and Countervailing Measures (SCM). Those agreements thus prohibit the use of such schemes, in the absence of any applicable WTO exemptions. The final part of the chapter analyses the negotiations regarding an energy agreement within the WTO, as well as the role of important and underexplored flexibilities within the WTO system, *i.e.*, the 'infant industries' exception to protect developing sectors and the inclusion of new subsidy exceptions in the SCM Agreement.

Part Four—Regulating Energy Transit and New Technologies

The fourth and last section of this volume examines the regulation of trade in energy and intellectual property issues in connection with the digital environment. *Beatriz Huarte Melgar* offers a broad picture of the legal challenges raised by the energy transit between States. She advocates that achieving energy security and energy independence became a central issue after the rescission of the provisional application of the Energy Charter Treaty by Russia in 2010, combined with the EU's intention to reset the negotiations on the Energy Charter Treaty Protocol on Transit. The chapter highlights the necessity for policymakers to strive in negotiations for legal alternatives to the regulation of energy transit.

Mikella Hurley then addresses the often discordant relationship between multilateral and preferential rules on the transit of energy. More precisely, she questions whether GATT Article XXIV authorises Members to offer more favourable terms to their PTA partners in this area. She concludes that this Article may offer a limited basis upon which PTA parties can choose to offer such treatment, provided that such action does not directly increase the restrictions imposed on the transit of energy goods for non-PTA Members.

In the final contribution to this volume, *Anna Giulia Micara* presents the rules on internet service providers' liability for trademark counterfeiting in the US and the EU. The chapter analyses recent case law concerning trademarks counterfeiting on the internet auction site eBay and in specific new business models, such as keyword advertising. The author concludes that legal certainty and the underlying balance between intermediaries and brand owners' interests urgently need to be further developed in this field.

This book is intended for a global audience, including established academics and practitioners as well as those at the start of their career, in the fields of public as well as private international law. We hope that the chapters presented here will help to push forward, through promoting and developing the rule of law, the—at times contentious—frontiers of international economic law.

List of Contributors

Freya Baetens
(*Cand.Jur./Lic.Jur.* (Ghent); LL.M. (Columbia); *Ph.D.* (Cambridge)) is Associate Professor of Law, Director of Studies and Head of the LUC Research Centre at Leiden University and Visiting Professor at the World Trade Institute (WTI) in Berne. Concurrently with her academic activities, she has assisted several international arbitration panels and regularly acts as counsel or expert in international disputes as an associate lawyer with VVGB (Brussels Bar). She is a Senior Officer on the Executive Board of the Society of International Economic Law (SIEL), a Fellow with the Centre for International Sustainable Development Law (CISDL) and Rapporteur of the International Law Association (ILA) Study Group on Preferential Trade and Investment Agreements. She is an editor of the Leiden Journal of International Law and member of the academic review board of the Cambridge Journal of International and Comparative Law. She has published on a wide range of topics, including treaty interpretation, state responsibility, equality, international dispute settlement, trade and investment matters, EU external relations, discrimination in international migration law, sustainable development, and interaction between legal regimes.

José Guilherme Moreno Caiado
is a Ph.D. candidate at the Graduate School in Law and Economics of the University of Hamburg (DFG Scholarship) and a fellow of the Dispute Settlement in Trade (DISSETTLE) project, dealing primarily with the international regulation of industrial subsidies. As a member of the Executive Board of the Society of International Economic Law, he is a co-organizer of the PEPA/SIEL Conferences, offering junior researchers in international economic law an opportunity to present their projects and strengthen their professional network. He holds a Master in Latin-American Integration from the São Paulo University (PROLAM/USP) as well as a legal specialization in trade law from the European Institute in Saarbrücken. His research and publications deal primarily with international trade law, export subsidies, product classification, and the economic analysis of international law. Before joining the University of Hamburg, he participated in the trainee program for lawyers of the Mission of Brazil to the WTO in Geneva.

Daniela Gomez Altamirano
is the Editorial Assistant for the Journal of International Economic Law at Georgetown University. She previously interned at the Trade Team of Berwin

Leighton Paisner LLP in Brussels, the Legal Service Unit of the European Commission and the Mexican Mission to the WTO. She participated in an Exchange Programme with the University of California Los Angeles (UCLA), obtained an LL.M. in International Economic Law and Policy (IELPO) from the University of Barcelona and a J.D. equivalent degree from the National University of Mexico, School of Law.

Filip Balcerzak
Abogado, LL.M., is a member of the Madrid Bar Association and the Warsaw Bar Association, where he is registered as a foreign lawyer practicing under the European Directives. He obtained his Law degree at the Adam Mickiewicz University of Poznań, where he currently continues his education at doctoral level. His law degree was recognised in Spain after he passed the required exams at the University of La Laguna. He also holds an LL.M. degree with specialisation in International Trade and Foreign Investment Law from the University of Ottawa.

Kuan-Chun Chang
is Associate Professor of Law jointly appointed by the National Chengchi University College of Law and the Department of Risk Management & Insurance. Previously, he was a visiting fellow at the Asian Law Institute, National University of Singapore, and a visiting lecturer at the Shanghai University of Finance and Economics. He obtained an LL.B. and an M.B.A. in Risk Management and Insurance from the National Chengchi University in Taipei, and LL.M. from the University of Pennsylvania, an LL.M in Banking and Financial Law from Boston University and an S.J.D. (with distinction) from the Georgetown University Law Center.

Matthäus Fink
is a doctoral candidate at the Institute of Public International Law and European Law of the Georg-August-University in Göttingen where he is also a member of the Scientific Advisory Board of the Göttingen Journal of International Law (GoJIL). He has published in the area of international investment law and environmental law and was invited to present his work at several international conferences. His current research deals with protected areas under international environmental law and international investment law.

An Hertogen
holds a Ph.D. in International Law from the University of Auckland and is currently an assistant editor for the legal blog *Opinio Juris*. She completed her

legal studies at the Catholic University of Leuven and received a Fulbright Scholarship to pursue an LL.M. at Columbia University. Before starting her Ph.D. research, she worked in leading law firms in Brussels and Auckland in the area of EU and competition law. Her current research interests include the tension between international and domestic law in issues of trade and environment, and issues of international monetary law.

Beatriz Huarte Melgar
is a guest lecturer at the Martin-Luther-Universität Halle-Wittenberg, where she pursues her doctoral degree under supervision of Professor Christian Tietje, with a scholarship of the Friedrich-Naumann-Stiftung für die Freiheit. She also attained a visiting research fellowship at the University of California, Los Angeles (UCLA). Previously she interned at MTC Healthcare Ltd. (Ireland) and Haupt Pharma AG (Germany). She has a master degree in European Studies from the Instituto Europeo in Bilbao, an LL.M. in EU law from the Universität des Saarlandes and a Licenciado en Derecho from the Universidad de Vigo.

Mikella M. Hurley
is currently pursuing a J.D. degree at the American University Washington College of Law, where she was the recipient of the 2012 Dean's Merit Scholarship. Previously she obtained a Masters degree in International Law from the Graduate Institute for International and Development Studies in Geneva and a B.A. degree in Religious Studies, with a minor in Classics Language, from Macalester College, St. Paul. She has also worked as a research and writing assistant for Professor Gabrielle Marceau and as programme officer (governance) and subsequently manager (transparency & accountability) for the GAVI Alliance.

Jan-Christoph Kuntze
works as Energy Advisor for the Deutsche Gesellschaft für Internationale Zusammenarbeit (GIZ) in Frankfurt. He holds a master degree in international law from the Graduate Institute of International & Development Studies in Geneva and a bachelor degree in international relations from the Technic University of Dresden. As a Mercator Fellow, he worked with the United Nations Conference on Trade and Development (UNCTAD) as well as the Directorate-General for Energy of the European Commission, and has extensive experience in European energy policy and international issues related to environment protection and development.

Rafael Leal-Arcas
completed his graduate legal education at Stanford, Columbia, the London School of Economics and the European University Institute in Florence. He is currently affiliated with the World Trade Institute (University of Bern) and with Queen Mary University of London (Centre for Commercial Law Studies). He is the author of several scholarly publications on international trade law, WTO law, international investment law, international environmental law, and EU law. A member of the Madrid Bar, he has been a Fellow at New York University, the World Trade Institute, Georgetown University, Harvard Law School, and others.

Anna Giulia Micara
is a post-doctoral fellow at the University of Milan, from which she also received a Ph.D. in International and European Law and an undergrad degree in political sciences. Her doctoral thesis dealt with issues of uniform protection of trademarks within the European Union and international trade. Her current research interests include, among other, intellectual property and international and European trade law, and she has published in renowned journals such as the Journal of World Intellectual Property and the Journal of Common Market Studies.

Tom Moerenhout
is a Research Fellow (Trade Programme) at the International Institute for Sustainable Development (Switzerland) while also pursuing a B.Sc. in Economics degree at the London School of Economics. Previously he obtained a Master degree in International Affairs from the Graduate Institute of International and Development Studies in Geneva as well as a Master degree in Comparative and International Politics and a Bachelor degree in Political Science from the Catholic University of Leuven (Belgium). He was also a Member of the Humanitarian Disaster Relief Team (Global Hope Network International).

Lars Schönwald
is currently a doctoral candidate and lecturer at the University of Passau. His doctoral thesis deals with legal aspects of European investments in the mining sectors of Sub-Saharan Africa. He teaches international economic law, international humanitarian law and general public international law, and he is involved in the coaching of Passau's Jessup Moot Court Team.

List of Abbreviations

ACHPR	African Charter of Human and Peoples' Rights
AG	Advocate General
APEC	Asia-Pacific Economic Cooperation
ASEAN	Association of Southeast Asian Nations
BIT	Bilateral Investment Treaty
CBD	Convention on Biological Diversity
CDO	Collateralized Debt Obligation
CER	Certified Emissions Reduction
CJEU	Court of Justice of the European Union
COP	Conference of the Parties of the CBD
CPC	Central Product Classification
CRA	Credit Rating Agency
CSR	Corporate Social Responsibility
CU	Customs Union
DMCA	Digital Millennium Copyright Act
ECD	E-commerce Directive
ECJ	European Court of Justice
ECT	Energy Charter Treaty
ECTP	Energy Charter Treaty Protocol on Transit
EIA	Environmental Impact Assessment
ERU	Emissions Reductions Unit
ESC	European Social Charter
ETS	Emission Trading Scheme
FET	Fair and Equitable Treatment
FITS	Feed-in Tariffs
FTA	Free Trade Agreement
GATS	General Agreement on Trade in Services
GATT	General Agreement on Tariffs and Trade
GHG	Greenhouse Gas
HIPC	Heavily Indebted Poor Countries
HRC	Human Rights Council
IATA	International Air Transport Association
IBRD	International Bank for Reconstruction and Development
ICAO	International Civil Aviation Organization
IIA	International Investment Agreement
IIL	International Investment Law

ILC	International Law Commission
IMF	International Monetary Fund
IOSCO	International Organization of Securities Commissions
ISP	Internet Service Providers
ITO	International Trade Organization
IUCN	International Union for Conservation of Nature
JNNSM	Indian Jawaharlal Nehru National Solar Mission
LCR	Local Content Requirement
LDCS	Least-Developed Countries
MEA	Multilateral Environmental Agreement
MEF	Major Economies Forum on Energy and Climate
MFN	Most-Favoured Nation
NRSRO	Nationally Recognized Statistical Rating Organization
NTD	Notice and Take-Down
OECD	Organization for Economic Co-Operation and Development
OHRLLS	UN Office of the High Representative for Least Developed Countries, Landlocked Developing Countries and Small Island Developing States
ORC	Other Regulations of Commerce
ORRC	Other Restrictive Regulations of Commerce
PA	Protected Area
PEPA	Postgraduate and Early Professionals and Academics network
PPP	Public-Private Partnership
PTA	Preferential Trade Agreement
PV	photovoltaic
REIO	Regional Economic Integration Organization
RMBS	Residential Mortgage-Backed Securities
SCM	Agreement on Subsidies and Countervailing Measures
SEC	US Securities and Exchange Commission
SIEL	Society of International Economic Law
SRSG	UN Special Representative of the Secretary General on the issues of Human Rights and Transnational Corporations and other Business Enterprises
TFA	Trade Facilitation Agreement
TPP	Trans-Pacific Partnership
TRIMS	Agreement on Trade-Related Investment Measures
TRIPS	Trade-Related Aspects of Intellectual Property Rights Agreement
TTIP	Trans-Atlantic Trade and Investment Partnership
UDHR	Universal Declaration of Human Rights
UNCLOS	UN Convention on the Law of the Sea
UNFCCC	UN Framework Convention on Climate Change

UN HABITAT	UN Human Settlements Programme
VCLT	Vienna Convention on the Law of Treaties
WGTDF	Working Group on Trade, Debt and Finance
WIPO	World Intellectual Property Organization
WTO	World Trade Organization

PART ONE

Facing Economic Crises and Uncertainties

CHAPTER 1

The Forgotten GATT Articles on Exchange Rates

An Hertogen[1]

1 Introduction

Historically, the International Monetary Fund (IMF) Articles of Agreement[2] were the main source of limits on states' monetary sovereignty.[3] However, few limits remain following the entry into force of the Second Amendment to the IMF Articles of Agreement in 1978.[4] This amendment legalized the de facto freedom to determine exchange rates that had arisen following US President Nixon's decision of 15 August 1971[5] to abandon the gold-dollar two-tier system

---

1 E-mail: anhertogen@fulbrightmail.org. Many thanks to Dr Holger Hestermeyer and Dr Simon Schropp for their comments during the PEPA/SIEL Conference in January 2012, to the participants at the Global SIEL Conference in July 2012 where this paper was presented as a poster, to the editors Dr Freya Baetens and José Caiado, the anonymous reviewers, and to John Ip. Any errors remain my own.

2 Articles of Agreement of the International Monetary Fund (adopted 22 July 1945, entered into force 27 December 1945) 2 UNTS 39 (IMF Articles of Agreement).

3 The concept of monetary sovereignty was expressed in *Case Concerning the Payment of Various Serbian Loans Issued in France* and *Case Concerning the Payment in Gold of the Brazilian Federal Loans Issued in France* (1929) PCIJ Series A No 20/21, 44. See Tullio Treves, 'Monetary Sovereignty Today' in Mario Giovanoli (ed) *International Monetary Law: Issues for the New Millenium* (OUP 2000) 111; Rosa María Lastra, *Legal Foundations of International Monetary Stability* (OUP 2006) 16–18. Treaty law and customary international law can restrict how sovereignty is exercised, see Dominique Carreau, *Souveraineté et Coopération Monétaire Internationale* (Editions Dujas 1970) 52; Charles Proctor and F.A. Mann, *Mann on the Legal Aspect of Money*, (OUP 2005) 500, 510.

4 IMF Board of Governors Resolution No 31–4, adopted 30 April 1976, entered into force on 1 April 1978. On the process of amendment, see Andreas F. Lowenfeld, *International Economic Law* (2nd edn OUP 2008) 631–33. From the beginning, the changes made by the Second Amendment have been critiqued as creating a 'non-system', see references in Paul R. Masson, 'The IMF: Victim of Its Own Success or Institutional Failure?' (2007) 62 International Journal 889.

5 Robert Gilpin and Jean M. Gilpin, *The Political Economy of International Relations* (Princeton UP 1987) 140; Andreas F. Lowenfeld, *International Economic Law* (OUP 2002) 526; Louis W. Pauly, 'Monetary Statecraft in Follower States' in David M. Andrews (ed), *International Monetary Power* (Cornell UP 2006) 194. For an historical overview see Barry J. Eichengreen, *Globalizing Capital: A History of the International Monetary System* (Princeton UP 2008).

 | DOI 10.1163/9789004270190_002

of convertibility,[6] and the failure by 1973 of attempts to save this 'par value' system that required governments to intervene in currency markets if needed to maintain the relative value of their currency.[7] Provided they do not adopt a gold standard,[8] do not apply unauthorized discriminatory or multiple currency practices[9] and do not manipulate their exchange rate,[10] IMF Members are free to decide whether to fix or float their exchange rate or whether to pick a policy in between these poles.

In the absence of legal obligations in the IMF Articles of Agreement, and with the arrival in 1995 of a strongly rule-based WTO, the debate about legal limits on exchange rate valuation has in recent years shifted towards the WTO. In 2011 and 2012, Brazil made three submissions[11] to the WTO's Working Group on Trade, Debt and Finance (WGTDF)[12] on the relationship between exchange rates and international trade. Its second submission asks for an examination of the

> available tools and remedies in the existing multilateral system, if any, to compensate for or otherwise redress those currency fluctuations that may impair commitments undertaken by Members in successive rounds of negotiations. In addition, addressing that issue may help prevent the overstretching of multilateral trade rules as regards, for instance,

6 In this system, the exchange rate of every currency was fixed relative to the US dollar and the US Treasury would buy and sell gold from and to other monetary authorities at a fixed price, see Lastra, *Legal Foundations* (n. 3) 356; Lowenfeld, *International Economic Law* (n. 4) 622–23.

7 Treves (n. 3) 114; Charles Proctor, 'USA v China and the Revaluation of the Renminbi: Exchange Rate Pegs and International Law', (2006) 17 EBLR 1333, 1337; Lowenfeld, *International Economic Law 2nd edn* (n. 4) 625–27.

8 IMF Articles of Agreement art. IV(2)(b).

9 Ibid., art. VIII(3). Discriminatory or multiple exchange rates exist when states apply different exchange rates depending on the state they are trading with or depending on the type of transaction (eg inflow or outflow).

10 Ibid., art. IV(1)(iii).

11 WGTDF, 'The Relationship between Exchange Rates and International Trade: Submission by Brazil' WT/WGTDF/W/53 (13 April 2011); WGTDF, 'The Relationship between Exchange Rates and International Trade: Submission by Brazil' WT/WGTDF/W/56 (20 September 2011); WGTDF, 'The Relationship between Exchange Rates and International Trade: Exchange Rate Misalignment and Trade Remedies: A Conceptual Note by Brazil' WT/WGTDF/W/68 (5 November 2012).

12 The WGTDF was chosen as the forum because of its focus on analysis rather than on negotiations, see WGTDF, 'Report of the Meeting of 10 May 2011' WT/WGTDF/M/22 (9 June 2011) 18.

> provisions on safeguards, antidumping, subsidies and countervailing measures, as well as bound tariffs.[13]

This chapter focuses on articles XII:3(a) and XV:4 GATT. These articles deal explicitly with situations in which states' domestic policies, including their exchange rate policies, affect trade. Only article XV:4, however, appears in a Brazilian submission.[14]

According to Article XII:3(a)

> [Members] undertake, in carrying out their domestic policies, to pay due regard to the need for maintaining or restoring equilibrium in their balance of payments on a sound and lasting basis and to the desirability of avoiding an uneconomic employment of productive resources. They recognize that, in order to achieve these ends, it is desirable so far as possible to adopt measures which expand rather than contract international trade.

This article thus recognizes that domestic policies can affect the balance of payments equilibrium and records an undertaking by WTO Members to avoid such policies.

Article XV:4 stipulates that

> [Members] shall not, by exchange action, frustrate the intent of the provisions of this Agreement, nor, by trade action, the intent of the provisions of the Articles of Agreement of the International Monetary Fund.

The goal of this chapter is to analyse whether these articles restrict a WTO Member in the exercise of its monetary sovereignty, should it be established that its exchange rate is undervalued and that this undervaluation reduces this Member's trade commitments vis-à-vis another WTO Member or increases the latter's trade commitments towards the former.

The Chapter is structured as follows. Part 2 discusses the tension between trade commitments and exchange rate undervaluation. Part 3 describes the difficulties WTO Members face invoking trade remedies such as countervailing duties against another Member's exchange rate undervaluation and explores possible explanations why articles XII:3(a) and XV:4 GATT have received little attention in practice. It will be argued that, with some clarifications, these

13 WGTDF 20 September 2011 (n. 11) 9.

14 WGTDF 5 November 2012 (n. 11) 5.

articles can be useful to WTO Members whose trade commitments are negatively affected by another Member's exchange rate undervaluation. Part 4 concludes.

2 The Tension Between Trade Commitments and Exchange Rate Undervaluation

Interest in the issue of exchange rate undervaluation and its impact on trade has waxed and waned since the middle of the 20th century. Following the competitive devaluations to counteract the negative effects of the Great Depression through export stimulation,[15] the par value system introduced under the IMF Articles of Agreement limited exchange rate fluctuations.[16] After this system collapsed in the 1970s, tensions arose between the US and Japan with the former accusing the latter of undervaluing the Yen to stimulate exports. These tensions ultimately led to the 1985 Plaza Agreement and the 1987 Louvre Accord in which the leaders of the G-5 co-operated to trigger a depreciation of the US dollar and an appreciation of other currencies to avert the spectre of protectionism in the US.[17]

In the past decade, the issue of exchange rate undervaluation, or at least 'competitive non-appreciation',[18] and its impact on trade resurfaced over allegations that the Chinese Renminbi is undervalued against the US dollar.[19] The issue expanded beyond the bilateral context of the US and China[20] following the onset of the Global Financial Crisis and various rounds of 'quantitative

15 Eichengreen (n. 5) 87.

16 See text accompanying footnotes 6 and 7.

17 See Benjamin C. Cohen, 'The Triad and the Unholy Trinity: Lessons for the Pacific Region (1993)' in Benjamin C. Cohen, *Global Monetary Governance* (Routledge 2008) 62–65.

18 Ted Truman, 'Message for the G20: SDR Are Your Best Answer' (*VoxEU*, 6 March 2009) <http://www.voxeu.org/debates/commentaries/message-g20-sdr-are-your-best-answer> accessed 20 June 2013.

19 See, for example, the work of the Fair Currency Coalition in the US, <http://www.faircurrency.org> accessed 20 June 2013. In July 2012, the IMF declared the Renminbi moderately undervalued, Lucy Hornby, 'IMF Softens Language on China Yuan Value as Issue Recedes' (*Reuters*, 25 July 2012) <http://www.reuters.com/art/2012/07/25/china-imf-idUSL4E8IP0JU20120725> accessed 20 June 2013. Since then, China has decided to allow the Renminbi to depreciate slightly: 'Update: China Govt Allowing Yuan To Depreciate, Papers Say' (*MNI News*, 5 August 2012) <https://mninews.deutsche-boerse.com/content/update-china-govt-allowing-yuan-depreciate-papers-say> accessed 20 June 2013.

20 François Godement, 'China: revisiting the issue of mercantilism' in Simon J. Evenett (ed), *The US-Sino Currency Dispute: New Insights from Economics, Politics and Law* (Centre for Economic Policy Research 2010) 188.

easing' in the UK and the US.[21] Brazilian leaders have been particularly vocal about undervaluation, warning about a 'monetary tsunami'[22] of capital flowing into economies with a higher interest rate from economies engaged in quantitative easing, and about an 'international currency war'[23] in which states try to lower their exchange rate to create a competitive advantage for their exporters and as a result grow their economy at the expense of other states. The issue is however relevant beyond Brazil, as other economies are also feeling the consequences of a strong currency.[24]

Exchange rate undervaluation can lead to trade tensions because, as Thorstensen, Marçal and Ferraz have argued, undervaluation reduces tariff protection in other states; when imports are cheaper in the importing state's currency, the *ad valorem* tariffs are lower too.[25]

Moreover, because the real exchange rate is the most important single price in open economies[26] exchange rate undervaluation makes imports more expensive while exports become cheaper.[27] This can have a negative impact on the competitiveness of other states producing competing goods.[28]

---

21 Quantitative easing is a tool of monetary policy that has been used by monetary authorities to further stimulate their economy when the conventional method of a lower interest rate is no longer available because the rate is at zero. It involves an expansion of their balance sheet and using these newly created funds to purchase bonds from financial institutions, see Jonathan Law and John Smullen (eds), 'Quantitative Easing', *A Dictionary of Finance and Banking* (2008).

22 'Brazil Blames "Monetary Tsunami" for Rising Real' (*Reuters*, 1 March 2012) <http://www.reuters.com/art/2012/03/01/brazil-currency-rousseff-idUSE5E7KG05Q20120301> accessed 20 June 2013.

23 Graham Bowley, 'As Dollar's Value Falls, Currency Conflicts Rise' *New York Times* (New York, 20 October 2010) B1; International Centre for Trade and Sustainable Development, 'Brazilian Finance Minister Warns of "International Currency War" ' (2010) 14(33) Bridges Weekly Trade News Digest. <http://ictsd.org/i/news/bridgesweekly/85803/> accessed 20 June 2013.

24 Ilene Grabel, 'War without end? Rich countries fire the latest shots in the global "currency war" ' (*Triple Crisis*, 19 August 2011) <http://triplecrisis.com/war-without-end-rich-countries-fire-the-latest-shots-in-the-global-currency-war/> accessed 20 June 2013.

25 Vera Thorstensen, Emerson Marçal and Lucas Ferraz, 'Exchange Rate Misalignment and International Trade Policy: Impacts on Tariffs' (2012) 46 JWT 597, 606.

26 UNCTAD 'Trade and Development Report 2007' UNCTAD/TDR/2007 (5 September 2007) 16.

27 Raj Bhala, 'Virtues, the Yuan, and the American Trade Empire' (2008) 38 HKLJ 183, 222 speaks of 'import suppression and export propulsion'.

28 Aaditya Mattoo, Prachi Misra and Arvind Subramanian, 'Beggar-thy-neighbours? Spillover Effects of Exchange Rates' (*VoxEU*, 23 March 2012) <http://www.voxeu.org/art/spillover-effects-exchange-rates> accessed 20 June 2013.

In theory, these changes in relative prices can improve a state's trade balance if exports increase and imports decrease sufficiently to offset the increased price of imports.[29] The adjustment to exchange rate undervaluation will not be immediate. At first, the trade balance will deteriorate as the price of imports increases and that of exports lowers while their volumes remain unchanged. Later, import volumes shrink and export volumes grow in response to the price signals.[30]

Staiger and Sykes have, however, argued that the theoretical predictions about the impact of exchange rate undervaluation on the trade balance are not always borne out in practice. Instead, they argue that the qualitative and quantitative effects of exchange rate misalignment on trade depend on a range of factors such as the flexibility of the prices of traded goods and services, and whether pricing occurs in the currency of the producer, the consumer or in a third currency such as the US dollar.[31]

Further research is required into the dynamic relationship between exchange rates and trade to overcome empirical hurdles that currently exist to the application of articles XII:3(a) and XV:4 GATT. In response to Brazil's first submission, the WGTDF instructed the WTO Secretariat to prepare a literature review,[32] which was completed at the end of September 2011[33] and updated in July 2012[34] following a two-day seminar organised by the WTO in March 2012.[35] The review establishes that the economic literature has focused on whether exchange rate *volatility* reduces incentives to trade, and that the answer to this question is ambiguous. Only in the past decade has attention shifted

29 This is known as the 'Marshall-Lerner condition', see Olivier Blanchard, *Macroeconomics* (Prentice Hall 1997) 240.

30 This dynamic is referred to as the 'J-curve', see ibid. 244.

31 Robert W. Staiger and Alan O. Sykes, '"Currency Manipulation" and World Trade' (2010) 9 WTR 583, 605. A more technical analysis supporting their argument can be found in Robert W. Staiger and Alan O. Sykes, '"Currency Manipulation" and World Trade' (*SSRN*, 13 June 2008) 4–25 <http://ssrn.com/abstract=1151942> accessed 20 June 2013.

32 WGTDF, 'Meeting of 10 May 2011' (n. 12) (50)–(51).

33 WGTDF, 'The Relationship Between Exchange Rates and International Trade: A Review of Economic Literature. Note by the Secretariat' WT/WGTDF/W/57 (27 September 2011).

34 WGTDF, 'The Relationship Between Exchange Rates and International Trade: A Short Update of Recent Economic Literature. Note by the Secretariat' WT/WGTDF/W/65 (18 July 2012).

35 WGTDF, 'Report of the Working Group on Trade, Debt and Finance for 2011 to the General Council' WT/WGTDF/10 (15 November 2011) 10. The material presented at the seminar can be found at 'WTO Seminar on Trade and Exchange Rates' (*WTO*, 27 and 28 March 2012) <http://www.wto.org/english/news_e/news12_e/devel_27mar12_e.htm> accessed 20 June 2013, and is summarized in WGTDF, 'Update' (n. 34).

to the question of how the *level* of an exchange rate affects trade flows. This research, the WTO Secretariat adds, 'is still in its infancy'.[36] Determining the impact of exchange rate levels on trade commitments is further complicated by the evolution towards 'made in the world' manufacturing, in which inputs, intermediate goods and final goods are traded internationally multiple times before reaching the final consumer.[37] Given the need for further research, the debate on how the level of the exchange rate affects trade will most likely continue for years.

3 The WTO and Exchange Rate Undervaluation

Given the link between exchange rate valuation and trade, the question arises whether the WTO Agreement restricts Members' conduct with respect to their exchange rates, or whether indeed 'the unpleasant truth may be that formal and enforceable international law has reached its limits'.[38]

Constraints on a WTO Member's exercise of its sovereignty can take the form of direct limits that prohibit specific policies. Another type of constraints is more indirect and allows other Members to respond when they are adversely affected by the former's policies. In the context of exchange rate undervaluation, the focus is often on the latter type of constraints as is visible in Brazil's second submission to the WGTDF which refers to, *inter alia*, safeguards, anti-dumping and countervailing measures.[39] Even though these indirect constraints can lead to a dispute about the legality of their application, they have the possible advantage of offering affected states immediate protection against the negative effects of undervaluation of a trading partner's currency. In contrast, violations of a direct limit need to go through time- and resource-intensive dispute settlement procedures before the affected state can get redress from the acting state. Even if the outcome is positive for the complaining state, by the time a decision is reached the economic damage from its trading partner's beggar-thy-neighbour behaviour may already have been done.

---

36 WGTDF, 'Review of Economic Literature' (n. 33) 31.

37 Ibid., 53.

38 Claus D. Zimmermann, 'Exchange Rate Misalignment and International Law' (2011) 105 AJIL 423, 476.

39 See text accompanying n. 13.

Whether trade remedies can be used successfully against undervalued exchange rates is, however, questionable.[40] Commentators disagree on whether exchange rate manipulation justifies countervailing duties.[41] To successfully apply these provisions, the economic effects of an undervalued exchange rate need to be 'translated' into WTO-speak.[42] However, things get lost in translation. While there is no space here to consider the argument in detail, I am of the opinion that an undervalued exchange rate fails to meet the legal test for a prohibited subsidy because any 'benefit' that might arise is not 'specific', as it applies across the economy rather than to a particular actor or industry.[43] Nor can it be deemed to be specific as an export subsidy under article 3 SCM Agreement because it is not *de jure* or *de facto* contingent upon exportation. The undervalued exchange rate is available regardless of exportation.[44] Even if exporters derive a benefit, this is not enough to find *de facto* export contingency.[45]

Trade remedies are further hampered by the difficulty to quantify the effects of undervaluation for the calculation of the appropriate amount of duties, as discussed in Section 2. There is, however, no need for such precise quantification when direct limits are involved, as a complainant will only need to show that there is prohibited undervaluation.[46]

40 Brazil's third submission also expresses doubt on the applicability of trade remedies to exchange rate undervaluation, see WGTDF, 5 November 2012 (n. 11) 7–8.

41 Some authors reject this possibility, eg Staiger and Sykes (n. 31) 31–33; Bryan Mercurio and Celine Sze Ning Leung, 'Is China a "Currency Manipulator"?: The Legitimacy of China's Exchange Regime Under the Current International Legal Framework' (2009) 43 Int'l Law 1257, 1294–97; Catharina E. Koops, 'Manipulating the WTO? Challenging Undervalued Exchange Rates Under WTO Rules' Amsterdam Center for International Law 2010 Research Paper Series 2–6 <http://ssrn.com/abstract=1564093> accessed 20 June 2013. Others admit that applying the agreement will be difficult, but do not exclude it completely, eg Marc Benitah, 'China's Fixed Exchange Rate for the Yuan: Could the United State Challenge It in the WTO as a Subsidy? (corrected version)' (*ASIL*, October 2003) <http://www.asil.org/insigh117.cfm> accessed 20 June 2013; Benjamin Blase Caryl, 'Is China's Currency Regime a Countervailable Subsidy? A Legal Analysis Under the World Trade Organization's SCM Agreement' (2011) 45 JWT 187, 217.

42 Robert W. Staiger and Alan O. Sykes, 'Currency Manipulation and World Trade: A Caution' in Evenett (n. 20) 110.

43 Joel P. Trachtman, 'Yuan to Fight About It? The WTO Legality of China's Exchange Regime' in Evenett (n. 20) 130.

44 Zimmermann (n. 38) 454.

45 SCM Agreement art. 3.1(a), fn. 4. See also Zimmermann (n. 38) 454–55.

46 Should a complaint be successful and advance to retaliation stage, there may be a need to quantify the effect of the undervaluation, Dukgeun Ahn, 'Is the Chinese exchange-rate regime 'WTO-legal'?' in Evenett (n. 20) 142.

Given the difficulties with fitting the trade effects of exchange rate undervaluation in the legal framework of trade remedies, the discussion below focuses on articles XII:3(a) and XV:4 GATT that directly limit WTO Members' exercise of their monetary sovereignty. Despite the *prima facie* relevance of these articles to the issue of exchange rate undervaluation, neither has been applied in practice, although article XV:4 has received attention in the literature.

In addition to the empirical uncertainty about the impact of exchange rate undervaluation on trade commitments,[47] I advance two further reasons why these articles may have been overlooked as a potential limit on WTO Members' exercise of their monetary sovereignty. A first reason is legal and arises out of the interpretive uncertainty surrounding the legal nature of the obligation in article XII:3(a) and the meaning of the central concepts in article XV:4. A second is institutional and relates to the allocation of competences between the IMF and the WTO. The analysis will consider each reason in turn, address whether they are indeed barriers to the application of these articles, and, if so, whether they can be overcome.

3.1 *Legal Barriers*

A first explanation for why the articles are often forgotten is that both suffer from interpretive uncertainty. The application of article XII:3(a) is hindered by uncertainty about the nature of the obligation, ie whether it imposes a binding obligation on WTO Members. In contrast, for article XV:4, uncertainty surrounds the scope of the obligation, ie the domestic policies prohibited by the requirement not to frustrate the intent of GATT provisions through exchange action.

3.1.1 Article XII:3(a) GATT

Article XII:3(a) is part of a provision allowing trade restrictions to safeguard the balance of payments.[48] Nevertheless, I argue that its scope of application exceeds the case of restrictions to safeguard the balance of payments. A conventional interpretation of this article, analysing the text in its ordinary meaning in its context and in the light of its object and purpose,[49] supports this conclusion.

First, 'domestic policies' is a general term that covers all policies adopted domestically. Given that exchange rate policies are adopted by monetary

47 See Section 2 above.

48 Developing states can also invoke the more generous exception in GATT art. XVIII, Section B.

49 Vienna Convention on the Law of Treaties (adopted 23 May 1969, entered into force 27 January 1980) 1155 UNTS 331 art. 31.

authorities who decide on the best policy for domestic purposes, it is hard to deny that they are domestic policies.

Second, looking at the context of the article, it is revealing that, contrary to 3(b) and 3(c), 3(a) does not refer to situations in which WTO Members are 'applying restrictions under this Article', but instead refers more broadly to 'domestic policies'. This again suggests that the article is not limited to trade restrictions enacted with the goal of safeguarding the balance of payments, but applies more broadly to all domestic policies that can affect equilibrium on the balance of payments, including those regarding the exchange rate valuation. Furthermore, if the provision were limited to situations of balance of payments problems, there would only be a mention to 'restoring equilibrium' rather than to 'maintaining and restoring'. Another indication that this provision is not limited to measures responding to a balance of payments crisis, but is of a preventative nature to avoid the specific consequences of domestic policies, is the reference to 'desirability of *avoiding* an uneconomic employment of productive resources'.[50]

Finally, although we know very little about the object and purpose of this particular article, we know that one of the aims of the GATT was to harness states' comparative advantage by eliminating mercantilist behaviour.[51] Exchange rate undervaluation arguably amounts to mercantilism,[52] an economic strategy whereby states pursue the accumulation of wealth at the expense of other states.[53]

If a Member maintains an undervalued exchange rate to stimulate exports, any resulting improvement of the trade balance occurs at the expense of that Member's trading partners. The increased prices of imports in the undervaluing Member will lower demand for these imports, affecting production in other Members. At the same time, the lower prices for exports will increase

50 GATT art. XII:3(a), emphasis added.

51 Donald M. McRae, 'The Contribution of International Trade Law to the Development of International Law' 260 Recueil des Cours de l'Académie de Droit International 99, 143. Whether current rules of trade liberalization achieve this outcome is debatable, but this question is beyond the scope of the current chapter.

52 Another reason why primarily Asian states adopted undervalued exchange rates was to accumulate foreign reserves following the 1997 Asian Financial Crisis and to reduce the need to rely on IMF funding. See Aaditya Mattoo and Arvind Subramanian, 'Currency Undervaluation and Sovereign Wealth Funds: A New Role for the World Trade Organization' (2008) Peterson Institute for International Economics Working Paper Series WP 08–2, 14 <http://www.iie.com/publications/wp/wp08-2.pdf> accessed 20 June 2013.

53 McRae (n. 51) 140. See also WTO, *Dictionary of Trade Policy Terms* (CUP 2003) 227.

demand abroad, to the further detriment of production overseas. Exchange rate undervaluation can thus lead to a surplus on the current account.[54]

The increased demand for a Member's exports will lead to an increased demand for its currency, which would in normal circumstances cause exchange rate appreciation. All things staying equal, this appreciation will increase the price of the goods on the international markets, lowering demand and rebalancing the current account. If a Member employs policies to avoid this adjustment, its actions are arguably contrary to article XII:3(a)'s requirement to pay due regard to the 'need for maintaining or restoring equilibrium in their balance of payments on a sound and lasting basis'. Policies to avoid appreciation could also be seen as 'an uneconomic employment of productive resources'. For example, the high reserve requirements imposed on Chinese banks to avoid the inflation that would otherwise result from the People's Bank of China's purchases of foreign assets to curtail the appreciation of the Renminbi[55] reduces the amount of capital available for investment.

The main uncertainty about the application of article XII:3(a) is whether the undertaking 'to pay due regard' to the specific ends of balance of payments equilibrium and economic employment of resources implies a binding obligation. Bhala argues that it is 'more exhortative than mandatory'.[56] I see no reason why the undertaking of WTO Members in article XII:3(a) would not be binding. However, the requirement 'to pay due regard' is only an obligation of conduct rather than an obligation of result.[57] At most, it requires Members to demonstrate that they have considered the goals of article XII:3(a), and the impact of their domestic policies thereupon.

It is unclear at what point domestic policies cross the line from conduct that pays 'due regard' to these goals, even if it does not achieve them, and conduct that does not pay due regard. To overcome this barrier, WTO Members need to be found willing to hold each other accountable when their domestic policies threaten the sound and lasting equilibrium on the balance of payments

54 See text accompanying n. 29 above.

55 See UNCTAD, 'Trade and Development Report 2011' UNCTAD/TDR/2011 (6 September 2011) 177. China thus has a deficit on the capital account to reflect its surplus on the current acount.

56 Raj Bhala, *Modern GATT Law: A Treatise on the General Agreement on Tariffs and Trade* (Sweet & Maxwell 2005) 1011.

57 In India–Quantitative Restrictions, India argued before the WTO Panel that the obligation to 'pay due regard' in art. XVIII:11, which is a parallel provision on the balance of payment exception for developing states, is not mandatory or enforceable, see *India–Quantitative Restrictions on Imports of Agricultural, Textile and Industrial Products* WT/DS90/R (6 April 1999) 3.229. However, the Panel and the Appellate Body did not analyze this argument.

or lead to an uneconomic employment of productive resources. Through the discussions, and any formal dispute settlement that may follow, criteria for the assessment of 'due regard' can be developed.

3.1.2 Article XV:4 GATT

In the absence of case law interpreting article XV:4,[58] there is significant uncertainty about its precise meaning, which is not helped by a large diversity of viewpoints in the literature. There are four unresolved issues: 1) the meaning of 'exchange action'; 2) the relationship between articles XV:4 and XV:9; 3) whether article XV:4 provides an independent basis for a legal claim; and 4) the meaning of 'frustrate'.

First, it is unclear which actions qualify as 'exchange action'.[59] The term is not used in the IMF Articles of Agreement[60] or anywhere else in the GATT. Other paragraphs of article XV GATT refer to 'exchange arrangements',[61] 'exchange restrictions',[62] 'exchange controls',[63] or 'action in exchange matters'.[64] Some authors restrict 'exchange action' to regulation of payments for current transactions, or currency convertibility,[65] and multiple exchange rates,[66] whereas

58 The possibility of a violation was raised in *Special Import Taxes Instituted by Greece* (1952) GATT BISD 1S/48, but a decision was never reached because the issue became moot, see John H. Jackson, *World Trade and the Law of GATT* (Bobbs-Merrill 1969) 485.

59 WTO (n. 53) does not define 'exchange action'.

60 IMF Articles of Agreement art. IV(1) refers to 'exchange arrangements' in its chapeau and to 'exchange policies' in subsection (iv). art. IV(3)(b) refers to 'exchange rate policies'.

61 GATT art. XV:2.

62 Ibid., art. XV:5 and XV:9(a) & (b).

63 Ibid., art. XV:9(a) & (b).

64 Ibid., art. XV:7.

65 Michael Waibel, 'Retaliating Against Exchange Rate Manipulation under WTO Rules' in Evenett (n. 20) 135; Erik Denters, 'Manipulation of Exchange Rates in International Law: The Chinese Yuan' (*ASIL*, November 2003) <http://www.asil.org/insigh118.cfm> accessed 20 June 2013. However, a later publication, co-authored by Denters, includes exchange rate manipulation under 'exchange action', Ioana Ciobănaşu and Erik Denters, 'Manipulation of the Chinese Yuan—May WTO Members Respond?' (*SSRN*, 12 December 2008) 11–13 <http://ssrn.com/abstract=1315290> accessed 20 June 2013.

66 Deborah E. Siegel, 'Legal Aspects of the IMF/WTO Relationship: The Fund's Articles of Agreement and the WTO Agreements' 96 AJIL 561, 567; Christoph Herrmann, 'Don Yuan: China's 'Selfish' Exchange Rate Policy and International Economic Law' in C. Herrmann and J. Philipp Terhechte (eds), *European Yearbook of International Economic Law 2010* (Springer-Verlag 2010) 46; Jorge Miranda, 'Currency Undervaluation as a Violation of GATT art. XV:4' in Evenett (n. 20) 117.

others define it more broadly to include manipulative currency practices[67] or any measure that relates to currency and capital.[68]

Using the Vienna Convention on the Law of Treaties' criteria for treaty interpretation,[69] the first inquiry is into the ordinary meaning of 'exchange action'. The Oxford English Dictionary defines 'action' as 'something that is done' or as 'the process or the act of doing'. This suggests a very broad concept,[70] which is confirmed by the provision's object and purpose. The drafters wanted to protect trade commitments against measures with respect to the exchange rate and they envisaged not just exchange controls and restrictions, but also manipulation of the exchange rate.[71]

'Exchange action' thus is arguably a broad concept,[72] but just how broad is it? For example, given the role assigned to market forces to determine the exchange rate, does 'exchange action' include any domestic macro-economic policy such as the US Federal Reserve's quantitative easing in response to the Global Financial Crisis, that affects the exchange rate indirectly through the response of market participants? To avoid overly restricting WTO Members' economic policies because of a potential effect on the exchange rate, the concept of 'exchange action' should not be given too wide an interpretation. Yet, it should still extend to any direct measure through which a state controls the level of its exchange rate, whether that is to support a fixed exchange rate or to manage a floating exchange rate. Measures that keep a currency deliberately undervalued should be included, because these undermine the GATT's liberalization commitments by affecting the tariff protection as well as by artificially reducing the price of the undervaluing Member's exports and increasing the price of its imports.

A second cause of uncertainty about article XV:4 GATT is its relationship with article XV:9 GATT.[73] The latter stipulates that the GATT does not preclude

---

67 WGTDF, 'Seminar at the WTO on International Trade and Exchange Rates: Statement by the French Delegation' WT/WGTDF/W/64 (25 May 2012) 2; Proctor, *USA v China* (n. 7) 1348; Ciobănaşu and Denters (n. 65) 11–13.

68 Mercurio and Leung (n. 41) 1286.

69 VCLT (n. 49) art. 31.

70 Miranda (n. 66) 117.

71 Jackson, *World Trade* (n. 58) 479.

72 Ahn (n. 46) 141; Miranda (n. 66) 119–21; Jonathan E. Sanford, 'Currency Manipulation: The IMF and WTO' (Congressional Research Service 2012) <www.fas.org/sgp/crs/misc/RS22658.pdf>.

73 This difficulty was recognized early on in GATT practice, but a group established in 1955 to clarify the relationship declined to add an interpretative note and preferred to leave the issue for a later time if and when a specific problem would arise, see Jackson, *World Trade* (n. 58) 485.

the use of exchange controls or exchange restrictions in accordance with the IMF Articles of Agreement[74] or the use of restrictions or controls on imports or exports to make exchange controls or restrictions effective.[75] The question is whether this exception makes XV:4 redundant. The reference to 'Nothing in this Agreement' at the start of XV:9 would indeed suggest as such, and this is reinforced by the fact that an original reference to 'Subject to paragraph 4' at the start of XV:9 was deleted during the Havana Conference.[76] Nevertheless, it is argued here that both paragraphs have a different scope of application. Article XV:9 is limited to exchange controls[77] and exchange restrictions,[78] whereas XV:4 deals with the broader category of exchange action, which encompasses—but is not limited to—exchange controls and exchange restrictions.[79] Multiple currency practices for example can be seen as exchange actions that are not however an exchange control or an exchange restriction.[80] Principles of effective treaty interpretation further dictate a broader scope to 'exchange action' to avoid XV:4's redundancy. Article XV:9 therefore at most provides a limited exception to XV:4.

A third uncertainty surrounding article XV:4 is whether it provides an independent basis for a legal claim or whether it instead requires violation of another GATT provision. The source for the uncertainty lies in the Ad Note to Article XV:4, which is as follows:

---

74 GATT art. XV:9(a).

75 Ibid., art. XV:9(b).

76 Bhala, *Modern GATT* (n. 56) 1175.

77 WTO (n. 53) 128 defines these as 'conditions or limits imposed by governments on the extent to which residents may have access to foreign exchange reserves'.

78 A decision of the IMF Executive Board clarified that 'The guiding principle in ascertaining whether a measure is a restriction on payments and transfers for current transactions under art. VIII, Section. 2, is whether it involves a direct governmental limitation on the availability or use of exchange as such.' See Decision 1034-(60/27) (1 June 1960) <http://www.imf.org/external/pubs/ft/sd/index.asp?decision=1034-%2860/27%29> accessed 20 June 2013.

79 Koops (n. 41) 12; Vera Thorstensen, Daniel Ramos and Carolina Muller, 'The "Missing Link" between the WTO and the IMF' (2013) JIEL 353, 377.

80 This interpretation makes GATT Ad Note art. VI, which allows countervailing duties when multiple currency practices constitute an export subsidy, less surprising. Siegel (n. 66) 593 is puzzled by this given that GATT art. XV:9(a) exempts practices applied consistently with the IMF Articles of Agreement. However, if multiple currency practices are neither an exchange restriction nor an exchange control, the exemption is not available.

> The word 'frustrate' is intended to indicate, for example, that infringements of the letter of any Article of this Agreement by exchange action shall not be regarded as a violation of that Article if, in practice, there is no appreciable departure from the intent of the Article. Thus, a contracting party which, as part of its exchange control operated in accordance with the Articles of Agreement of the International Monetary Fund, requires payment to be received for its exports in its own currency or in the currency of one or more members of the International Monetary Fund will not thereby be deemed to contravene Article XI or Article XIII. Another example would be that of a contracting party which specifies on an import licence the country from which the goods may be imported, for the purpose not of introducing any additional element of discrimination in its import licensing system but of enforcing permissible exchange controls.

Some authors argue that the reference to an infringement of the letter of an article implies that the exchange action must violate the letter *and* intent of a GATT provision.[81] I disagree.

The Ad Note clarifies that an infringement of the letter of a GATT provision is not a *sufficient* condition for 'frustration' and that an appreciable departure of the intent of the article is a *necessary* condition. Article XV:4 can thus exculpate technical violations of another GATT article through exchange actions if compatible with that article's intent. However, we cannot infer from the Ad Note that infringement of the letter is also a necessary condition.

Moreover, the conclusion that an appreciable departure of the intent is not only a necessary, but also a sufficient condition, is more plausible. Article XV:4 itself refers only to the frustration of the intent. The reference to the letter of a GATT provision in the Ad Note is only by way of an example.[82] According to Zimmermann, the example covers all exchange actions, and illustrates how frustration of the intent of the IMF Articles of Agreement through trade action

81 See, for example, Koops (n. 41) 10; Annemaria Viterbo, *International Economic Law and Monetary Measures: Limitations to States' Sovereignty and Dispute Settlement* (Edward Elgar 2012) 310; and Zimmermann (n. 38) 471, who also argues that GATT art. XV:4 was only intended to apply to non-IMF Members until they became an IMF Member or negotiated a special exchange agreement with other WTO Members as provided in GATT art. XV:6.

82 Ahn (n. 46) 141; Trachtman (n. 43) 129 points out that this broader interpretation may be available.

should be interpreted.[83] In the absence of any case law, we cannot know for certain how the use of the example is intended, but in my opinion, it is more reasonable to interpret the reference to the example as just one possibility of frustration rather than as using exchange action as an example for trade action. The reasons for this are first, the placement of the words 'for example' in the first sentence, rather than at the start of the second sentence. Second, the drafters presumably only discussed exchange action because they were more concerned about frustration of the GATT than about that of the IMF Articles of Agreement.

The conclusion that article XV:4 provides an independent basis for a claim is important with respect to undervalued exchange rates. Leaving article XII:3(a) out of consideration, no GATT provision contains specific obligations concerning a WTO Member's exchange rate valuation. Yet, undervalued exchange rates can erode existing trade liberalization commitments. While they do not fit within the legal definition for an export subsidy, their economic effect is the same,[84] making them prime candidates for a finding that the GATT's intent has been frustrated, and thus that article XV:4 has been violated.

This conclusion leads us to the final barrier to the application of article XV:4 GATT: the difficult question of the intent behind the GATT and its provisions.[85] The examples in the Ad Note could be interpreted as suggesting that an exchange action in compliance with the IMF Articles of Agreement does not frustrate the GATT's intent.[86] The Second Amendment of the IMF Articles of Agreement has reinstated IMF Members' monetary sovereignty, prohibiting only a limited set of policies.[87] If this interpretation of the Ad Note's definition is correct, the GATT's intent will only rarely be frustrated.[88] However, had the GATT's drafters intended this, they could simply have extended the exception in article XV:9 GATT to include all exchange action and not just exchange controls or exchange restrictions compatible with the IMF Articles of Agreement.

83 Zimmermann (n. 38) 471.

84 Mattoo and Subramanian (n. 52) 5.

85 Simon Lester, 'GATT art. XV:4 and Intent' (*International Economic Law and Policy Blog*, 23 November 2009) <http://worldtradelaw.typepad.com/ielpblog/2009/11/gatt-art-xv4-and-intent.html> accessed 20 June 2013.

86 Bhala, *Modern GATT* (n. 56) 1172 interprets the Ad Note in this way.

87 See text accompanying footnotes 4–10.

88 Bhala, *Modern GATT* (n. 56) 1173.

3.2 *Institutional Barriers*

A second barrier to the application of articles XII:3(a) and XV:4 GATT is institutional. It is debated to what extent the WTO can get involved in exchange rate issues or whether these belong exclusively to the IMF's jurisdiction.[89] Likewise, in the WGTDF's discussions of Brazil's submissions, some Members questioned the WTO's jurisdiction and pointed to the need not to duplicate the work of the IMF and the G-20.[90]

The three institutions created at the 1944 Bretton Woods Conference were originally given separate responsibilities. The International Bank for Reconstruction and Development (IBRD), better known as the World Bank, was to focus on development, the International Monetary Fund on monetary matters and the International Trade Organization (ITO), from which the GATT was salvaged when the United States refused to sign up to the ITO, on trade.[91]

Nevertheless, the different focus does not justify the artificial separation between trade and exchange rates.[92] The text of the GATT does not support a strict separation. Article XV:2 GATT requires the WTO to consult with the IMF on the factual determination of whether an exchange rate is indeed undervalued when it examines the legality of trade restrictions for balance of payment restrictions. It thus provides for a synergy between the two regimes, rather than requiring Panels to leave anything exchange rate related to the IMF.[93]

Furthermore, articles XII:3(a) and XV:4[94] indicate that the GATT's drafters were aware of the potential impact of exchange rate fluctuations on trade. This suggests that it is appropriate to bring the matter of exchange rate undervaluation within the WTO's jurisdiction if the undervaluation affects trade, independently of obligations under the IMF Articles of Agreement.

89 Koops (n. 41) 2; Waibel (n. 65) 136.

90 WGTDF, 'Meeting of 10 May 2011' (n. 12) 52–53; WGTDF, 'Report to the General Council' (n. 35) 7; WGTDF, 'Report of the Meeting of 26 November 2012' WT/WGTDF/M/26 (25 January 2013) 7, 8, 12, 16, 20, 23, 29.

91 Rosa María Lastra, 'The International Monetary Fund in Historical Perspective' (2000) 3 JIEL 507, 507–08; Mitsuo Matsushita, Thomas J. Schoenbaum and Petros C. Mavroidis, *The World Trade Organization: Law, Practice, and Policy* (OUP 2006) 1; Lowenfeld, *International Economic Law 2nd edn* (n. 4) 24; Thorstensen and others (n. 79) 356.

92 See also Lucas Ferraz, Emerson Marçal and Vera Thorstensen, 'Effects of Exchange-Rate Misalignmentson Tariffs' (*VoxEU*, 4 December 2011) <http://www.voxeu.org/indexphp?q=node/7382> accessed 20 June 2013.

93 Zimmermann (n. 38) 462; Thorstensen and others (n. 79) 374.

94 As well as GATT art. II:6 and para. 2 of the Ad Note to art. VI:2 and 3.

The GATT's drafters' failure to deal with undervaluation in more depth can be explained by the existence at the time of the 'par value' system of exchange rates.[95] Because states' obligations under the IMF Articles of Agreement restricted the possibility of undervaluation, the GATT did not need to address the question of undervaluation. If anything, the collapse of the par value system in the 1970s has increased the significance of articles XII:3(a) and XV:4 GATT. Although exchange rate adjustment is now considered the primary tool to address imbalances,[96] few states leave the task of determining the exchange rate entirely to the foreign exchange markets. Instead, central banks regularly intervene in international currency markets to influence the value of their currency.[97] The articles intended to avoid exchange rate policies undermining trade liberalization commitments thus continue to be relevant in the post-Bretton Woods era.

4 Conclusion

This chapter has focused on two GATT articles that are often overlooked in discussions on exchange rate undervaluation and trade. Three potential obstacles to the application of these articles were considered: the empirical uncertainty about the impact of exchange rate undervaluation on trade commitments; the legal uncertainty; and the institutional barriers that have their roots in the long abandoned IMF's par value system. It was argued that the articles remain relevant despite the tremendous changes in the international monetary system since the 1970s.

Neither article provides a ready-made solution for the trade effects of exchange rate undervaluation, due to barriers created by significant empirical and legal uncertainty in the application of the articles. This chapter has offered

95 Bhala, *Modern GATT* (n. 56) 303–06, 1169; Thorstensen and others (n. 79) 354. See text accompanying footnotes 6 and 7 for more on the par value system.

96 John Howard Jackson, *The World Trading System: Law and Policy of International Economic Relations* (MIT Press 1997) 242–43; Matsushita, Schoenbaum and Mavroidis (n. 91) 463, 465.

97 UNCTAD, *TDR 2011* (n. 55) 163; Richard Portes, 'Currency Wars and the Emerging-Market Countries' (*VoxEU*, 4 November 2010) <http://www.voxeu.org/index.php?q=node/5740> accessed 20 June 2013. Even Brazil has admitted to operating a 'dirty float', see Joe Leahy, 'Brazil admits tight hold over exchange rate' *Financial Times* (London, 24 October 2012) <http://www.ft.com/cms/s/0/3185f656-1dfa-11e2-8e1d-00144feabdc0.html#axzz2AehH0wR8> accessed 20 June 2013.

some possible clarifications to both articles to enable the WTO to respond when exchange rate undervaluation affects trade commitments.

These clarifications do not necessarily require an amendment of the GATT. What the articles lack is visibility. If WTO Members would challenge other Members' exchange rate policies on this basis, a dynamic process of interpretation and clarification can start.[98] This process does not have to entail using the WTO's dispute settlement procedures. Discussions such as the one instigated by Brazil in the WGTDF are informal methods towards clarifying the applicable law that can evolve into more formal methods.

98 Space considerations do not allow for a discussion of this process, but see Wayne Sandholtz and Kendall W. Stiles, *International Norms and Cycles of Change* (OUP 2009); Jutta Brunnée and Stephen J. Toope, *Legitimacy and Legality in International Law: An Interactional Account* (CUP 2010).

CHAPTER 2

An Optimal Global Regime for Regulating Credit Rating Agencies in the Post Financial Crisis Era—From the Perspective of the Appropriate Role of the Rating Agencies in the Capital Market

Kuan-Chun Johnny Chang

1 Introduction

Credit rating agencies (CRAs) are in the business of providing credit ratings for securities and other debt-related instruments. Theoretically, the purpose of CRAs is to help investors to deal with the problematic aspects of the principal-agent relationship and asymmetric information by providing an easily understandable reference on a particular financial product's likelihood of default, thus assisting in setting a market price for the product in question.[1] However, CRAs have been widely criticized as key contributors to the recent global financial crisis, especially in light of their role in the expansion of the market for asset-backed securities.[2] In the case of the subprime mortgage crisis that triggered the financial market meltdown, CRAs gave triple A ratings[3] to 75 percent of those subprime mortgages that lost sizable value only months after the ratings were issued. According to a report of the Senate Investigation Committee:

> During the first half of 2007, despite the news of failing subprime lenders and increasing subprime mortgage defaults, Moody's and S&P continued to issue AAA credit ratings for a large number of residential

1 Deryn Darcy, 'Credit Rating Agencies and the Credit Crisis: How the "Issuer Pays" Conflict Contributed and What Regulators Might Do About It' (2009) 2009 CLMBLR 605, 606.

2 Kristina St. Charles, 'Regulatory Imperialism: The Worldwide Export of European Regulatory Principles' (2010) 19 MNJIL 399.

3 According to Moody's Rating system, obligations rated 'Aaa' are judged to be of the highest quality, with minimal credit risk. See Moody's Investor's Service, *Moody's Rating symbols and Definitions* (2009) 8 <https://www.moodys.com/sites/products/AboutMoodysRatingsAttachments/MoodysRatingsSymbolsand%20Definitions.pdf> accessed 27 August 2013.

 | DOI 10.1163/9789004270190_003

> mortgage-backed securities (RMBS) and collateralized debt obligation (CDO) securities…[Not long after], [b]eginning in July 2007, Moody's and S&P downgraded hundreds and then thousands of RMBS and CDO ratings, causing the rated securities to lose value and become much more difficult to sell, and leading to the subsequent collapse of the RMBS and CDO secondary markets. The massive downgrades made it clear that the original ratings were … deeply flawed.[4]

The accountability of CRAs has been questioned by market participants ever since. It is commonly agreed that such poor performance arose from the rating industry's issuer-pay business model, from which CRAs derive most of their revenues.[5] This fact alone indicates that CRAs had a conflict of interest and turned a blind eye to the high levels of risk associated with structured products and derivatives.[6]

To tackle the problem of conflicts of interest and restore CRAs' accountability, regulatory regimes worldwide have adopted the disclosure-based approach, which mandates that CRAs must provide additional information regarding potential conflicts of interest.[7] Regulators have also attempted to prevent excessive entanglement between CRAs and issuers.[8] Nevertheless, the rating industry's issuer-pay business model is difficult to change because revenues paid by issuers remain CRAs' primary source of income for rating a wide range of debt issues. This structure increases the possibility that CRAs will be

4 US Senate Primary Subcommittee on Investigation, *Wall Street and the Financial Crisis: Anatomy of a Financial Collapse* (Majority and Minority Report Staff Report 2010) 263–64.

5 Marwan Elkhoury, Credit Rating Agencies and Their Potential Impact on Developing Countries, United Nations Conference on Trade and Development (Discussion Paper No 186 2008) 14 <http://www.unctad.org/en/docs/osgdp20081_en.pdf> accessed 27 August 2013; Thomas J. Pate, 'Triple-A Ratings Stench: May the Crediting Agencies be Held Accountable?' (2010) 14 BARRYLR 25, 33.

6 Claire A. Hill, 'Why Did Rating Agencies Do Such a Bad Job Rating Subprime Securities?' (2010) 71 UPTLR 585, 593.

7 Stéphane Rousseau, 'Enhancing the Accountability of Credit Rating Agencies: The Case for a Disclosure-Based Approach' (2006) 51 MCGLJ 617, 652–53; US Securities & Exchange Commission, 'Fact Sheet: Strengthening Oversight of Credit Rating Agencies' (17 September 2009) <http://www.sec.gov/news/press/2009/2009-200-factsheet.htm> accessed 27 August 2013.

8 For example, a regulation prohibits CRA analysts from providing advisory services while rating the issuer simultaneously. For details, see US Securities & Exchange Commission, *Report on the Role and Function of Credit Rating Agencies in the Operation of the Securities Markets* (2003) 23 <http://www.sec.gov/news/studies/credratingreport0103.pdf> accessed 27 August 2013.

willing to risk their reputational capital by giving inaccurate, untruthful, or less-than-full disclosure. On the other hand, due to regulators' lack of expertise, CRA ratings remain indispensible in maintaining the flow of information in the capital markets. This fact lessens the incentive to regulate, primarily because of the fear that over-regulation may negatively affect both investors' and issuers' reliance on CRA ratings. Following this line of thought, this chapter argues that the globally-chosen, disclosure-based firewall method falls short of resolving issues associated with conflicts of interest. It suggests that an optimal regulatory system can be established only through identification of the fundamental role assigned to CRAs by market participants and regulators.

Based on the preceding notion, section 2 of this chapter will introduce the causes of CRAs' problems with conflicts of interest; sections 3, 4 and 5 will observe global approaches in dealing with such problems and comment on their effectiveness; section 6 will examine the appropriate role of the CRA in the capital markets; section 7 will present proposals for regulatory reform in accordance with the identified status of the CRA; and section 8 will conclude.

2 CRAs and the Conflicts of Interest Problem

Credit rating agencies suffer from conflicts of interest that may distort their judgment. A securities rating is critical to the issuer because it dictates the interest rates that the issuer will need to pay to its investors—the higher the credit rating, the more eager the investors and the lower the interest rate; likewise, the lower the credit rating, the more hesitant the investors and the higher the interest rate.[9] This situation was particularly obvious when it came to complex structured financial products such as RMBS, because their profitability depended so heavily on their credit rating.[10] Thus, issuers typically pressure CRAs to issue the highest rating possible.[11]

Conflicts of interest that may influence the sound judgment of the CRA arise in two ways. First, rating agencies receive payment for their ratings from the issuers of the securities rather than the investors. Such issuer-pays model shifts the focus of a rating from protecting investors to meeting the issuers'

9 A. Brooke Murphy, 'Credit Rating Immunity? How The Hands-off Approach Toward Credit Rating Agencies Led to the Subprime Credit Crisis and the Need for Greater Accountability' (2010) 62 OKLR 735, 750.

10 Elizabeth Devine, 'The Collapse of an Empire: Rating Agency Reform in the Wake of the 2007 Financial Crisis' (2011) 16 FDMJCFL 177, 188.

11 Ibid.

expectations in order to ensure payment for future analyses.[12] Second, 'the rating agencies themselves were active participants in the creation of the faultily-structured products, not objective third-party arbiters.'[13] To illustrate, through their consulting services, CRAs assist issuers in structuring highly complex financial products to maximize their ratings, which in turn lowers the interest rate paid to investors and the resulting cost of capital.[14] If the CRA performs the appropriate tests and determines that an investment-grade rating is not available for a certain bound, the analyst can notify the issuer of the bond, allowing the issuer to restructure the RMBS.[15] The opportunity to retrospectively tailor the RMBS's structure is an unavoidable business strategy for the CRA under these circumstances, as issuers are free to take their bonds to other rating agencies if they do not receive a satisfactory rating from the initial CRA.[16]

Allowing issuers multiple opportunities to restructure the bonds in order to receive a most favorable credit rating violates the fundamental principle that stipulates that a bond's rating must be a fair and accurate representation of its creditworthiness.[17] What is more disturbing is that the initial insufficiency of a bond and its subsequent restructuring is never reflected in the rating, nor is it disclosed to investors through any other means.[18]

3 Present Global Approach to Countering Conflicts of Interest—The Reputational View

It has been argued that it is inappropriate to invoke legal or regulatory forces to control ratings quality, because CRAs accumulate their reputation through issuing high-quality ratings.[19] As a consequence of this argument, even though

12 Aaron Lucchetti & Serena Ng, 'How Rating Firms' Calls Fueled Subprime Mess' *Wall Street Journal* (New York, 15 August 2007) A1.

13 Devine (n. 10) 189.

14 Benjamin H. Brownlow, 'Rating Agency Reform: Preserving the Registered Market for Asset-Backed Securities' (2011) 15 NCBNKI 111, 124.

15 Aaron Unterman, 'Innovative Destruction-Structured Finance and Credit Market Reform in the Bubble Era' (2009) 5 HBLJ 53, 61.

16 Pate (n. 5) 33.

17 Murphy (n. 9) 751.

18 US Securities & Exchange Commission, *Summary Report of Issues Identified in the Commission Staff's Examinations of Select Credit Rating Agencies* (2008) 9 <http://www.sec.gov/news/studies/2008/craexamination070808.pdf> accessed 27 August 2013.

19 John P Hunt, 'Credit Rating Agencies and the 'Worldwide Credit Crisis': The Limits of Reputation, the Insufficiency of Reform, and a Proposal for Improvement' (2009) CLMBLR 109, 188.

it could in theory be optimal for a CRA to 'cheat' and be indifference with its reputation under some circumstances, the CRA bears the risk of loss of reputation.[20] Investors realize that an agency's opinion diminishes information asymmetries in that it is designed to accurately certify issuers' creditworthiness, therefore, the value of such certification depends on a CRA's reputation for accuracy, independence, and integrity.[21] Moreover, because of the inherent value the reputation CRAs built, it provides them an economic incentive to behave in a diligent and ethical manner, even in the absence of regulation.[22] To build and maintain their reputations, CRAs should be expected to make a solid effort in providing high-quality services, because should a CRA have a reputation for erroneous or biased analysis, investors will discount the value of the ratings assigned. Such doubts regarding the accuracy or independence of the ratings of a particular CRA will lead issuers to seek a more credible agency to determine their creditworthiness.[23] Therefore, the reputation of CRAs is an economic incentive for the CRAs to behave diligently and ethically, regardless of the regulatory framework.

4 Disclosure-Based Approach and Erection of the Firewall—Common Grounds for Present Global Regulations

4.1 *The Revised IOSCO Code of Conduct*

The revised International Organization of Securities Commissions' (IOSCO) Code of Conduct Fundamentals for Credit Rating Agencies (Code of Conduct) suggests the following means to address the issue of conflicts of interest. First, a CRA is required to adopt written internal procedures and mechanisms to

> (1) identify, and (2) eliminate, or manage and disclose, as appropriate, any actual or potential conflicts of interest that may influence the opinions and analyses a CRA makes or the judgment and analyses of the individuals a CRA employs who have an influence on ratings decisions.[24]

---

20 Ibid.

21 Claire A. Hill, 'Regulating the Rating Agencies' (2004) 82 Wash. U.L.Q. 43, 50–51.

22 Rousseau (n. 7) 638.

23 Ibid.

24 IOSCO, Code of Conduct Fundamentals for Credit Rating Agencies 2008, 2.6.

Such disclosures should be 'complete, timely, clear, concise, specific and prominent.'[25]

A CRA also bears the duty to disclose the general nature of its compensation arrangements with rated entities, including its rating services and other arrangements unrelated to its ratings services, such as compensation for consulting services.[26] 'Reporting lines for CRA employees and their compensation arrangements should be structured to eliminate or effectively manage actual and potential conflicts of interest.'[27] Besides, a CRA should ensure that its analysts will not be compensated or evaluated on the basis of the amount of revenue the CRA derives from issuers that its analysts rate or with which analysts regularly interact.[28] A CRA should also refrain from having employees who are directly involved in the rating process, initiate, or participate in discussions regarding fees or payments with any entity they rate.[29]

In addition, CRA employees are prohibited from participating in or otherwise influencing the determination of the CRA's rating of any particular entity or obligation if an employee:

> a. Owns securities or derivatives of the rated entity, other than holdings in diversified collective investment schemes; b. Owns securities or derivatives of any entity related to a rated entity, the ownership of which may cause or may be perceived as causing a conflict of interest, other than holdings in diversified collective investment schemes; c. Has had a recent employment or other significant business relationship with the rated entity that may cause or may be perceived as causing a conflict of interest; d. Has an immediate relation (ie, a spouse, partner, parent, child, or sibling) who currently works for the rated entity; or e. Has, or had, any other relationship with the rated entity or any related entity thereof that may cause or may be perceived as causing a conflict of interest.[30]

4.2 *The United States*

In 2006, the US Congress passed the Credit Rating Agency Reform Act, which required the US Securities and Exchange Commission (SEC) to establish clear guidelines for determining which credit rating agencies qualify as a Nationally

25 Ibid., 2.7.
26 Ibid., 2.8.
27 Ibid., 2.11.
28 Ibid.
29 Ibid., 2.12.
30 Ibid., 2.13.

Recognized Statistical Rating Organization (NRSRO).[31] It also gives the SEC the power to regulate NRSROs' internal processes regarding record-keeping, to guard against conflicts of interest, and to make the NRSRO determination subject to a Commission vote.[32] On February 2, 2009, the SEC published the text of new rules and amendments to existing rules

> to increase the transparency of the NRSROs' rating methodologies, strengthen the NRSROs' disclosure of ratings performance, prohibit the NRSROs from engaging in certain practices that create conflicts of interest, and enhance the NRSROs' recordkeeping and reporting obligations to assist the Commission in performing its regulatory and oversight functions.[33]

The February Final Rules adopted three amendments to Rule 17g-5, which regulates conflicts of interest.[34] The first amendment added paragraph (c)(5), which prohibits an NRSRO from issuing or maintaining

> a credit rating with respect to an obligor or security where the NRSRO or its affiliate made recommendations to the obligor or the issuer, underwriter, or sponsor of the security about the structure of the security, the assets, the liabilities, or the activities of the obligor or issuer of the security.[35]

The second amendment added paragraph (c)(6), which prohibits a person within an NRSRO who 'has responsibility for participating in determining credit ratings or for developing or approving ratings from participating in discussions, negotiations, or arrangements'.[36] The third amendment added paragraph (c)(7), which prohibits an NRSRO from allowing a 'credit analyst who participated in determining or monitoring the rating to receive gifts, or other

31 Credit Rating Agency Reform Act 2006, 15E (a)(2)(C).

32 Ibid., 15E (c) & (h).

33 Press release US Securities & Exchange Commission, 'SEC Approves Measures to Strengthen Oversight of Credit Rating Agencies' (3 December 2008) <http://www.sec.gov/news/press/2008/2008-284.htm> accessed 27 August 2013.

34 17 CFR, 240.17 g-5 (2009).

35 US Securities & Exchange Commission, *Amendments to Rules for Nationally Recognized Statistical Rating Organizations Release* (No 34-59342; File No S7-13-08, 2 February 2009) <http://www.sec.gov/rules/final/2009/34-59342fr.pdf> accessed 27 August 2013.

36 Ibid.

benefits, from the obligor being rated or from the issuer, underwriter, or sponsor of the securities being rated.'[37]

On July 21, 2010, the Dodd-Frank Wall Street Reform and Consumer Protection Act was signed into law, prescribing several financial reforms. This outline addresses reforms relating to asset securitizations and credit rating agencies.[38] The Bill provided that when a former employee of an NRSRO is hired by an issuer, underwriter or sponsor of a security rated by the NRSRO and that employee was involved in 'determining the credit ratings' of such entities or their securities, the rating agency must review its ratings for any such entity or securities in which such employee participated during the one-year period prior to the rating action to determine whether any conflicts exist.[39] Considering that the SEC is required to make this information publicly available,[40] it is noteworthy that each NRSRO is mandated to

> report to the SEC the names of certain former employees of the agency who, within the previous five years, became an employee of any issuer, underwriter, or sponsor of a security rated by such agency, and who participated in the rating process during the twelve months prior to such employment.[41]

4.3 *European Union*

In October 2007, EU Finance Ministers agreed to a set of conclusions on the financial crisis, which included a proposal to assess the role played by credit rating agencies and to address any relevant deficiencies.[42] After controversial discussions in the European Parliament and the European Council, the Regulation on Credit Rating Agencies (CRA Regulation) was adopted by the Parliament on April 23, 2009, and was approved by the Council of Ministers on May 5, 2009.[43]

---

37 Ibid.

38 Michael S. Gambro, 'The Dodd-Frank Wall Street Reform and Consumer Protection Act: Reforms to the Asset-Backed Securitization Process and The Regulation of Credit Rating Agencies' (2011) 1873 PLI/Corp 43, 45.

39 Dodd-Frank Wall Street Reform and Consumer Protection Act 2010, Section 932(a).

40 Ibid.

41 Ibid., 4.

42 Europa Press Release, 'Approval of new Regulation will raise standards for the issuance of credit ratings used in the Community' (23 April 2009) <http://europa.eu/rapid/pressReleasesAction.do?reference=IP/09/629> accessed 27 August 2013.

43 Ibid.

For mitigating the conflicts of interest, the CRA Regulation introduced a disclosure-based approach as well as created a firewall between rating activities and consulting services. Article 6 provides that:

> [A] credit rating agency shall take all necessary steps to ensure that the issuing of a credit rating or a rating outlook is not affected by any existing or potential conflict of interest or business relationship involving the credit rating agency issuing the credit rating or the rating outlook, its managers, rating analysts, employees, any other natural person whose services are placed at the disposal or under the control of the credit rating agency, or any person directly or indirectly linked to it by control.[44] A credit rating agency shall ensure that employees who are directly involved in the credit rating process shall not be allowed to initiate or participate in negotiations regarding fees or payments with any rated entity, related third party or any person directly or indirectly linked to the rated entity by control.[45]

In addition, pursuant to Section c of Annex I of the CRA Regulation, credit rating analysts and other employees directly involved in the credit rating process, as well as persons closely associated with them, are prohibited from

> buying, selling, or engaging in any transaction involving any financial instrument issued, guaranteed, or otherwise supported by any rated entity within the area of primary analytical responsibility of the analyst, other than holdings in diversified collective investment schemes.[46]

Furthermore, an employee is prohibited from participating in or otherwise influencing the determination of a credit rating of any particular rated entity if this employee or any person closely associated with them:

> a) owns financial instruments of the rated entity, other than holdings in diversified collective investment schemes; b) owns financial instruments

44 Commission of the European Communities, 'Proposals for a Regulation of the European and of the Council amending Regulation (EC) No 1060/2009 on credit rating agencies' (COM 2011 747 final 15 Nov 2011) 26 <http://ec.europa.eu/internal_market/securities/docs/agencies/COM_2011_747_en.pdf> accessed 27 August 2013.

45 Regulation (EU) No 462/2013 of the European Parliament and of the Council amending Regulation (EC) No 1060/2009 on credit rating agencies (2013) OJ L 146.

46 Ibid., 37.

of any entity related to a rated entity, the ownership of which may cause or may be generally perceived as causing a conflict of interest, other than holdings in diversified collective investment schemes; c) has had a recent employment or other business relationship or any other relationship with the rated entity that may cause or may be generally perceived as causing a conflict of interest.[47]

The CRA regulation further requires CRAs to identify and eliminate or, where appropriate, manage and disclose any actual or potential conflicts of interest that may influence the analyses and judgments of those analysts who participate in determining a credit rating as well as persons approving credit ratings.[48] Disclosure of the general nature of its compensation arrangements is also mandatory.[49]

4.4 *Comparisons*

Both the US and EU regulations embrace detailed provisions pertaining to disclosure and transparency, but the disclosures required by the EU CRA Regulation are more far-reaching than those required by the US Rating Agency Reform Act.[50] Both require, among other things, the disclosure of conflicts of interest, organizational structure, codes of conduct, a list of the largest twenty clients by revenue, and methodologies.[51] The EU CRA Regulation additionally requires disclosure of the general nature of compensation arrangements, material modifications made to systems, resources and procedures, a list of all ancillary services provided by the CRA, as well as disclosure of various policies.[52] 'While perhaps burdensome, these added disclosures do not create any specific hurdles for CRAs' because the 'revised IOSCO Code of Conduct already recommends CRAs make many of these disclosures.'[53] The US regulation also requires CRAs to maintain records associated with many of these items.[54]

---

47 Ibid.

48 Ibid., 36.

49 Ibid., 40.

50 Charles (n. 2) 439.

51 See Regulation (EC) No 1060/2009 (n. 45) annex I, § E(I)(5); 15 USC. § 78o-7(a)(1)(B)(iii) (2006).

52 Regulation (EC) on credit rating agencies (n. 45) annex I, § E(I)(4).

53 Charles (n. 2) 439. Also see IOSCO, Code of Conduct Fundamentals for Credit Rating Agencies 2008, 2.8, 3.3, 3.9 and 3.10.

54 For details, see 17 CFR § 240.17g-2(a) (2009).

5 Some Critiques on Present National and International Regimes

5.1 *Critiques to the Reputational View*

The reputational view fails in three aspects. First, due to the oligopolistic market structure of the ratings industry, the impact of the disciplining force of market competition is limited.[55] Concerns for reputation only slightly influence CRAs' conduct because reputation is assessed mainly in relation to competitors; this means that the performance of a CRA in relation to other CRAs accounts for their reputation.[56] Such a structure offers incentives for CRAs to adjust their rating to the ratings of other major CRAs and thus, to undermine the control function of market discipline.[57] Second, it is unclear whether the market is or has been particularly sensitive to any ratings agency capture by issuers or to the rating agencies' failure to issue accurate ratings.[58] The prerequisite for the market to launch any kind of disciplinary action is to fully realize how inferior a CRA's performance is before the market reacts in any type of punitive fashion.[59] Given the difficulty of assessing whether or not a particular credit rating agency is truly biased or not, the sensitivity of the market may be extremely low.[60] Third, economists have pointed out that:

> The premiums that reputable firms earn also serve a crucial role in inducing such sellers to maintain their reputations. Without premiums for high-quality items, sellers would find that a fly-by-night strategy of quality reduction would be profit maximizing. The reason is that, in markets with reputations, sellers can always increase profits in the short-run by reducing the quality of their products. After all, quality reductions will yield immediate cost savings, while the adverse effect on reputation will arise only in the longer run. Since positive profits can be earned via the fly-by-night strategy, it would always dominate, unless positive profits could also be earned via the faithful strategy of quality maintenance.[61]

---

55 Andreas Kruck, *Private Ratings, Public Regulations: Credit Rating Agencies and global Financial Governance* (Palgrave Macmillan 2011) 76.

56 Ibid.

57 Ibid.

58 Timothy E. Lynch, 'Deeply and Persistently Conflicted: Credit Rating Agencies in the Current Regulatory Environment' (2009) 59 CWRLR 227, 253.

59 Ibid.

60 Ibid.

61 Carl Shapiro, 'Premiums for High Quality Products as Returns to Reputations' (1983) 98 Q J ECON 659, 660.

5.2 *Disclosure-Based Approach is Insufficient to Resolve Conflicts of Interest*

Empirical studies suggest that when CRAs are dominated by brand names, competing entities in the industry may not be able to effectively signal the quality of their ratings by disclosing past performance information in the form of large volumes of non-standardized data.[62] Since such disclosures require extensive processing before being usable as a diagnostic tool for assessing and comparing the quality of different producers, it seems unlikely to alter the choice makers' tendency to use brand names as the heuristic model for inferring the quality of competing brands.[63] Therefore, even though global regulations unanimously require CRAs to disclose their potential conflicts of interest, the behavior of both investors and CRAs is difficult to change.

In addition, the presumption of disclosure-based regulation is that free market forces, particularly the risk of losing money, will encourage prudent investors to perform their own due diligence before they buy shares or interests in certain financial products. In this sense:

> While this assumption is often true during rigorous economic conditions when investors are skeptical about potential profits and naturally adverse to risk, it often does not apply during a prolonged boom economy when free market forces are less influential and investors blindly ride market momentum and forgo due diligence procedures.[64]

Moreover, rating-dependent regulations might lessen regulators' incentive to monitor a CRA, including its inherent conflicts of interest, and are likely to mislead investors through a mirage that the rating represents the guarantee of the government.[65] Because CRA ratings are incorporated into financial regulations and into private contracts and investor guidelines, this could create a source of demand for ratings that is not tied directly to their quality: for example, an issuer may demand a rating because investors need the rating to fulfill regulatory or other requirements, even if neither party believes that the rating

62 Lynn Bai, 'The Performance Disclosures of Credit Rating Agencies: Are They Effective Reputational Sanctions?' (2010) 7 NYUJLB 47, 95.

63 Ibid.

64 F. Phillip Hosp, 'Problems and Reforms in Mortgage-Backed Securities: Handicapping the Credit Rating Agencies' (2010) 79 MSLJ 531, 567.

65 European Commission, 'Public Consultation on Credit Rating Agencies' (5 November 2010) 5–8 <http://ec.europa.eu/internal_market/consultations/docs/2010/cra/cpaper_en.pdf> accessed 27 August 2013.

is a high-quality assessment of creditworthiness.[66] Because financial market regulators on their own have limited ability to collect and process the necessary information to access the credit risk of all borrowers they seek to regulate, public regulators have chosen to delegate these tasks to the CRAs.[67] Such practices are prevalent on both national and international levels.[68] The relationship between public regulators and CRAs is supposed to be a principal-agent relationship, but the following situation constantly contradicts this concept: (1) the absence of unequivocal instructions to CRAs to perform risk assessments on behalf of financial regulators; (2) the fact that public regulators do not create a new entity to perform this duty, (3) the fact that regulators simply rely on preexisting actors (CRAs) and rating processes.[69]

Last, investors are heterogeneous and differ in their abilities to understand and evaluate information.[70] Before an investor is able to adequately discount the value of a rating based on risks posed by conflicts of interest, he or she must make an assessment of the rating's informational value prior to taking the conflict into account.[71] To achieve this goal, an investor must understand the transaction that the agency is rating. This is so because even if the CRA discloses in detail its ratings methodologies and procedures in, this information is meaningless to someone who does not understand the transaction itself.[72] Investors may possess little or no ability to discount the value of ratings despite the disclosure of conflicts, and as a result, investors often fail to scrutinize the

66 Lucchetti (n. 12).

67 Kruck (n. 55) 71.

68 For instances, in the U.S., Rule 3a-7 under the Investment Company Act exempts structured-finance vehicles from the Act as long as the securities that are issued receive one of the four highest ratings from an NRSRO and meet other requirements. In EU, the use of external ratings is explicitly envisaged by the Capital Requirements Directive 48 (EC) relating to the taking up and pursuit of the business of credit institutions (2006) OJ L 177. Moreover, according to Pillar one of Basel II, The credit risk is calculated according to two alternative approaches: the Standardized Approach and the Internal Ratings Based Approach to risk weighting under the Standardized Approach, banks measure credit risk based on external credit assessments provided by external credit assessment institutions such as CRAs and export credit agencies. For details, see Basel Committee on Banking Supervision, 'International Convergence of Capital Measurements and Capital Standards' (June 2006) 12, 19. Also see Aldo Caliari, 'Assessing Global Regulatory Impacts of The US Subprime Mortgage Meltdown: International Banking Supervision and the Regulation of Credit Rating Agencies' (2010) 19 TRNATLCP 145, 154.

69 Kruck (n. 55) 71.

70 Darcy (n. 1) 652.

71 Ibid., 655.

72 Ibid.

informational value of ratings.[73] In fact, the disclosed information containing complex transactions, structures and analytical methods may be too detailed for many investors to understand and assimilate.[74] The recent financial crisis revealed that most investors, including large institutional investors, rely heavily on CRAs because they have only limited expertise to properly perform due diligence on complex investments such as mortgage-backed securities.[75] Since structured transactions are far more complex than traditional corporate securities, and structured finance products have become even more complex over time, perhaps the core problem lies in investors' ability to understand the underlying structured transactions, rather than their failure to apprehend the full risk of the issuer pays conflict.[76]

6 The Appropriate Role of CRAs in the Capital Market

Because the disclosure-based approach may encounter some impediments in regulating conflicts of interest, this chapter argues that other supplemental methods must be introduced to address this issue in accordance with the appropriate role of CRAs in the capital market.

CRAs are private financial service firms that estimate the credit-worthiness of borrowers or financial instruments.[77] By rating a wide range of different borrowers with the same scale and then publishing these risk assessments, they have established an important standard for credit risk.[78] Therefore, the criteria CRAs use to evaluate creditworthiness are in effect access rules for financial markets—a high-quality credit rating will allow for unhindered access to the most liquid capital markets, and vice versa.[79] The rating also has an influence on the cost of borrowing, as the interest to be paid will be lowest for holders

73 Ibid., 657.

74 Steven L. Schwarcz, 'Rethinking the Disclosure Paradigm in a World of Complexity' (2004) U ILLLR 1, 5.

75 Hosp (n. 64) 567.

76 Darcy (n. 1) 655.

77 Kruck (n. 55) 23.

78 Dieter Kerwer, (2001) 'Standardising as Governance: The Case of Credit Rating Agencies' 3 <http://ssrn.com/abstract=269311> accessed 27 August 2013.

79 Dieter Kerwer, 'Holding Global Regulators Accountable: The Case of Credit Rating Agencies' (2005) 4 <http://www.polwiss.edu.tum.de/fileadmin/tueds03/www/Publikationen/Kerwer/Kerwer_2005_-_Holding_global_regulators_accountable_-_Rating.pdf> accessed 27 August 2013.

of the highest rating.[80] Thus, a further component of CRAs is that their ratings have in fact become compulsory.[81] Although in principle, no one is forced to be rated by CRAs, in reality, it has become rather difficult to escape their influence.[82] In addition, private credit ratings have been employed to make the regulation of financial market risk more detectable.[83] CRAs are coercive regulators to the extent that they have become instrumental in public regulation.[84]

Given that the regulatory use of CRAs transforms them into quasi-public regulators, accountability is the first and foremost requirement pertaining to their role. Unfortunately, the financial crisis has proven that there appears to be an accountability gap, which constitutes an imbalance between the power held by CRAs and the process by which they are held responsible.[85] This gap is difficult to close merely through disclosure or segregation of consulting and rating services. Some suggest that CRAs' regulatory role should be eliminated.[86] Under such a plan, reliance on CRA ratings would be reduced, and CRAs would play a lesser role in regulating the market place.[87] While such a plan paves an appropriate course, the problem is that there is no agency or body to fill the regulatory void that the removal of the regulatory role of CRAs would result.[88] Hence, instead of adopting the relatively radical approach of removing CRAs from their regulatory role, the following proposal offers two possible additions to the regulatory framework that will help to restore the integrity of the financial marketplace in the US.

7 Proposals for Regulatory Reform

7.1 *Subjecting CRAs to Civil Liabilities*

In order to increase the accountability of the rating agencies and, theoretically, the quality of their work, one possibility is to allow for increased litigation and

---

80 Timothy J. Sinclair, *The New Masters of Capital: American Bond Rating Agencies and the Politics of Creditworthiness* (Cornell university Press 2005) 5.

81 Kerwer (n. 79) 4.

82 Ibid.

83 The World Bank, 'Credit Rating Agencies: No Easy Regulatory Solution' (2009) 2 <http://rru.worldbank.org/documents/CrisisResponse/Note8.pdf> accessed 27 August 2013.

84 Kerwer (n. 79) 4.

85 Rousseau (n. 7) 643.

86 The World Bank (n. 83) 6.

87 Ibid.

88 Joseph DeCampo, 'Credit Rating Agencies' (2009) 29 RBNKFL 69, 77.

legal liability as a check against the rating agencies' power.[89] Litigation, or at least the potential threat of litigation, would incentivize rating agencies to review ratings more vigorously.[90] Critics of this proposal point out that the disadvantages of increased liability include the potential for less accurate ratings, increases in the cost of services, and disproportionate remedies for liability.[91] They also argue that because it is difficult to determine when exactly a rating is 'bad' and therefore, difficult to know when a CRAs' determination warrants punishment, civil liability requires substantial government oversight, particularly in devising performance standards.[92]

Nonetheless, the issue of the lack of standards can be addressed through the introduction of a specific provision addressing the civil liability of credit rating agencies in the CRA regulations. Accordingly, CRAs could be held liable if they intentionally or negligently violate the provisions of the CRA regulations, leading to an incorrect rating upon which investors have based investment decisions.[93] Section 933a of the Dodd-Frank Act of the US provides a standard of review for private lawsuits against CRAs—the plaintiff must only plead that the agency knowingly or recklessly failed to conduct a reasonable investigation of factual elements of a rated security or verification of such elements.[94] Related regulation should also address the following issues: (1) whether the provision imposing civil liability applies only to a credit rating agency giving a higher than appropriate rating to a security in which an investor chose to invest, or if such a provision should also cover situations in which a credit rating agency has given a lower than appropriate rating and the investor chose not to invest; and (2) whether unsolicited ratings should be included as potential liabilities under the umbrella CRAs' fraudulent conduct, in that such ratings, if incorrect, may cause damage to investors who relied on them.[95]

However, a potential obstacle to the imposition of civil liabilities on CRAs in the US is the degree to which the Supreme Court's First Amendment precedent affects investor lawsuits against CRAs.[96] The US Supreme Court excused publishers from liability for defamation claims absent a showing of 'actual malice'.

89 Caitlin M. Mulligan, 'From AAA to F: How the Credit Rating Agencies Failed America and What can be done to Protect Investors' (2009) 50 BCLR 1275, 1297.

90 Ibid.

91 John C. Coffee, *Gatekeepers: The Professions and Corporate Governance* (OUP 2006) 303.

92 Milosz Gudzowski, 'Mortgage Credit Ratings and the Financial Crisis: the Need for a State-Run Mortgage Security Credit Rating Agency' (2010) 2010 CLMBLR 245, 280.

93 EC Consultation (n. 65) 24.

94 Dodd-Frank Act 2010 (n. 39) Section 933(b).

95 EC Consultation (n. 65) 24.

96 Murphy (n. 9) 767.

To reach this decision, the court reasoned that protection by means of such a standard for liability was necessary to encourage reporting on matters of public concern.[97] Commentators have argued that CRAs are not simply giving their opinion about the creditworthiness of an offering, but, rather, are helping to design and sell a financial product.[98] This role is more appropriately viewed through the lens of the professional-client-speech doctrine than as a contribution to the marketplace of ideas.[99] In *In re Fitch, Inc. v. UBS PaineWebber, Inc.*,[100] the Federal Court of Appeals for the Second Circuit found that the rating agency (Fitch) took an active role in the planning of the transactions in cause, a role that is inconsistent with traditional journalism.[101] The court distinguished between the role of credit rating agencies and other journalists based on two compelling characteristics: first, credit rating agencies typically issue credit ratings only when they are hired and paid by an issuer; and second, the role of a credit rating agency is far more active than that of a reporter.[102] Thus, if a credit rating agency plays an active role in structuring the deal, courts should recognize the credit rating agency's speech for what it is—professional speech—and deny the credit rating agency the protection of the actual malice standard.[103] Advocates further assert that

> allowing [CRAs] to be held to the traditional standards of liability for the claims asserted against them—primarily negligence, negligent misrepresentation, and fraud—advances the government's interest in maintaining an effective financial market. Conversely, if [CRAs] receive the heightened protection of the actual malice standard, the interest in securing a stable economy becomes vulnerable.[104]

7.2 *Performance-Based Sanctions*

Phillip Hosp proposed a handicapping system that 'ties the past performance of a rating agency with the regulatory benefits derived from its credit rating.'[105] Handicapping the CRAs resembles golf handicaps, in which a numerical

---

97 *New York Times Co v Sullivan*, 376 US 254, 279–280 (1964).

98 Jonathan W. Heggen, 'Not Always the World's Shortest Editorial: Why Credit-Rating-Agency Speech Is Sometimes Professional Speech' (2011) 96 IALR 1745, 1764.

99 Ibid.

100 *In re Fitch Inc v UBS PaineWebber Inc*, 330 F.3d 104 (2003).

101 Ibid., 110.

102 Ibid., 109–110.

103 Ibid., 1766.

104 Ibid., 773.

105 Hosp (n. 64) 570.

advantage is given or a disadvantage imposed accounts for past performance.[106] Hosp further elaborated that:

> [t]he purpose of the handicap is to level the playing field between golfers of different skill levels. It accomplishes this by giving less skilled golfers a scoring advantage over their competitors. The size of the advantage is determined by the difference between the two golfers' playing ability. If the difference of the average scores between the two golfers is five strokes, then the handicapping system will subtract five shots from the lesser player's score ... The value of golf's handicapping system to the credit rating industry lies in its ability to predict each golfer's future performance based on their past performance. The system effectively alters the value of each stroke depending on each player's ability.[107]

In applying this to credit ratings, Hosp suggested the regulator to create CRA handicaps in order to forecast the likelihood of an issuer's rating. The information that is currently required to be disclosed is the main indicator used to calculate the future performance of a CRA's rating.[108] Such information includes the accuracy of the CRA's past ratings, the CRA's accuracy in rating similar types of debt or securities, and the timeliness of its downgrades.[109] After obtaining a CRA's handicap through the preceding calculation, the regulator would incorporate the handicap into its regulatory structure by adjusting the CRA's credit ratings in conformity with the handicap.[110] That means, when an issuer contracts with a CRA to rate one of its mortgage-backed securities (hereinafter the MBS), after conducting the rating process, the CRA issues an AA credit rating on the security's senior tranche.[111] Then, the handicapping system comes into play. The initial AA rating would be called the 'gross rating' (ie, unadjusted rating).[112] After the CRA issues the gross rating, the [regulator] would apply that CRA's handicap to determine the 'net rating' (ie, adjusted rating). If such CRA has a negative track record in rating other MBSs or has delay in downgrading its ratings, the handicap could potentially reduce the gross rating from AA to A.[113]

106 Ibid.

107 Ibid., 570.

108 Ibid.

109 Ibid.

110 Ibid.

111 Ibid., 570–71.

112 Ibid., 571.

113 Ibid.

Handicapping credit ratings would allow investors to compare CRAs more accurately than they now can under the disclosure-based approach, because market participants would be able to understand the handicaps, which are represented by letters or numbers that easily reflect the competence of a CRA—much like the ratings themselves.[114] Unlike disclosure requirements, under the handicapping system, disclosure of rating methodologies is not necessary. This would prevent CRAs from pirating models and mathematical formulas developed by other CRAs, which would, in turn, encourage CRAs to invest in those models and formulas.[115] This system would also 'incentivize CRAs to accurately measure risks of particular investments, which would counterbalance any conflicts of interest within the issuer-paid business model.'[116] In other words, this proposal would impose a tangible cost to the CRAs in the form of lost profits that would counterbalance any gains derived from issuing inflated ratings.[117] Furthermore, with separate handicaps for different types of securities, the regulator would level the playing field among small CRAs and large CRAs.[118] The best-case scenario would be that smaller CRAs could outperform larger CRAs if they develop superior modeling techniques by concentrating on a particular field within the financial system.[119]

This chapter argues that the handicapping system based on the performance statistics invokes a sanction to deter conflicts of interest in the credit rating industry. Such system stimulates rating agencies' incentive to engage in a degree of self-regulation and to scrutinize new offerings more closely and to downgrade in a more proactive manner.

Such a system would also benefit new players entering the credit rating industry build a track record that enables them to compete with established agencies. It is effective in fostering competition so as to gradually change the oligopolistic market structure of the ratings industry.

8 Concluding Remarks

Credit ratings are necessary for risk-sensitive regulation and for reducing information asymmetries and principal-agent problems in financial markets.

114 Ibid., 572.

115 Ibid., 571.

116 Ibid.

117 Darcy (n. 1) 663.

118 Hosp (n. 64) 574.

119 Ibid.

Unfortunately, the 2007 financial crisis has revealed that the accountability gap of CRAs derived from the conflict of interest incurred by the CRAs' fee structure, issuer-paid-fees. While current global regulations have adopted the disclosure-based approach to mitigate the problem, this approach is not fully effective because of the existence of widespread rating-dependant financial regulations and market participants' lack of expertise in interpreting the content of disclosed information. Since CRAs have been recognized as quasi-public regulators in the capital market, it is essential as well as urgent to institute further measures to ensure and facilitate the accountability of CRAs. This chapter advocates that civil liability and performance-based sanctions in collaboration with the disclosure-based method are two feasible alternatives to counter these conflicts of interest.

Despite recent regulatory reforms and proposals for further improvements on the supervision of CRAs, rating has its limitations. To further monitor CRAs, it is always the regulator's duty to educate investors on the nature and function of credit ratings and their limitation, and to inform investors that ratings are not the sole factor in investment decisions.[120] Through such education, users of rating information, particularly investors, will be equipped with knowledge to oversee the performance of the CRAs so as to further the market discipline which may serve as an supplement for the performance sanction. In addition, improving investors' understanding of their rights against CRAs will increase their willingness and capability to pursue CRAs' liability once the damages occurs due to the false rating.

120 Piero Cinquegrana, 'The Reform of the Credit Rating Agencies: A Comparative Perspective' ECMI Policy Brief No 12/ February 2009, 10 <http://www.ceps.eu/ceps/download/3805> accessed 27 August 2013.

PART TWO

Confronting Environmental Challenges

CHAPTER 3

Protected Areas under the Convention on Biological Diversity in International Investment Law: Conflicts and Solutions

Matthäus Fink

1 Introduction

The tension between International Investment Law (IIL) and the protection of the environment has gained attention both in practice[1] and in academia.[2] One tool of environmental protection is the designation of protected areas (PAS). In itself a traditional measure for protection of the environment,[3] PAS

1 See for example: *Santa Elena v Costa Rica*, ICSID Case No ARB/96/1 (17 February 2000), 39 ILM 317 (*Santa Elena v Costa Rica*); *Tecmed v United States of Mexico*, ICSID Case No ARB(AF)/00/2 (29 May 2003); *Metalclad v United States of Mexico*, ICSID Case No ARB(AF)/97/1 (30 August 2000) (*Metalclad v Mexico*); *Methanex v United States of America*, UNCITRAL (9 August 2005), 44 ILM 1345; *Chematura v Canada*, PCA (2 August 2010); *Vattenfall v Germany*, ICSID Case No ARB/09/6 (registered 17 April 2009, settled via mutual agreement 11 March 2011). Recently: *Marion Unglaube v Republic of Costa Rica*, ICSID Case No ARB/08/1, Award 16 May 2012 & *Reinhard Hans Unglaube v Republic of Costa Rica*, ICSID Case No ARB/09/20, Award 16 May 2012 (*Unglaube v Costa Rica*). Unless otherwise indicated, all awards are available at <www.italaw.com> last accessed 27 August 2013.

2 T. Waelde and A. Kolo, 'Environmental Regulation, Investment Protection and 'Regulatory Taking' in International Law' (2001) 50 ICLQ 811; O. Fauchald, 'International Investment Law and Environmental Protection' (2006) 17 YBIEL 3; M.-C. Cordonier-Segger, M. Gehring and A. Newcombe (eds), *Sustainable development in world investment law* (Wolters Kluwer 2010); Kyla Tienhaara, *The Expropriation of Environmental Governance: Protecting Foreign Investors at the Expense of Public Policy* (CUP 2009); Jorge Viñuales, 'Foreign investment and the environment in international law: an ambiguous relationship' (2010) 80 BYBIL 244.

3 For historical illustrations, see Alexander Gillespie, *Protected Areas and International Environmental Law* (Nijhoff 2007) 7–9; Nele Matz, 'Protected Areas in International Nature Conservation Law: Can States Obtain Compensation for their Establishment?' (2003) 63 ZaöRV 693, 699–700.

 | DOI 10.1163/9789004270190_004

are envisaged *inter alia* in the Convention on Biological Diversity[4] (CBD).[5] The establishment of PAs can potentially cause conflicts with obligations under IIL. States have concluded treaties containing protections of foreign investors.[6] These treaties guarantee certain protection standards, such as 'fair and equitable treatment' or 'no expropriation, without compensation'.[7] This system

4 Convention on Biological Diversity (adopted 11–22 May 1992, entered into force 29 December 1993) 1760 UNTS 79 (CBD). The CBD has 193 parties. Two protocols were established, which do not have direct relevance in the present context: Cartagena Protocol on Biosafety to the Convention on Biological Diversity (adopted 29 January 2000, entered into force 11 September 2003) 2226 UNTS 208 (Cartagena Protocol); Nagoya Protocol on Access to Genetic Resources and the Fair and Equitable Sharing of Benefits Arising from their Utilization to the Convention on Biological Diversity (adopted 29 October 2010, open for signature until 1 February 2012) UN Doc UNEP/CBD/COP/DEC/X/1 (Nagoya Protocol).

5 Due to space limitations, this chapter addresses only PAs under the CBD (n. 4). PAs are further enshrined in the following treaties: Convention on the Conservation of European Wildlife and Natural Habitats (open for signature 19 September 1979, entered into force 1 June 1981) 1284 UNTS 210; Convention on the Conservation of Migratory Species of Wild Animals (adopted 23 June 1979, entered into force 1 November 1983) 1651 UNTS 333; Convention on wetlands of international importance especially as waterfowl habitat (adopted 2 February 1971, entered into force December 1975) 996 UNTS 245. For an overview see Gillespie (n. 3) 9–25. PAs are also considered under the Climate Regime; United Nations Framework Convention on Climate Change (adopted 9 May 1992, entered into force 21 March 1994) 1771 UNTS 107. See therefore: Gillespie (n. 3) 9–12, 199–201. Finally, PAs are also enshrined in European Union Law. But, as these instruments enjoy a different legal status as compared to international law, they are excluded in this chapter. Also the UNESCO World Heritage Convention is not part of the present analysis, as it does not include provisions on PAs as such.

6 According to the *World Investment Report 2011* states have concluded 2807 bilateral investment treaties and 308 other investment treaties. The latter includes free trade agreements which contain investment provisions. See UNCTAD, *World Investment Report 2011* (2011) 100.

7 This contribution deals only with these two protection standards. Other protection clauses such as 'full protection and security', 'most-favoured nation' and 'non-discrimination', which are typically found in international investment agreements (IIA), will not be considered due to space limitations. Although they may differ on specific points, they generally have a very similar object and purpose (see Rudolf Dolzer and Christoph Schreuer, *Principles of International Investment Law* (OUP 2008) 21. This contribution will refer to some IIAs and model bilateral investment treaties: North American Free Trade Agreement (adopted 17 December 1992, entered into force 1 January 1994) 32 ILM 605 (1993) (NAFTA); Dominican Republic-Central American Free Trade Agreement (adopted 5 August 2004, entered into force January 2006) available at <http://www.ustr.gov/trade-agreements/free-trade-agreements/cafta-dr-dominican-republic-central-america-fta/final-text> accessed 27 August 2013 (CAFTA-DR); Energy Charter Treaty (adopted 17 December 1994, entered into force April 1998) 2080 UNTS 100 (ECT); Model BIT Germany (2008); Model BIT USA (2012); Model BIT Canada (2004); Model BIT France (2006). All Model BITs are available at <www.italaw.com> accessed 27 August 2013.

of investment protection has been criticized for its deficient consideration of public purposes and too investor-friendly arbitration awards.[8]

The mentioned tension and the questions in this contribution can be illustrated referring to the recent case *Unglaube v. Costa Rica*.[9] German investors purchased land property at the north-west coast of Costa Rica with direct access to the beach in 1988. They developed slots for the construction of holiday houses and small hotels. As the beach is one of the rare nesting spots for the endangered leatherback turtles, Costa Rica established a marine PA in 1995, which extends 125m inlands including the property of the investors.[10] However, Costa Rica failed until the release of the Award in May 2012 to formally expropriate and compensate the investors.[11] Consequently the investors were indeed still the owners of the property, but could not make use of it, because Costa Rican authorities stopped issuing permits and the further development of the respective area. The tribunal decided that these actions of Costa Rica constituted a de-facto expropriation and awarded the investors compensation.[12] Regrettably neither the Respondent State nor the tribunal referred to Article 8 CBD. Germany and Costa Rica are both parties to the CBD and Costa Rica could have argued that it designated the PA for fulfilling its obligations under Article 8 CBD.[13] Also in other investment disputes aroused the question of violations of investment protection standards through the designation or the impact of PAs.[14]

---

8 See for example: Gus van Harten, David Schneiderman *and others*, 'Public statement on the international investment regime' (31 August 2010) available at <http://www.osgoode.yorku.ca/public_statement> accessed 15 August 2013. See for a recent critic by NGO's: Seattle to Brussels Network & Network for Justice in Global Investment, 'Call for an alternative investment model' (November 2011) available at <www.s2bnetwork.org/fileadmin/dateien/downloads/Statement-ENG.pdf> accessed 27 August 2013. For a recent critic with regard to investment protection clauses within the planed Trans-Pacific Partnership agreement, see E Evatt and others, 'An Open Letter from Lawyers to the Negotiators of the Trans-Pacific Partnership Urging the Rejection of Investor-State Dispute Settlement' (8 May 2012) available at <http://canadians.org/trade/documents/TPP-Jurists-letter-0512.pdf> accessed 27 August 2013. Compare, critical: M. Sornarajah, 'Mutations of Neo-Liberalism in International Investment Law' (2011) 3 TL&D 203.

9 *Unlgaube v Costa Rica* (n. 1).

10 Ibid. 37ff. Only the principal facts of the case were outlined for illustration purposes.

11 Ibid., 316.

12 Ibids 202–223 and 318, 325 and 332.

13 It is worthy to note that the CBD (n. 4) was binding upon both States since August 1994. The investment treaty between the two States entered into force in April 1998.

14 *Empresas Lucchetti, SA and Lucchetti Peru, SA v The Republic of Peru*, ICSID Case No ARB/03/4 (7 February 2005), which dealt with a dispute concerning a pasta factory near close to an PAs established under the Ramsar convention, but the tribunal declined

The overall question in the contribution is whether, and to what extent, the law and policy of PAs for biodiversity protection can be taken into account in IIL, as connected to the problem of conflicts between the two regimes of international law.[15] The premise of this analysis is that States are parties to one investment treaty as well as to the CBD. On the one hand, they have agreed in the CBD to protect biological diversity, while on the other hand, they are obliged to comply with certain investment protection standards. This chapter addresses conflicts of treaty norms and explores possible solutions in the relationship between the two regimes. In the following section, the framework of PAs under the CBD will be set out. Then, the exiting conflicts with protection standards of IIL will be addressed. This raises the question of possible solutions for considering PAs in IIL, which is the main focus of this contribution. The outlook explores alternative avenues to deal with the described conflicts before a final conclusion is set out.

2 Protected Areas for the Protection of Biodiversity

2.1 *The Legal Framework of PAs*

The CBD prescribes in Article 8 *in situ* conservation as a tool for the protection of biodiversity, pursuant to which States shall establish—as far as possible and appropriate—a system of PAs.[16] The notion of PAs is defined in Article 2 of the

jurisdiction. Further *Santa Elena v Costa Rica* (n. 1) where parties were in dispute about the amount of compensation for a designation of a PA, but the home state of the investors—United States of America—was and still is not party to the CBD (n. 4). The same counts for *Metalclad v Mexico* where Mexico stopped a waste factory *inter alia* through an ecological reserve, *Metalclad v Mexico* (n. 1) paras 69, 97–98, 109–111.

15 The contribution does not deal with issues of investment law in CBD (n. 4) law, because of the institutional mechanisms of arbitration in the investment regime. Furthermore the contribution focuses on treaty law and excludes customary law, because of the marginal role of the latter in the present context. The contribution adopts the notion of 'regime' as used by the International Law Commission (ILC) in its fragmentation report: 'New types of specialized law do not emerge accidentally but seek to respond to new technical and functional requirements. (...) Each rule-complex or 'regime' comes with its own principles, its own form of expertise and its own 'ethos', not necessarily identical to the ethos of neighbouring specialization.'; ILC, *Fragmentation of International Law: Difficulties arising from the Diversification and Expansion of International Law—Report of the Study Group of the International Law Commission* (finalized by Martti Koskenniemi 2006 UN Doc A/CN/4/L682, 14) para. 15.

16 The relevant passages of art 8 of the CBD (n 4): 'Each Contracting Party shall, as far as possible and as appropriate: (a) Establish a system of protected areas (...); (b) Develop,

CBD as 'a geographically defined area which is designated or regulated and managed to achieve specific conservation objectives'.[17] This wide definition covers all categories of protected areas established by the International Union for Conservation of Nature (IUCN). IUCN is a non-state international environmental organization and supports international environment protection efforts. It played a crucial role preparing drafts of the CBD.[18] The IUCN developed a system of categories for PAs depending on the degree of conservation and permitted industrial and agricultural use,[19] which is not binding for States, but instead serves as an international parameter for classifying PAs.

Annex I of the CBD, which deals with identification and monitoring, specifies in its Article 1 when ecosystems and habitats should be identified for protection. Key factors are high biodiversity, a large number of threatened species, as well as social, economic and cultural importance. Under a systematic interpretation,[20] PAs are thereby concretized. The *chapeau* of Article 8 of the CBD emphasizes State Parties′ leeway regarding PAs as the designation of PAs has to be carried out 'as far as possible' and 'as appropriate'. Thus, *Klemm* concludes that '[t]he Parties are therefore free to protect whatever areas they choose'.[21] As there are no binding requirements and conditions in the CBD and the Annex when a State has to establish a PA, this conclusion appears convincing. Furthermore the CBD does not create an organ with the power to determine where, when and how PAs should be designated. However, the obligation

---

where necessary, guidelines for the selection, establishment and management of protected areas (…); (c) Regulate (…) biological resources important for the conservation of biological diversity (…), with a view to ensuring their conservation and sustainable use; (d) Promote the protection of ecosystems, natural habitats and the maintenance of viable populations of species in natural surroundings; (…) (f) Rehabilitate and restore degraded ecosystems (…).'

17 CBD (n. 4) art. 2.

18 Philippe Sands and others, *Principles of International Environmental Law* (CUP 2012) 88.

19 For an overview, see Alexander Gillespie, 'Defining Internationally Protected Areas' (2008) 11 J Int Wildl Law Pol 240; Nigel Dudley and Sue Stolten (eds), *Defining Protected Areas: An international conference in Almeria, Spain* (IUCN 2008) 46–77.

20 Art. 31 (1), (2) Vienna Convention Law of Treaties (adopted 23 May 1969, entered into force 27 January 1980) 1155 UNTS 331 (VCLT). Art. 31 (2) VCLT sets out that 'Annexes' are part of a systematic interpretation. See Mark Villiger, *Commentary on the 1969 Vienna Convention on the Law of Treaties* (Nijhoff 2009) 427, 10.

21 Cyrille de Klemm, *Biological diversity conservation and the law: legal mechanisms for conserving species and ecosystems* (IUCN—Gland 1993) 162. For the general wide discretion of CBD (n. 4) rules, see Désirée McGraw, 'The CBD—Key Characteristics and Implications for Implementation' (2002) 11 RECIEL 17, 18–23; Sam Johnson, 'The Convention on Biological Diversity: The Next Phase' (1997) 6 RECIEL 219.

of member States to establish a system of PAs and to protect certain ecosystems and habitats remains. Consequently, others point out that Article 8 of the CBD contains the 'main set of obligations to conserve biological diversity'.[22] *Wolfrum* acknowledges the fundamental importance of PAs for the purposes of the CBD, but points out that States have some discretion.[23] *Beyerlin* also speaks of 'classical obligations' with regard to Article 8 of the CBD.[24] Taking into account the purpose of the convention—to conserve biological diversity (Article 1 of the CBD)—Article 8 of the CBD is more than a programmatic norm and obliges States to establish PAs.[25] Therefore, Article 8 of the CBD contains a legal obligation of member States concerning PAs, with a leeway for implementation.

A concretization of Article 8 of the CBD occurs through decisions of the Conference of the Parties (COP) of the CBD.[26] COP decisions can be used for the interpretation of Article 8 of the CBD as a form of subsequent practice.[27]

22 Lyle Glowka and others, *A guide to the convention on biological diversity* (IUCN—Gland 1994) 39. Positive also: Elisa Morgera & Elsa Tsioumani, 'Yesterday, Today, and Tomorrow: Looking Afresh at the Convention on Biological Diversity' (2011) 21 Yearbook of International Environmental Law 3–40.

23 Rüdiger Wolfrum, 'The Protection and Management of Biological Diversity' in F. Morrison & R. Wolfrum (eds), *International, Regional and National Environmental Law* (Kluwer 2000) 355, 358, fn. 13 and 359.

24 Ulrich Beyerlin, 'Erhaltung und nachhaltige Nutzung' als Grundkonzept der Biodiversitätskonvention' in N. Wolf and W. Köck (eds), *10 Jahre Übereinkommen über die biologische Vielfalt—Eine Zwischenbilanz* (Nomos 2004) 55, 63. In this direction also: Catherine Tinker, 'A "New Breed" of Treaty: The United Nations Convention on Biological Diversity' (1995) 13 Pace Envtl. L. Rev 191, 202–204.

25 Furthermore, the bullet point 9 of the Preamble highlights the fundamental meaning of *in-situ* conservation: '(…) Noting further that the fundamental requirement for the conservation of biological diversity is the in-situ conservation of ecosystems and natural habitats and the maintenance and recovery of viable populations of species in their natural surroundings, (…)'.

26 Art. 23 I CBD (n. 4) establishes the COP and Article 23 IV i) CBD empowers it to '(c)onsider and undertake any additional action' for the achievement of the purposes of the CBD. Furthermore, the COP can adopt amendments and annexes to the CBD (see Arts. 29 and 30 CBD). Such instruments must in any event be subsequently ratified by States Parties. For an evaluation of the COP 2010, see Stuart Harrop, "Living In Harmony With Nature"? Outcomes of the 2010 Nagoya Conference of the Convention on Biological Diversity' (2011) 23 J Environmental Law 117; Morgera & Tsioumani (n. 22).

27 Art. 31 (3) b) VCLT. For the use of COP decisions as subsequent practice, see Jutta Brunée, 'COPing with Consent: Law-Making Under Multilateral Environmental Agreements' (2002) 15 LJIL 1, 31; Geir Ulfstein, 'Treaty Bodies' in D. Bodansky, J. Brunnée and E. Hey (eds), *The Oxford Handbook of International Environmental Law* (OUP 2007) 877, 884;

COP decisions have repeatedly emphasized the role of PAs for the fulfilment of the purposes of the CBD, calling for additional designations of PAs.[28] COPs urged member States to restore endangered ecosystems.[29] In 2004 the COP VII adopted a program for PAs, establishing a working group to support and to review its implementation.[30] The program fosters the role and implementation of PAs. The mentioned criteria of Annex I of the CBD were again highlighted as guidance for the designation of PAs.[31] COP X in 2010 emphasized that States should take into account criteria developed by other international institutions such as the IUCN list of endangered species.[32] The COP decisions thereby clarify the scope of Article 8 of the CBD to some extent, stipulating that a State is at the very minimum obliged to take some sort of positive action if endangered species live in a certain area and biodiversity is at stake. However, a hard law obligation to designate specific PAs is not contained in the CBD.[33]

2.2 *Policy and Programs for PAs*

Indeed, there are several policy initiatives under the CBD and other instruments for PAs. In the working program for PAs the COP VII urged States to '[...] establish or expand protected areas in any large, intact or relatively unfragmented or highly irreplaceable natural areas [...]'.[34] The COP acknowledged the role of PAs for the fulfilment of the 'Millennium Development Goals'.[35] In 2010 the COP X proclaimed the goal to cover 17% of terrestrial areas with

---

Hermann Ott, *Umweltregime im Völkerrecht* (Nomos 1998) 171–200; Morgera & Tsioumani (n. 22).

28 Consideration of Arts. 6 and 8 of the Convention, UNEP/CBD/COP/III/19 (17 November 1995) 11; Implementation of Arts. 6 and 8 of the Convention, UNEP/CBD/COP/III/38 (15 November 1996) 48; Protected areas (Arts. 8 (a) to (e)), UNEP/CBDCOP/DEC/VII/28 (13 April 2004); Protected Areas, UNEP/CBD/COP/DEC/X/31(29 October 2010).

29 Implementation of Arts. 6 and 8 of the Convention, UNEP/CBD/COP/III/38 (15 November 1996) para. 6.

30 Protected areas (Arts. 8 (a) to (e)), UNEP/CBDCOP/DEC/VII/28 (13 April 2004).

31 Ibid., 15.

32 Protected areas (Arts. 8 (a) to (e)), UNEP/CBDCOP/DEC/VII/28 (13 April 2004); Protected Areas, UNEP/CBD/COP/DEC/X/31 (29 October 2010) para. 1 (h).

33 Similar: Wolfrum (n. 23) 355, 358, fn. 13.

34 Protected areas (Arts. 8 (a) to (e)), UNEP/CBDCOP/DEC/VII/28 (13 April 2004) Annex, para. 1.1.2.

35 Protected areas (Arts. 8 (a) to (e)), UNEP/CBDCOP/DEC/VII/28 (13 April 2004) para. 1. See further: Carolina L. Diaz, 'Biodiversity for Sustainable Development: The CBD's Contribution to the MDGs' (2006) 15 RECIEL 30. For the 'Millennium Development Goals' see United Nations Millennium Declaration, UNGA Res. 55/2 'Millennium Declaration' (8 September 2000) GAOR 55th Session Supp. 49 vol 1, 4.

PAs by 2020.[36] The same COP considered the important role of PAs in the fight against climate change and urged States to adopt corresponding measures.[37] Beyond the CBD, PAs are enshrined in several international environmental treaties to protect different ecological values.[38] The IUCN's recent *World Parks Congress*[39] recognized the significant role of PAs for environmental protection and urged States to strengthen efforts for PAs.[40] These policy initiatives are not legally binding,[41] but show that the establishment of PAs is part of the international environmental protection agenda. Furthermore, these initiatives lead to foster the will of States to designate PAs.

2.3 *PAs Serve Community Interests*

In the Preamble of the CBD, Member States 'affirm that the conservation of biological diversity is a common concern of humankind'. The concept of 'common concern of humankind' does not as such entail any specific legal obligations for States[42] as reflected in the acknowledgment of sovereign rights over biological resources in the CBD Preamble. Nonetheless, the concept of

---

36 The Strategic Plan for Biodiversity 2011–2020 and the Aichi Biodiversity Targets, COP 10, Dec X/2 (18–29 October 2010) Target 11. Currently 12,9% of the earth territory are covered by PAs, see <http://www.cbd.int/protected/implementation/>. For an analysis of the Strategic Plan see, Morgera & Tsioumani (n. 22). Critically with regard the Strategic Plan, see Harrop (n. 26).

37 Protected Areas, UNEP/CBD/COP/DEC/X/31 (29 October 2010) paras 14–18.

38 See (n. 4). For the relevance of the concept of sustainable development and PAs and other goods protected by PAs, see Barbara Lausche, *Guidelines for Protected Areas Legislation* (IUCN-Gland 2011) 16–17.

39 The IUCN is the leading organization concerning PAs and establishes a coherent platform for different PAs policies. It organizes the *World Parks Congress* once in a decade. The 5th and latest took place in Durban / South-Africa from 8–17 September in 2003. The next *World Parks Congress* will be held in 2014. For the relationship of IUCN to CBD see above, p. 49.

40 IUCN, *Benefits Beyond Boundaries: Proceedings of the Vth IUCN World Parks Congress* (Gland, Switzerland 2005) 219–223. The Congress elaborated a wide range of recommendations for governments, see ibid. 139–218.

41 *Morgera & Tsioumani* consider the Strategic Plan Biodiversity 2011–2020 and the Aichi Biodiversity Targets of an 'inspirational document', Morgera & Tsioumani (n. 22).

42 Jutta Brunnée, '"Common Interest"—Echoes from an Empty Shell? Some Thoughts on Common Interest and International Environmental Law' (1989) 49 ZaöRV 791, 808; Jutta Brunnée, 'Common Areas, Common Heritage and Common Concern' in D. Bodansky, J. Brunnée and E. Hey (eds), *The Oxford Handbook of International Environmental Law* (OUP 2007) 550, 566; P. Birnie, A. Boyle and C. Redgwell, *International Law & the Environment* (OUP 2009) 130; Frank Biermann, '"Common Concern of Humankind": The Emergence of a New Concept of International Environmental Law' (1996) 34 AVR 426.

'common concern' itself suggests that States are not entirely free with regard to such 'common concerns',[43] as it manifests the character of a community interest.[44] Community interests are understood as interests and values shared across borders which require transnational cooperation.[45] The protection of the environment is considered to be a community interest.[46] Biodiversity can only be protected by common and worldwide efforts; the same applies to the protection of the atmosphere and the climate. PAs are important and efficient tools to achieve these goals. They play a crucial role within the transformation of carbon-dioxide. Rare flora and fauna can find a refugium within PAs. Indeed biodiversity has less of the transboundary character as for example climate issues. However, biodiversity is acknowledged as universal good by the CBD. Thus, the designation of PAs serves not only individual State's interests, but also community interests. The following section will now deal with the question, if there could arise conflicts between Article 8 of the CBD and obligations of International Investment Law.

3 Conflicts with International Investment Law?

3.1 *The Notion of 'Conflict' in International Law*

What does 'conflict' mean? A strict view sees a 'conflict' between two norms of international law only when the compliance with one norm automatically

---

43 Birnie, Boyle and Redgwell ibid. 130; Brunnée ibid. 550, 566.

44 This is supported by various affirmations in the Preamble and the CBD (n. 4) itself (see art. 1 and 2 CBD; points 1, 2, 8, 23 Preamble). For a differentiation of the concept of 'common concern of humankind' from the concepts of 'Common Areas' and 'Common Heritage' see, Brunnée ibid. 550–553, 557, 561, 564.

45 See Bruno Simma, 'From Bilateralism to Community Interest in International Law' (1994) 250 RdC 217, 233, 244; Isabel Feichtner, 'Community Interests' in Rüdiger Wolfrum (ed.) *The Max Planck Encyclopedia of Public International Law* (OUP 2008–) 4 <www.mpepil.com> accessed on 9 December 2011.

46 *Case Concerning the Gabcikovo-Nagymaros Project* (Hungary v Slovakia) (Merits) (1997) ICJ Rep. 136, para. 153; *Case Concerning Pulp Mills on the River Uruguay* (Argentina v Uruguay) (Merits) (2010) ICJ Judgment; Andreas Paulus, *Die internationale Gemeinschaft im Völkerrecht* (Beck 2001) 267, 284; Philippe Sands, *Principles of International Environmental Law* (CUP 2003) 3–5; Alexandre Kiss and Dinah Shelton, *Guide to International Environmental Law* (Brill 2007) 13–14; Thomas Cottier & Sofya Matteotti-Berkutova, 'International environmental law and the evolving concept of common concern of mankind' in T Cottier, O Nartova and S Bigdeli (eds), *International trade regulation and the mitigation of climate change* (CUP 2009) 21, 28.

violates the other norm.[47] This understanding excludes constellations where one norm grants States a certain margin, while the other norm does not provide discretion. Thus States mostly comply with the latter norm. Perpetuation of this could however lead to the ineffectiveness of the other norm,[48] which as a consequence loses acceptance among States.[49] Further, this strict understanding excludes the correlation between a prohibitive norm and a permissive rule.[50] Nowadays, a wider notion of conflict is accepted, according to which a 'conflict' also exists when norms contradict as to their purposes or their implementation.[51] As this broader notion of conflict includes different levels of tensions between norms, it is useful for a comprehensive analysis and is thus adopted in this contribution.

3.2 *Conflicts with the Standard of Fair and Equitable Treatment*

Almost every IIA contains the protection standard of fair and equitable treatment (FET).[52] Although there is no accepted general definition, some key elements have been developed in arbitral practice and in academia.

---

47 Wilfrid Jenks, 'The Conflict of Law-Making Treaties' (1957) 30 BYBIL 401, 426; Gabrielle Marceau, 'Conflicts of Norms and Conflicts of Jurisdictions, The Relationship between the WTO Agreement and MEAs and other Treaties' (2001) 35 J World Trade 1181, 1182–83.

48 Nele Matz, *Wege zur Koordinierung völkerrechtlicher Verträge völkervertragsrechtliche und institutionelle Ansätze* (Springer 2006) 12 (Matz, Koordinierung völkerrechtlicher Verträge).

49 Ibid.

50 See Erich Vranes, 'The Definition of Norm Conflict in International Law and Legal Theory' (2006) 17 EJIL 395.

51 Matz, Koordinierung völkerrechtlicher Verträge (n. 48) 12; ILC Fragmentation Report (n. 15) paras 25–26; Vranes ibid. 395, 418; Ralf Michaels and Joost Pauwelyn, 'Conflict of Norms or Conflict of Laws?: Different Techniques in the Fragmentation of International Law' in T. Broude and Y. Shany (eds), *Multi-sourced equivalent norms in international law* (Hart 2011) 21, 40; Anne van Aaken, 'Fragmentation of International Law: The Case of International Investment Protection' (2006) XVII FYBIL 90, 91.

52 See (n. 7) art. 10 I 2 ECT; art. 1105 I NAFTA; art. 10.5 I CAFTA-DR; art. 2 II Model BIT Germany; art. 5 I, II (a) Model BIT USA; art. 5 I Model BIT Canada; art. 3 Model BIT France. See also: Dolzer and Schreuer, *Principles IIL* (n. 7) 119. They point out the existence of differences in the formulation of FET; see ibid. 121–122. Every IIA must, in any event, be interpreted individually. However, for the purpose of the present contribution, a general reference to FET is useful. Thus, as an example for FET reference is made to art. 2 II Model BIT Germany (n. 7): 'Each Contracting State shall in its territory in every case accord investments by investors of the other Contracting State fair and equitable treatment (...) under this Treaty.'

The protection of legitimate expectations lies at the core of FET.[53] Thus, the violation of investor-state contracts as well as the cancellation of permits could result in a violation of the FET standard.[54] If as a consequence of establishing a PA for biodiversity protection, a State does not fulfil its entire obligations of an investor-state contracts because of the restrictions grounded in the PA, it could lead to a violation of FET. Or if the State revokes granted permits for certain business activities, because they would endanger the PA, it could also constitute an infringement of FET. These are possible constellations where conflicts could emerge with PAs under the CBD. There are, however, no requirements to such extent in the CBD. The CBD does not directly regulate aspects of foreign investment concerning PAs. But if a State were at first to allow a foreign investor to carry on its business and subsequently establishes a PA in the same geographical area, it could frustrate the foreign investor's legitimate expectations. States could amend or change national legislation concerning PAs to achieve the CBD's aim of protection of biodiversity. Such measures could lead to restrictions of previously granted rights or permits of foreign investors. Thus, the implementation of Article 8 of the CBD could cause conflicts with the FET standard.

---

53 From case law: *Tecmed S.A. v United Mexican States*, ICSID Case No ARB(AF)/00/2, Award 29 May 2003, para. 154; *International Thunderbird Gaming Corporation v Mexico*, UNCITRAL, Award 26 January 2006, Dissenting Opinion by Arbitrator Thomas Wälde, paras 21–58; *Saluka v Czech Republic*, Partial Award, 17 March 2006, para. 302; *EDF (Services) Limited v Romania*, ICSID Case No ARB/05/13, Award 8 October 2009, para. 216. From academia: Ioana Tudor, *The fair and equitable treatment standard in the international law of foreign investment* (OUP 2008) 163–169; Todd Grierson-Weiler and Ian Laird, 'Standards of Treatment' in P. Muchlinski, F. Ortino and C. Schreuer (eds), *The Oxford Handbook of International Investment Law* (OUP 2008) 259, 275–277; Dolzer and Schreuer (n. 7) 119, 133–140; Stephan W. Schill, 'Fair and Equitable Treatment, the Rule of Law, and Comparative Public Law' in S.W. Schill (ed), *International Investment Law and Comparative Public Law* (OUP 2010) 151, 163–166.

54 From case law: *Metalpar S.A. and Buen Aire S.A. v Argentine Republic*, ICSID Case No ARB/03/5, Award 6 June 2008, para. 185; *Total S.A. v The Argentine Republic*, ICSID Case No ARB/04/01, Decision on Liability, 27 December 2010, para. 117. See also: Moshe Hirsch, 'Between fair and equitable treatment and stabilization clause: Stable legal environment and regulatory change in international investment law' (2011) 12 JWIT 783, 784, 792ff; K. Vandevelde, 'A unified theory of fair and equitable treatment' (2010) 43 NYU J Int'l L & Pol 43, 66.

3.3 *Conflicts with 'No Expropriation without Compensation'*

International Investment Law provides that a State has to compensate the foreign investor in case of expropriation.[55] It does not forbid expropriations. States have the right to expropriate,[56] but they have to adhere to conditions such as a public purpose, non-discrimination, due process and compensation. The critical question is: when does an act of State constitute an expropriation? To further complicate matters, IIAs very often also cover indirect expropriations.[57] In the arbitral practice, two different tendencies in determining expropriations can be identified: the *public purpose* and *sole effects* doctrines. The *sole effects* doctrine only considers the effects of States' acts,[58] whereas the *public purpose* doctrine ascribes an important role to the public purpose of States' acts.[59] Recently, the principle of proportionality is invoked to assess whether an expropriation has taken place.[60] This matrix analyzes whether

---

55 See (n. 7) art. 13 ECT; art. 1110 NAFTA; art. 10.7 CAFTA-DR; art. 4 II Model BIT Germany; art. 6 I and Annexes A and B Model BIT USA; art. 13 I Model BIT Canada; art. 5 II Model BIT France. This is also protected under customary international law; see Ian Brownlie, *Principles of Public International Law* (OUP 2008) 544. For a typical clause, see art. 13 (1) ECT: 'Investments of Investors of a Contracting Party in the Area of any other Contracting Party shall not be nationalized, expropriated or subjected to a measure or measures having effect equivalent to nationalization or expropriation (hereinafter referred to as 'Expropriation') except where such Expropriation is: (a) for a purpose which is in the public interest; (b) not discriminatory; (c) carried out under due process of law; and (d) accompanied by the payment of prompt, adequate and effective compensation.'

56 Dolzer and Schreuer (n. 7) 89–90; see Ian Brownlie ibid. 533.

57 See treaties (n. 7). This contribution uses the term 'indirect expropriation'. In literature and in practice other terms are used as well for describing the same concept: 'creeping expropriation', 'de facto expropriation' or 'regulatory expropriation'; see August Reinisch, 'Expropriation' in P. Muchlinski, F. Ortino and C. Schreuer (eds) *The Oxford Handbook of International Investment Law* (OUP 2008) 407, 421–422.

58 See *Metalclad v United Mexican States* (n. 1) paras 102–103, 108. The *Metalclad* case is one of the most cited regarding the danger of IIL to environmental protection. However, one has to keep in mind that the Tribunal in that case focused on a violation of FET. The statements regarding expropriation were of merely supplementary character.

59 See for example *Methanex v United States of America* (n. 1) Part IV—Chapter D—p. 4, paras 7–8. This doctrine is also discussed under the term 'police power', see Dolzer and Schreuer (n. 7) 109.

60 *Tecmed v United Mexican States* (n. 1) para. 122. For an analysis, see Xiuli Han, 'The Application of the Principle of Proportionality in Tecmed v Mexico' (2007) 6 Chinese JIL 635. Also: Alec Sweet, 'Investor-State Arbitration: Proportionality's New Frontier' (2010) 4 Law & Ethics of Human Rights 48; Erlend Leonhardsen, 'Looking for Legitimacy: Exploring Proportionality Analysis in Investment Treaty Arbitration' (2012) 3 JIDS 89, 114 ff.; Caroline Henckels, 'Indirect Expropriation and the Right to Regulate: Revisiting

the State's measure was proportionate. This balancing exercise can incorporate *effective* and *public purpose* elements.[61] Some States have included certain clauses in their IIAs to define what an indirect expropriation is.[62] Nevertheless, it ultimately depends upon the facts in the specific case. As *Ratner* points out, it is not possible to define absolute criteria in an abstract way for the determination of an expropriation, but instead such determination grounds on a case-by-case basis.[63]

In the present context, it is questionable whether there is a conflict with Article 8 of the CBD. As Article 8 does not call for an expropriation to designate PAs, there is no conflict under a strict understanding of conflict. But as demonstrated above, Article 8 of the CBD obliges States to establish a system of PAs and restore ecosystems. If a State does in fact fulfil its duty for the protection of biodiversity through a designation of a PA, then such a measure could constitute an expropriation under IIL. If the State formally takes the title of property, it has to pay compensation. In such a constellation a conflict with IIL arises only, when the State does not pay compensation. But the more likely scenario is that States establish PAs without taking the formal property title. Instead the State enacts laws that restrict the allowed use in the respective area and pays no compensation to investors. These measures could constitute an indirect expropriation. These constellations show the tension between the individual property rights of foreign investors and the (community) interests of the greater public. Thus, under a wider notion of conflict of norms, such conflict

---

Proportionality Analysis and the Standard of Review in Investor-State-Arbitration' (2012) 15 JIEL 223, 230 ff.

61 For an overview, see Benedict Kingsbury and Stephan W. Schill, 'Public Law Concepts to Balance Investors Rights with State Regulatory Actions in the Public Interest—the Concept of Proportionality' in S.W. Schill (ed), *International Investment Law and Comparative Public Law* (OUP 2010) 75, 89–96; Markus Perkams, 'The Concept of Indirect Expropriation in Comparative Public Law—Searching for Light in the Dark' in S.W. Schill (ed) ibid. 107. General with regard to the principle of proportionality, Aharon Barak, *Proportionality—Constitutional Rights and Their Limitations* (CUP 2012).

62 See Annexes A and B Model BIT US; Annex B. 13 (1) Model BIT Canada. For a review of investment treaty practice concerning environmental issues, see Kathryn Gordon and Joachim Pohl, 'Environmental Concerns in International Investment Agreements: a survey' (2011) *OECD Working Papers on International Investment, No 2011/1*, OECD Investment Division, available at <www.oecd.org/daf/investment> accessed 27 August 2013.

63 Steve Ratner, 'Regulatory Takings in Institutional Context: Beyond the Fear of Fragmented International Law' (2008) 102 AJIL 475, 526–528.

can be assumed to exist between Article 8 of the CBD and the obligation not to expropriate without compensation.

3.4 *Interim Conclusion*

This section has shown that there could be conflicts between the rule advocating the establishment of PAs under the CBD and protection standards under IIL. A strict understanding of the notion 'conflict' would deny the existence of such conflicts, as the CBD does not oblige States to expropriate or otherwise violate the rights of foreign investors. Furthermore the CBD grants wide leeway in its implementation, which is in itself a typical feature of international environmental law.[64] Thus, the conflicts often occur in the implementation phase. The following sections will therefore scrutinize how international law can deal with these conflicts.

4 Possible Solutions: Considering PAs in International Investment Law

With regard to solving of the described conflicts, this section considers the following legal instruments: systemic interpretation of IIL (I), other tools within IIL such as conflict-clauses and a reduction of the amount of compensation (II) and general conflict maxims (III).[65]

4.1 *Systemic Interpretation: The Role of Article 31(3)(c) VCLT*

In the debate about fragmentation in international law the interpretation rule of Article 31(3)(c) of the Vienna Convention on the Law of Treaties (VCLT) assumes a prominent role:[66] 'There shall be taken into account, together with

64 See Ulrich Beyerlin, 'Different Types of Norms in International Environmental Law—Policies, Principles, and Rules' in D. Bodansky, J. Brunnée and E. Hey (eds), *The Oxford Handbook of International Environmental Law* (OUP 2007) 425, 426–433; Catherine Tinker, 'Responsibility for Biological Diversity Conservation' in C. Ku & P. Diel (eds), *International Law—Classic and Contemporary Readings* (Lynne Rienner 2009) 371, 372.

65 The order in which the tools are considered is guided by the principle of 'accommodation'—therefore 'systemic interpretation' is discussed first—and by the principle of 'special first', which leads first to the analysis of instruments within investment law before dealing with general conflict rules.

66 See ILC Fragmentation Report (n. 15) paras 410–480; Campbell McLachlan, 'The Principle of Systemic Integration and Article 31(3)(c) of the Vienna Convention' (2005) 54 ICLQ 279; Anne van Aaken, 'Defragmentation of public international law through interpretation: a methodological proposal' (2009) 16 IJGLS 438; Richard Gardiner, *Treaty Interpretation* (OUP 2008) 250.

the context: [...] any relevant rules of international law applicable in the relations between the parties.'

Hanqin calls it 'a 'master key' to the house of international law',[67] but others are rather more sceptical.[68] However, the so-called 'systemic interpretation' may constitute one useful tool to deal with the conflicts between PAs under the CBD and IIL.

4.1.1 Prerequisites: Article 8 CBD as a Relevant and Applicable Rule for Investment Law

To use this rule of interpretation for the analysis of international investment agreements Article 8 of the CBD must fulfil the requirements set out in Article 31(3)(c) VCLT. First of all, Article 8 of the CBD is a 'rule of international law'.[69] Furthermore, the CBD must be 'applicable'. Under the premise that States of the investment treaty under consideration are parties also to the CBD,[70] Article 8 of the CBD is 'applicable'.[71] In this regard the discussion within

67 ILC Fragmentation Report (n. 15) para. 420.

68 Hugh Thirlway, 'The law and procedure of the International Court of Justice 1960–1989, Part 3' (1991) 62 BYBIL 1, 58; Jörg Kammerhofer, 'Systemic integration, legal theory and the International Law Commission' (2010) XIX FYBIL 157; Jörg Kammerhofer, 'Law-Making by Scholarship? The Dark Side of 21st Century International Legal "Methodology" ' in J. Crawford and S. Nouwen (eds), *Select Proceedings of the European Society of International Law* (Hart, forthcoming January 2012); Nele Matz-Lück, 'Harmonization, Systemic Integration, and 'Mutual Supportiveness' as Conflict-Solution Techniques: Different Modes of Interpretation as a Challenge to Negative Effects of Fragmentation?' (2008) XVII FYBIL 39, 47–48; Melanie Samson, 'High Hopes, Scant Resources: A Word of Scepticism about the Anti-Fragmentation Function of Art. 31(3)(c) of the Vienna Convention on the Law of Treaties' (2011) 24 LJIL 701.

69 The criteria 'rule of international law' in art. 31(3)(c) VCLT includes all sources of international law as enshrined in art. 38 (1) ICJ Statute; see Villiger (n. 19) 25.

70 See p. 48 above.

71 However, it does not necessarily follow that the CBD is applicable in investment proceedings. The applicable law for investment disputes is determined in the IIA or agreed by the parties. If such determination does not exist, the procedural rules of the institution establish the applicable law. For example, art. 42 ICSID sets out that: '(T)he Tribunal shall apply the law of the Contracting State party to the dispute (including its rules on the conflict of laws) and such rules of international law as may be applicable.' (Convention on the Settlement of Investment Disputes Between States and Nationals of Other States (opened for signature 18 March 1966, entered into force 14 October 1966) 575 UNTS 159). On the applicable law in investment disputes, see Ole Spiermann, 'Applicable Law' in P. Muchlinski, F. Ortino and C. Schreuer (eds), *The Oxford Handbook of International Investment Law* (OUP 2008) 89.

the WTO, if all WTO members must also be party to the other agreement,[72] is not of relevance for the context at hand, as the parties of the IIA are both also bound by the CBD. Additionally, the participation of the foreign investor in the dispute raises the question, if the CBD could still be held 'applicable', because the investor is not party to that treaty. But the treaty which is interpreted is one between States. The foreign investor is not party the IIA. The protection standards were agreed between states. Therefore, it is not an obstacle that the investor is not party to the CBD. Thus, Article 8 CBD can be classified as 'applicable' in the sense of Article 31(3)(c) VCLT.

The core question is, however, whether Article 8 of the CBD is 'relevant' for the IIA. According to *Villiger* a rule is 'relevant' if it 'concern[s] the subject-matter of the treaty'.[73] *Gardiner* adds rules 'which in any way affect that interpretation'.[74] The ICJ in the *Oil Platforms* case did not consider this relevance criterion of Article 31(3)(c).[75] A systematic argument supports a lower understanding of 'relevant' than 'same subject-matter', because the latter term is used in Articles 30 and 59. Finally, the *Oxford Dictionary of English* defines 'relevant' as 'appropriate to the matter in hand',[76] which speaks in favour of a broader understanding than 'same subject-matter'. The implementation of Article 8 of the CBD through the designation of PAs can have an impact on foreign investor rights, if they are located in the affected zone.[77] Therefore, Article 8 of the CBD is a 'relevant' rule pursuant to the meaning of Article 31(3)(c) VCLT. Hence, subsequently it will be discussed how the interpretation of standards of IIL can 'take into account' Article 8 of the CBD.

4.1.2 Considering PAs within 'Fair and Equitable Treatment'

FET is a quite vaguely formulated standard[78] and is therefore open to interpretation. Thus, a systemic interpretation according to Article 31 (3) c) VCLT is

---

72 See only *European Communities—Measures Affecting the Approval and Marketing of Biotech Products* wt/DS291–293/R (29 September 2006) paras 7.68–7.71; Oliver Dörr, 'art 31' in O. Dörr & K. Schmalenbach (eds), *Vienna Convention on the Law of Treaties—A Commentary* (Springer 2012) 566–567.

73 Villiger (n. 19) 25.

74 Richard Gardiner, *Treaty Interpretation* (OUP 2008) 260.

75 *Case Concerning Oil Platforms* (Islamic Republic of Iran v United States of America) (Merits) (2003) ICJ Rep. 161, paras 39–41. This case is often mentioned to illustrate the use of art. 31(3)(c) VCLT. It is regrettable that the ICJ did not elaborate on the criterion of 'relevant' in art. 31(3)(c) VCLT.

76 C. Soanes and A. Stevenson, *Oxford dictionary of English* (OUP 2005) 1487.

77 See above, p. 54ff.

78 Tudor, *The fair and equitable treatment standard* (n. 53) 3, 35, 132.

not excluded *a priori*. As Article 8 of the CBD does not contain a rule regarding the treatment of foreign investors, a direct reference to it within FET does not appear operational. But the protection of legitimate expectations under FET can work as a link to Article 8 of the CBD. The foreign investor has to respect the national legal order[79] and Article 8 of the CBD requires States to establish PAs for biodiversity protection. Truly, it depends on the facts in the individual case. However, the foreign investor can foresee a designation of PAs, when investing in zone where measures of biodiversity protection could be issued. This does not mean that Article 8 of the CBD is given priority. Through the systemic interpretation it forms but one element of defining the investors' expectations. In other words, the CBD can serve as one factor influencing the determination of the legitimate expectations. Hence, such a systemic interpretation of the FET standard can be a viable way to consider PAs under Article 8 of the CBD in IIL.

4.1.3 Considering PAs within the 'No Expropriation without Compensation' Standard

As the CBD does not contain rules concerning expropriation, a systemic interpretation seems at first glance far away. There are however options, where the status of PAs under the CBD can be considered in the interpretation of the standard of 'no expropriation without compensation'. Firstly, Article 8 of the CBD can be taken into account for the identification of a public purpose,[80] which is required for a lawful expropriation. The designation of a PA for the protection of biodiversity according to Article 8 of the CBD serves public and even community interests of States.[81] Secondly, when it comes to the criterion of 'non-discrimination',[82] Article 8 of the CBD can serve as an element of differentiation. If the PA can fulfil its purpose only in the zone of the foreign investor, such foreign investor is not in the same circumstances as other investors. If on the other hand, the PA can be established also in other areas, all investors are in that regard in same circumstances. These two points, 'public purpose' and

79 See recently: '(P)rudent investment practice requires that any investor exercise due diligence before committing funds to any particular investment proposal. An important element of such due diligence is for investors to assure themselves that their investments comply with the law. Such due diligence obligation is neither overly onerous nor unreasonable.', *Alasdair Ross Anderson and others v Republic of Costa Rica*, ICSID Case No ARB(AF)/07/3, Award, 19 May 2010, para. 58. Similar: *Unglaube v Costa Rica* (n. 1) para. 258. See also and with further references: Dolzer and Schreuer (n. 7) 133ff.

80 For the criteria of a lawful expropriation see above (p. 56).

81 See above (pp. 52–53).

82 See above (p. 56).

'non-discrimination', show how a harmonizing interpretation of the expropriation criteria can be used to handle the present conflicts.

Regarding the task of identifying an indirect expropriation,[83] a systemic interpretation can also take into consideration Article 8 of the CBD. With reference to the *public purpose* doctrine[84] for example, the empowerment of States to establish PAs for the protection of biodiversity pursuant to Article 8 of the CBD could serve as an additional argument for the regulatory power of states.[85] When adopting a proportional analysis,[86] Article 8 of the CBD further serves as one argument in balancing the individual investor's rights and the public interest. Under both concepts, Article 8 of the CBD does not automatically lead to the impossibility of finding an indirect expropriation. While in such a way Article 8 of the CBD can be taken into account, in severe cases a designation of PAs under Article 8 of the CBD could well constitute an expropriation. To sum up, a systemic interpretation of the 'no expropriation without compensation' standard is possible in the above elaborated manner.

4.1.4 Interpretation of 'Carve-Out' and 'Exception'-Clauses

In some IIAs, States have adopted so-called 'carve-out' clauses to define acts which do not constitute a violation of an IIA: 'Except in rare circumstances, non-discriminatory regulatory actions by a Party that are designed and applied to protect legitimate public welfare objectives, such as public health, safety, and the environment, do not constitute indirect expropriations.'[87]

While some commentators welcome these developments,[88] *Schwebel* sees an endangerment of the fundamental purpose of IIAs.[89] 'Carve-out' clauses

83 Ibid.

84 For the *public purpose* doctrine above (p. 56).

85 For the general regulatory power within investment law see Dolzer and Schreuer (n. 7) 109.

86 See above (pp. 56–57).

87 See above (n. 7). Annex B art. 4 b) Model BIT USA. Such formulations can be found in other IIAs: Annex B. 13 (1) c) Model BIT Canada; Interpretation declaration NAFTA; CAFTA-DR. The typical European IIA does not contain such clauses. Gordon and Pohl observe that '(t)hese clauses remain relatively rare (...)'; see Gordon and Pohl (n. 62) 22.

88 Muthucumaraswamy Sornarajah, *The international law on foreign investment* (CUP 2010) 363–399; Tienhaara (n. 2) 343–345.

89 Stephen Schwebel, 'The United States 2004 Model Bilateral Investment Treaty: An Exercise in the Regressive Development of International Law' in G. Aksen and others (eds), *Global reflections on international law, commercial and dispute resolution: liber amicorum in honour of Robert Briner* (ICC Publication 2005) 815.

typically do not mention other international treaties so they cannot serve directly for the resolution of the conflicts discussed here.[90] Nevertheless, the designation of PAs under Article 8 of the CBD falls under the term 'environment' as a legitimate public welfare objective. The CBD can thereby confirm the non-existence of an indirect expropriation. Furthermore, when considering the criteria 'non-discriminatory', the CBD could be a decisive factor for differentiation as discussed earlier.[91] Hence, such 'carve-out' clauses can in fact be applicable to the conflicts discussed here.

'Exception'—[92] or 'reserving policy space'[93]—clauses concretize States' right to enact regulation for public purposes. They are similar to 'carve-out' clauses, but function at the level of justification.[94] They could serve to deal with the conflicts at hand: PAs under the CBD are designated for the protection of 'animal and plant life' and the 'conservation of living resources'. Both aspects are incorporated in Article 8 of the CBD. In this regard, the CBD is a relevant and applicable rule in the meaning of Article 31(3)(c) VCLT and can thus be taken into account for the interpretation of the exception clauses.

---

90 For an analysis of clauses regarding the relationship to other treaties, see below (p. 64).

91 See above (p. 61).

92 For state practice, see Suzanne Spears, 'The Quest for Policy Space in a New Generation of International Investment Agreements' (2010) 13 JIEL 1037, 1060–1062. *Sornarajah* sees in such state practice the renunciation of the neo-liberal conception of IIL; see Muthucumaraswamy Sornarajah, 'Mutations of Neo-Liberalism in International Investment Law' (2011) 3 TL&D 203, 230.

93 See Gordon and Pohl (n. 62) 16.

94 For example, art. 10 No 1 Model BIT Canada states sets out: 'Subject to the requirement that such measures are not applied in a manner that would constitute arbitrary or unjustifiable discrimination between investments or between investors, or a disguised restriction on international trade or investment, nothing in this Agreement shall be construed to prevent a Party from adopting or enforcing measures necessary: (a) to protect human, animal or plant life or health; (b) to ensure compliance with laws and regulations that are not inconsistent with the provisions of this Agreement; or (c) for the conservation of living or non-living exhaustible natural resources.' Similar clauses are included in the following treaties: art. 1114 (1) NAFTA; art. 12 (4) Model BIT USA. Of the used treaties, the followings have no such clause: German Model BIT; Model BIT France. Other IIA which contain an exception clause: art. 22 (1) (b) and (c) COMESA; art. 10.9 (3) (c) (Chapter 10) (signed 22 November 2006, not yet in force); art. 25 Norwegian Model BIT (available at: www.italaw.com, last access 17 December 2011; not yet in force). For the characterization as 'justification' see Spears, Policy Space IIA (n. 92).

Another point of interest is the burden of proof. A state invoking an exception has to prove the existence of its requirements.[95] For this reason, the *International Institute for Sustainable Development* opposes such a clause.[96] However, if States allow investors to establish an invest within their territory in the first place, it seems reasonable to impose on them the burden of proof for invoking exceptions. The exception clauses thus represent a balanced instrument between investor rights and States' regulatory rights.

4.1.5 Interim Conclusion

To sum up, Article 31(3)(c) VCLT is not a magic key to solve the present conflicts. Nevertheless, it is one technique of handling the conflicts between IIL and Article 8 of the CBD. A systemic interpretation can therefore form one important legal tool to consider aspects of Article 8 of the CBD in IIL.

4.2 *Conflict-Clauses in International Investment Agreements*

In treaty practice special conflict-clauses could indicate a path for the solution of conflicts between IIA and the CBD. There are clauses which define the relation of the IIA to other treaties regarding most-favouring treatment: 'This Treaty shall not derogate from any of the following that entitle an investor of a Party or a covered investment to treatment more favorable than that accorded by this Treaty: [...] 2. International legal obligations of a Party [...]'.[97] But the CBD does not contain more favourable treatment standards concerning foreign investors than an IIA. The CBD has no direct rules with respect to

95 This is an accepted rule of procedural law. See Chittharanjan Amerasinghe, *Evidence in international litigation* (Nijhoff 2005) 88; Markus Benzing, *Das Beweisrecht vor internationalen Gerichten und Schiedsgerichten in zwischenstaatlichen Streitigkeiten* (Springer 2010) 645, 670. With special reference to environmental concerns: Caroline Foster, *Science and the Precautionary Principle in International Courts and Tribunals—Expert Evidence, Burden of Proof and Finality* (CUP 2011) 185. Further, with regard to the comparable art. XX lit. b) GATT/WTO it is accepted that the invoking state has the burden of proof. See Peter-Tobias Stoll and Lutz Strack, 'Article XX lit b' in R. Wolfrum, P.-T. Stoll and H. Hestermeyer (eds), *Max Planck commentaries on world trade law—Trade in Goods* (Vol. 5, Nijhoff 2011) 509, 34. A differentiation between state-state and state-investor disputes is not indicated.

96 Howard Mann and others, *Model International Agreement on Investment for Sustainable Development: Negotiators' Handbook* (International Institute for Sustainable Development 2006) 18. They argue for 'carve-out' clause, because than the burden of proof lies on the investor.

97 See above (n. 7), art. 16 Model BIT USA. For similar provisions see art. 1108 NAFTA; Annex III Model BIT Canada; art. 7 I Model BIT Germany; art. 16 ECT.

the treatment of foreign investors. Thus, such conflict-clauses have no impact in the present context. Another type of conflict clauses in IIAs directly defines the relationship between the IIA and other treaties, focusing on trade-related obligations contained in those other treaties.[98] Similar direct conflict clauses with respect to obligations of other treaties like environmental or human rights agreements are not contained in IIA.[99] Therefore, in treaty practice no conflict clause can be identified which could serve in the determination of the relationship between the IIA and the CBD norms regarding PAs. It remains questionable whether such clauses are really suitable because when negotiating an IIA, States cannot define any possible conflict in advance. Thus, it is difficult to define the relationship to particular obligations of other international treaties.[100] Finally, a hierarchy based on such a clause might lead to the complete non-application of one treaty. A 'smoother' accommodation between the two regimes could instead be reached through the above-described harmonizing interpretation.

4.3 *The Limited Role of General Conflict Rules*

The general conflict-resolution maxims *lex specialis derogat legi generali* and *lex posterior derogat legi priori* may clarify the relationship between the rules of IIL and PAs under the CBD. The former asserts that a special rule has priority over a general rule, the latter that a later treaty is given precedence to an earlier

98 See above (n. 7). For example, art. 104 NAFTA contains a clause regarding trade-related obligations in certain Multilateral Environmental Treaties (MEA). The wording of art. 104 NAFTA: '1. In the event of any inconsistency between this Agreement and the specific trade obligations set out in: a) the Convention on International Trade in Endangered Species of Wild Fauna and Flora, done at Washington, March 3, 1973, as amended June 22, 1979, b) the Montreal Protocol on Substances that Deplete the Ozone Layer, done at Montreal, September 16, 1987, as amended June 29, 1990, c) the Basel Convention on the Control of Transboundary Movements of Hazardous Wastes and Their Disposal, done at Basel, March 22, 1989, on its entry into force for Canada, Mexico and the United States, or d) the agreements set out in Annex 104.1, such obligations shall prevail to the extent of the inconsistency, provided that where a Party has a choice among equally effective and reasonably available means of complying with such obligations, the Party chooses the alternative that is the least inconsistent with the other provisions of this Agreement.' This clause is based on the fact that Free Trade Agreements as NAFTA contain trade obligations and thus requires the definition of its relation to relevant MEAs.

99 The author is not aware of any such direct conflict rules. A reason could be seen in the fact that other international treaties, e. g. CBD (n. 4), do not contain directly investment related obligations. Thus, *prima facie* such conflict rules are not required.

100 For this problematic issue of treaty negotiation, see ILC Fragmentation Report (n. 15) paras 270–271; Matz, Koordinierung völkerrechtlicher Verträge (n. 48) 273.

treaty—provided that they both deal with the same subject-matter. Both maxims are considered to be part of international law[101] and extensively discussed by the International Law Commission (ILC) in its fragmentation report.[102]

Concerning the first maxim, it is questionable whether it is possible to determine whether the IIA or the CBD forms the more special rule. As the CBD covers PAs for biodiversity and does not contain specific or general rules concerning foreign investors, the relationship between the two does not fit within the category of 'general and specific' rules. Neither the CBD includes a general rule that is specified in IIL, nor the other way around. Thus, the IIA cannot be regarded as *lex specialis* to the CBD, or *vice versa*.

The crucial question regarding the second maxim is whether the IIA and the CBD concern the 'same subject matter'.[103] Only if such content can be identified does the later treaty gain priority. The ILC speaks of 'pointing into the same direction'.[104] Regarding Article 59 VCLT, which contains the *lex posterior* rule, arbitral tribunals have held a strict view with respect to 'same subject-matter'.[105] As mentioned before, neither does the CBD contain provisions regarding foreign investors, nor do IIAs incorporate rules concerning PAs for the protection of biodiversity. Thus, both treaties cannot be said to 'point into the same direction'. The ILC itself stated that both conflict rules work better within one regime.[106] Hence, both conflict rules have a limited role in the present context.

4.4 *Interim Conclusion*

The different tools discussed offer different methods to consider PAs under the CBD in the context of IIL. The systemic interpretation of certain criteria discussed above can serve as a linking element between the two regimes. The interpretation of exception-clauses in particular can deploy a systemic

101 See ILC Fragmentation Report (n. 15) paras 56 and 225. The *lex posterior* maxim is codified in Arts. 30 and 59 VCLT. Both arts constitute international customary law, see Villiger (n. 19) 21 and 728, 15. In *Enron v Argentina* the tribunal uses the maxim *lex specialis* explicitly and thus expresses its fundamental acceptance of that conflict maxim for IIL; see Enron v Argentina, ICSID Case No ARB/01/3 (22 May 2007) para. 334 <www.italaw.com> accessed 27 August 2013.

102 See ILC Fragmentation Report (n. 15) paras 46–222 and 223–323.

103 This criterion stems from Arts. 30(1) and 59(1) VCLT.

104 ILC Fragmentation Report (n. 15) para. 23.

105 Art. 59 VCLT plays a role in investment disputes within the EU, if EU member States have signed a IIA (so called 'Intra-EU-BITS). See *Eureko v Slovak Republic*, PCA Case No 2008–13, Award on Jurisdiction (26 October 2010) 63–72, especially paras 241, 245 and 250 <www.italaw.com> accessed 27 August 2013.

106 ILC Fragmentation Report (n. 15) para. 255.

connection to the CBD but one must nevertheless keep in mind the mentioned limits. Conflict-clauses in the existing treaty practice do not help with regard to the determination of the relationship between IIL and the CBD. The general conflict rules play only a limited role in the context at hand and all the mentioned tools have its deficiencies in considering PAs under the CBD in IIL. Therefore, alternative conflict resolution methods ought to be considered.

5 Outlook: Alternative Methods to Deal with Conflicts

5.1 *Prevention of Conflicts: The Role of Environmental Impact Assessments*

Environmental Impact Assessments (EIA) can play a significant role in the prevention of conflicts of norms concerning foreign investor treatment. An EIA is a process of evaluation of the positive and negative impacts of a particular project on the environment,[107] for example, before the foreign investor is granted access to the host country. In particular it could be scrutinised whether the potential zone of investment could also be designated as PA. The EIA would ensure the foreign investor a place where a PA is unlikely to be established. Conducting an EIA ensures that investors and States are aware of possible impacts on the site so EIAs can play a preventive role in the conflicts discussed here. This leads to the question of the legal status of EIAs. International law calls for an EIA in the transboundary context.[108] Indeed does the CBD contain a rule on EIA, but it is basically left to the discretion of Member States.[109]

107 See Astrid Epiney, 'Environmental Impact Assessment', in Rüdiger Wolfrum (ed.), *The Max Planck Encyclopedia of Public International Law* (OUP 2008) MN 1 <www.mpepil.com> 27 August 2013. For an overview of the typical procedure of an EIA, see Neil Craik, *The International Law of Environmental Impact Assessment* (CUP 2010) 23–37.

108 See the so called 'Espoo-Convention': Convention on Environmental Impact Assessment in a Transboundary Context (adopted 25 February 1991, entered into force 10 September 1997) 1989 UNTS 309. The ICJ stated in the *Pulp Mills Case* that the conducting of an EIA in a transboundary context is part of international customary law; *Case concerning Pulp Mills on the River Uruguay* (Argentina v Uruguay) (2010) ICJ Judgment, para. 204. The Court did not mention any further requirements as part of such obligation. Instead the Court held that is up to each State to determine how an EIA is to be conducted.

109 See art. 14 CBD (n. 4): '1. Each Contracting Party, as far as possible and as appropriate, shall: (a) Introduce appropriate procedures requiring environmental impact assessment of its proposed projects that are likely to have significant adverse effects on biological diversity with a view to avoiding or minimizing such effects and, where appropriate, allow for public participation in such procedures; (...)'.

Other instruments provide for the conduction of EIAs at the national level as well.[110] But there are no provisions concerning EIAs in IIA.[111] *De lege ferenda* an inclusion of EIA in IIA could be an effective way to minimize conflicts in the context at hand.[112] Taking into account the described practice above, such an inclusion of an obligation to conduct an EIA in IIA does not appear unrealistic. Such a requirement of conducting an EIA could be included in the section with regard to the protected investments under an IIA. Thus, a foreign investor could only claim violations of the IIA, if an EIA had previously been conducted. This would lead to the described preventive role of EIAs for the present conflicts.

5.2 *Institutional Coordination between the Two Regimes*

Another method of preventing or resolving the conflicts of norms could be found in an institutional coordination. At the international level institutional linkages between the two regimes could be enhanced. Within the institutional framework of the CBD exist some special working groups—one in particular concerning PAs[113]—but none which address foreign investments. Hitherto the attention of the actors within the CBD has been focused on the relationship with other environmental treaties.[114] The investment regime, on the other hand, does not even have a common institutional framework to serve as a contact point. Thus, a direct institutional coordination is unrealistic. Instead, the use of existing procedural means should be strengthened.

---

110 In the European Union: Directive (EC) 85/337 Environmental Impact Assessment (1985) OJ L 175. In the aftermath EU member states adopted corresponding national laws. The African Court on Human and Peoples Rights', based an EIA on rights to life in case of major industrial projects; see *The Social and Economic Rights Action Center and the Center of for Economic and Social Rights v Nigeria* (the *Ogoniland Case*), African Court on Human and Peoples Rights', Case No 155/96 (30th Session, 13–27 October 2001) 273.

111 An indirect role can be seen in the requirement of conducting an EIA to obtain financial support by the World Bank for certain investor projects. See Katja Böttger, *Die Umweltpflichtigkeit von Auslandsdirektinvestitionen* (Nomos 2002) 93.

112 Similar suggestion with regard to general environmental protection: Valentina Vadi, 'Environmental Impact Assessment in Investment Disputes: Method, Governance and Jurisprudence' (2010) XXX Polish Yearbook of International Law 169, 202. Regarding the impact of human rights *Simma* has suggested a kind of human rights audit of investment treaties, Bruno Simma, 'Foreign Investment Arbitration: a Place for Human Rights?' (2011) 60 ICQL 573.

113 See supra (n. 30).

114 See Lee Kimball, 'Institutional Linkages between the Conservation on Biological Diversity and other International Conventions' (1997) 6 RECIEL 239; Matz, Koordinierung völkerrechtlicher Verträge (n. 48) 194 ff.

For example, the arbitral tribunals could use such possibilities to consult experts,[115] who could support the investment tribunal in assessing technical and scientific issues of PAs concerning biodiversity protection. Another option is the admission of *amicus curiae* briefs, which lies within the competence of the tribunal to allow them.[116] These instruments could serve for a modest form of communication between the two regimes.

5.3 *PAs for Community Interests: Financial Recourse for Their Designation?*

Finally, a subsequent instrument can be considered: are there instruments for financial recourse, if an investment tribunal condemns a State to pay compensation for its designation of PAs under the CBD? The CBD provides a fund for its implementation,[117] but this would not cover the eventual compensation due to a foreign investor. In any case, the CBD-fund as well as other funds has limitations with respect to the amount of financial support.[118] Also under general customary law there is no a rule for invoking compensation for the designation of PAs by one State against the international community.[119] Therefore, *de lege ferenda* States could establish a fund for States, which establish PAs for

115 See Tomoko Ishikawa, 'Third party participation in investment treaty arbitration' (2010) 59 ICLQ 373, 393, 402, 405.

116 Ibid., 373; Cristian Tams & Alessandra Asteriti, 'Transparency and Representation of the Public Interest in Investment Treaty Arbitration' in S.W. Schill (ed), *International Investment Law and Comparative Public Law* (OUP 2010) 787, 789–795.

117 See Arts. 20 and 21 CBD (n. 4). See therefore Glowka (n. 22) 100; Yibin Xiang & Sandra Meehan, 'Financial Cooperation, Rio Convention and Common Concerns' (2005) 14 RECIEL 212, 214f.

118 For the CBD (n. 4), see Glowka ibid; Xiang & Meehan ibid. For another example, see the *Global Environment Facility* (GEF). It is a fund created in 1991 to assist countries in their efforts to protect the environment. According to art. 39 CBD it serves as the interim financial institution for the CBD. For further information, see Laurence Boisson de Chazournes, 'The Global Environment Facility (GEF): A Unique and Crucial Institution (2005) 14 RECIEL 193; David Freestone, 'The establishment, role and evolution of the global environment facility: Operationalising common but differentiated responsibility?' in T.M. Ndiaye and R. Wolfrum (eds), *Law of the sea, environmental law and settlement of disputes: liber amicorum judge Thomas A. Mensah* (Nijhoff 2007) 1077; Nele Matz, 'Financial Institutions between Effectiveness and Legitimacy—A Legal Analysis of the World Bank, Global Environmental Facility and Prototype Carbon Fund' (2005) 5 International Environmental Agreements 265, 282–286. For the requirements under GEF for the CBD see Decision I/2, Annex I, Report of the First Meeting of the COP to the CBD, UNEP/CBD/COP/I/17 (1994) p. 33.

119 See Matz, *Protected Areas* (n. 3) 714–716.

community interests such as biodiversity protection. The costs of the community measure would be shared and the designating State would not have to bear all the costs alone. This would also strengthen the CBD's underlying purpose of the correlative nature of obligations to protect biodiversity and the aim in the CBD to receive financial support.[120] Such a financial recourse would establish a subsequent solution of the conflict between PAs under the CBD and IIL. With regard to the likelihood of establishing such a fund, one must keep in mind the crucial role of environment protection, which States recognize and implement more and more. This shift is manifested in the willingness to contribute financial resources for environmental protection measures, at least by some States. Also from an economical viewpoint, the value of nature is accepted through studies and impacts the will of States.[121] Taking into account the already existing structures of funds for environmental measures, the suggested fund appears not as a far-out possibility.

6 Conclusion

This contribution has shown the extent to which certain legal instruments and techniques can deal with conflicts between PAs under Article CBD and IIL. As the CBD has wider margins of implementation than IIA, States eventually tend to adhere more to IIL. Nevertheless, there are several means to consider PAs for the protection of biodiversity in IIL. As the protection of biodiversity through PAs serves community interests, investment tribunals and States should use these techniques. This would strengthen the acceptance of the criticised system of IIL and could lead to an equilibrated balance between the two regimes in international law.

120 See for that purpose: Wolfrum (n. 23) 355.

121 See for example the Ecosystem-approach, Secretariat of the Convention on Biological Diversity, *The Ecosystem Approach* (Montreal 2004); Millennium Ecosystem Assessment—World Resources Institute, *Ecosystems and Human Well-being: Opportunities and Challenges for Business and Industry* (Washington 2005); The Economics of Ecosystems and Biodiversity for National and International Policy Makers, *Chapter 8—Recognising the value of protected areas* (2009) available at <www.teebweb.org> accessed 10 August 2013.

CHAPTER 4

The EU Emission Trading Scheme as Applied to Aviation: Extraterritorial Measure Justified under GATT Article XX

Daniela Gómez-Altamirano[1]

1 Introduction

In response to environmental concerns and due to the absence of any effective international agreement, countries have unilaterally undertaken climate change policies. An example of a unilateral policy measure is the Emission Trading Scheme (ETS) developed by the European Union in light of its obligations under the Kyoto Protocol.[2]

Under its ETS, the EU has developed a market-based instrument that encourages a specific behaviour through market signals rather than through explicit directives regarding pollution control levels, including instruments such as tradable allowances and pollution charges.[3]

This system, however, places the EU and countries applying ETSs at a competitive disadvantage when compared with foreign energy-intensive industries facing uneven greenhouse gas constraints. The competitive disadvantage causes an increase in the level of emissions generated outside the region applying the system, the so called 'carbon leakage', which tends to undermine the effectiveness of a domestic climate mitigation policy.

As a result, countries have been put under increased pressure to develop some form of 'border adjustment' that will complement ETSs, thereby levelling the playing field and avoiding carbon leakage. Arguments justifying such trade measures generally refer to competitive concerns, weakening of environmental

---

1 E-mail: dgomez.altamirano@gmail.com. The author would like to thank participants at the 2012 Society of International Economic Law (SIEL) Biennial Conference at National University of Singapore for their insights and comments on this work.

2 Directive (EC) 2003/87 of the European Parliament and of the Council establishing a scheme for greenhouse gas emission allowance trading within the Community (2003) OJ L 275.

3 Robert Stavins, 'Experience with Market-Based Environmental Policy Instruments' (FEEM Working Paper No. 52.2002) < http://papers.ssrn.com/sol3/papers.cfm?abstract_id=199848> accessed 27 August 2013.

 | DOI 10.1163/9789004270190_005

efficiency, and further incentives for countries to join an international environmental agreement.[4]

In 2008, as part of its policy on climate change and in an effort to address the growing impact of aircraft emissions on global warming, the EU included aviation activities in its greenhouse gas emissions allowance-trading scheme.[5]

As of January 2012, all airlines, including those from third countries, are required to acquire and surrender emission allowances for the carbon emissions generated by their flights departing from and arriving to airports located in the EU, *ie* between EU airports and between EU and non-EU airports.[6]

The inclusion of the aviation industry in the EU's ETS has sparked a global debate among the EU Member States, other countries including India, China,[7] the United States,[8] the aviation industry and environmentalists. In this regard, the International Civil Aviation Organization (ICAO) has adopted resolutions urging contracting states not to implement emission trading systems on aircraft operators except on the basis of mutual agreement between those states.[9]

Litigation has also been initiated. A consortium of US airlines, supported by the International Air Transport Association (IATA) lodged a complaint claiming that the EU is in breach of a number of principles of customary international law and of various international agreements including the Chicago

4 Monjon and Quirion, *Which design of a border adjustment for the EU ETS? A quantitative assessment*, Centre International de Recherche sur l'Environnement et le Développement (CIRED).

5 Directive (EC) 2008/101 of the European Parliament and of the Council amending Directive (EC) 2003/87 so as to include aviation activities in the scheme for greenhouse gas emission allowance trading within the Community (2008) OJ L8/3.

6 In November 2012 the European Commission made a proposal to exempt from enforcement flights into and out of Europe operated in 2010, 2011, and 2012 to provide negotiation time for the ICAO General Assembly in autumn. 2013. The European Parliament and the Council approved the proposal on. 24 April 2013. The decision entered into force with immediate effect. See Decision (EU) 377/2013 of the European Parliament and of the Council derogating temporarily from Directive (EC) 2003/87 establishing a scheme for greenhouse gas emission allowance trading within the Community (2008) OJ L 113.

7 China, opposing to the EU scheme, has already blocked the order of Airbus A230s from Hong Kong Airlines.

8 The US House of Representatives has voted to make it illegal for US airlines to comply with the EU carbon cap on aviation.

9 Consolidated Statement of Continuing ICAO Policies and Practices Related to Environmental Protection, ICAO Assembly Resolution A36–22 (28 September 2007) para. 6(c). See also the ICAO Working Paper, *Inclusion of International Civil Aviation in the European Union Emissions Trading Scheme (EU ETS) and its impact*, C-WP/13790 (17 October 2011).

Convention, the Kyoto Protocol and the Open Skies Agreement.[10] Submitting preliminary ruling on this case, the Court of Justice of the EU (ECJ) found that the directive including aviation activities in the EU's ETS cannot be characterized as an extra-territorial measure and is therefore valid and completely legal.[11]

The objective of this chapter is not to analyse the aviation EU-ETS Directive in light of the EU obligations under the aforementioned international agreements, but to discuss to what extent the EU measure, as applied to third countries, could be justified under World Trade Organization rules.

Because the core point of this chapter is to analyse the implications of the extraterritorial nature of the Aviation Directive and its consistency under WTO rules, it will focus only on the legal and factual requirements under which the EU airline carbon cap could be applied as a justification under Article XX of the GATT. However, it is important to outline the arguable claims that could be made in an attempt to prove a violation of the Aviation Directive with WTO provisions. The arguments are elaborated in a section below.

The following general questions are to be answered in order to conduct the legal analysis: Can the EU regulate non-EU airlines in relation to greenhouse gas emissions generated in other states' territories and over the high seas? Is this an exercise of extra-territorial jurisdiction, and if so, should it be permissible in the service of a common environmental goal? To what extent is this measure contrary to or supported by existing multilateral agreements on climate change, and what is the relevance of such agreements for WTO rules? Are extraterritorial unilateral trade measures a legitimate means to combat environmental issues? If legitimate, under what conditions should they be applied?

2 How Does the EU Directive on Aviation Work?

As of January 2012 all aircraft operators, including those from third countries, are required to monitor and report their emissions and to surrender emission allowances for the carbon emissions generated by their flights departing from and arriving to airports located in the EU, *ie* between EU airports and between EU and non-EU airports. There are some limited and specific exemptions, such as those for countries with 'equivalent measures' in place, for operators with

10 Case C-366/10, *Air Transport Association of America, American Airlines, Inc, Continental Airlines, Inc, United Airlines, Inc v The Secretary of State for Energy and Climate Change* (2010) OJ C260/9.

11 Preliminary ruling, ibid.

fewer than 243 flights to or from the EU for 3 consecutive 4-month periods, and for operators with less than 10,000 tonnes of emissions per reporting year, which are outside the scope of the scheme. According to the EU Directive, the rationale behind this exception is to avoid placing disproportionate administrative burdens on airlines operating limited services including airlines from developing countries.

The EU ETS is a so-called 'cap and trade' system that imposes an emission cap on industries covered by the scheme, such as aviation. Emission allowances are allocated to each operator within a regulated industry for each reporting year. At the end of each reporting year, the operator is required to surrender allowances equal to its total emissions for the reporting year. In case of non-compliance, the operator is subject to a penalty. Operators that emit more than their allocated emissions must procure additional allowances for surrender by (i) purchasing allowances at auction, (ii) purchasing allowances from other EU ETS participant, or (iii) purchasing carbon offset credits such as certified emissions reductions (CERs) and emissions reductions units (ERUS).

Each EU Member State has transposed the requirements of the EU Directive into national law in order to set out in detail by national legislation in each State what operators must do in order to apply for free allowances, how they can comply with the monitoring and reporting requirements, and the process of surrendering allowances for compliance. Aircraft operators are allocated to the Member State to and from which most of their flights operate. For instance, given the importance of London's Heathrow Airport as a hub for flights into and out of Europe, a large number of airlines have been assigned to the UK.

Regarding the allocation and auctioning of allowances, the EU ETS is divided into two trading periods for airlines: from 2012 to 2013 and from 2013 to 2020. For the first trading period, the total amount of aviation allowances available to the airline industry is capped at 97% of the annual average emissions for the historical aviation emissions, *ie* for the years 2004–2006. During the 2012–2013 trading period, 85% of the total available allowances will be allocated to airlines free of charge and Member States will auction the remaining 15%. Finally, for the 2013–2020 trading period the total amount of available allowances decreases to 95% of historical aviation emissions; 82% of the total available allowances will be allocated free of charge; 15% will be auctioned and 3% will be set aside in a special reserve for new entrants and fast-growing airlines.

The free allowances are distributed on an annual basis by Member States who are also responsible for the auctioning of allowances. Operators will be able to purchase allowances at special auctions for airlines or at auctions open to all sectors subject to the EU ETS.

The figures expressed above were designed in consideration of the historical nature of the overall aviation cap and the growth of international aviation since 2006. Given the increase of the aviation sector from 2006 to date, the allowances available to airlines free of charge, together with those that can be purchased at auctions, will be insufficient to meet actual traffic levels. Thus, most airlines will inevitably have to become net purchasers of emissions allowances only by sustaining their current operations.[12]

Moreover, operators may also have to comply with the monitoring and reporting of emissions requirements. By 31 March 2012, aircraft operators must collect their emissions data and prepare an annual emissions report. The report must be verified by an independent, accredited verifier and submitted to the competent authority in their designated Member State for approval.

The EU Directive provides for a penalty of €100 per tonne of CO_2 emitted for which an allowance is not surrendered. As a last means of compliance, Member States can also request an operating ban on persistent offenders. Interestingly, individual Member States have also provided for additional penalties in their national legislation by implementing the EU Directive.[13]

3 Arguable Inconsistency of the EU Aviation Measure with WTO Agreements

The question of whether the EU Directive could be scrutinized under the General Agreement on Trade in Services (GATS) is significant, as this measure is directly related to air transport services. An even more important question is that of whether the GATS Annex on Air Transport Services exempts the Aviation Directive from regulation under the GATS in respect to what is

12 In 2012, the EU Directive on Aviation will cost airlines around US$2.86 billion and in 2015 these costs are likely to increase to US$4.3 billion. Merill Lynch, 'Aviation in EU ETS; An Incentive for Efficiency' (2008) <http://www.ml.com/media/113530.pdf> accessed 27 August 2013.

13 For instance, the UK has put in place penalties in the form of fines for failing to submit an emission, failing to monitor or report emissions, failing to comply with an emissions plan or with notices issued by the competent authority going beyond the EU Directive. Whenever a fine is not paid within six months or an operating ban is ordered by the EU, the UK competent authority can detain any aircraft operated by the operator in question. Furthermore, if there is persistent non-payment or an operating ban is in place for more than 56 days, the UK competent authority can potentially sell the aircraft without leave of the court.

covered by the scope of 'traffic rights'. If it is concluded that the requirement in the Aviation Directive that non-EU airlines are to hold allowance to cover their CO_2 emissions is a measure affecting 'traffic rights', then an analysis under the non-discrimination principles may be conducted.

Moreover, it could also be argued that the EU Directive has implications for goods transported by airlines as air cargo. The Aviation Directive could indirectly affect trade in situations where airlines pass the cost on in their cargo rates. In such a scenario GATT could also govern the EU directive. For instance, the Aviation Directive is likely to be in violation of GATT Article I should the EU exempt some countries from complying with the Directive under the 'equivalent measures' exemptions and also in the event of discrimination between products according to the distance between their place of origin and the EU territory. Where this results in different cargo rates for goods, the EU could provide more favourable treatment to imports of goods from these WTO Members.

Under the national treatment principle, it could be argued that even when the EU Directive applies to both EU and non-EU airlines there could be a de facto violation of GATT Article III:2 as imported goods will be subject to higher taxes than domestic goods. However, if the EU Directive is considered not to be a tax or charge but rather an internal regulation, then it will be subject to Article III:4. In this regard, it could be argued that by increasing the cost of bringing imported goods to sale in the EU, it has affected the internal sale of those imported goods. The additional costs faced by imported goods would constitute the less favourable treatment.[14]

4 Could the EU Airline Carbon Cap Be Justified Under the GATT General Exceptions?

As noted above, assuming that the EU measure is challenged in a WTO dispute settlement proceeding and found to be inconsistent with GATT obligations, the EU may seek to justify its action under a GATT general exception. Some commentators describe Article XX as an 'environmental charter' since it allows trade restrictions related to the protection of the environment.[15]

---

14 For further explanation on arguments regarding the legality of the EU-ETS as applied to aviation under WTO rules, see Lorand Bartels, 'The WTO Legality of the EU's Emission Trading Scheme (ETS) as Applied to Aviation' (2011) ICTSD Programme on Trade and Environment Issue Paper No 6; and Joshua Meltzer, 'Climate Change and Trade—The EU Aviation Directive and The WTO' (2012) 15(1) JIEL 111.

15 Michael J. Trebilcock and Robert Howse, *The Regulation of International Trade* (Routledge 2005) 514.

Article XX requires a two tier-test. First, whether the trade measure at issue is provisionally justified under one of the substantive exceptions; and second, whether the measure satisfies the Article's '*chapeau*'.[16] Article XX has not yet been addressed as a justification for climate change mitigation under the WTO dispute settlement system. However, the most likely substantive exceptions in this context are Article XX(b), covering measures 'necessary to protect human, animal, or plant life or health', and Article XX(g), for measures 'relating to the conservation of exhaustible natural resources.'[17]

The relevance of both subparagraphs of Article XX for the EU measure is simple. Article XX(b) arguably covers policies aimed at reducing carbon emissions because of the possible adverse effects of global warming for humans, animals, and plants. As for Article XX(g), it could be argued that this subparagraph covers such environmental policy aiming at the conservation of the earth's atmosphere, which may be considered an exhaustible natural resource.

Whereas Article XX(b) or Article XX(g) applies to the EU measure, the analysis will have to include the alleged policy goal, the relationship of the measure to the goal, and details of the measure's implementation. In this regard, WTO case law suggests that the policy objective underlying these exceptions is not at issue; rather, it is the trade measure and how it is related to the policy objective that has to be examined under this provision.[18]

4.1 *Is the EU Measure Necessary to Protect Human, Animal, or Plant Life or Health?*

For a measure to be justified under Article XX(b), the policy objective must be legitimate and the measure must be necessary to protect human, animal, or plant life or health.

4.1.1 Policy Objective of the Measure at Issue

According to the text of the EU Directive, its purpose is to promote the reduction of greenhouse gas emissions in a cost-effective and economically efficient manner.[19] From this statement, it could be argued that the policy objective embedded in the EU measure is to protect human, animal, or plant life or health by combating global warming.

16 Appellate Body Report, *United States—Standards for Reformulated and Conventional Gasoline* (*US-Gasoline*) wt/DS2/AB/R (20 May 1996) 22.

17 Because the 'necessity' requirement in art. XX(b) sets a higher standard, measures falling under both paragraphs are typically argued under art. XX(g).

18 Appellate Body Report, *US Gasoline* (n. 16) 29–30.

19 Directive (EC) 2008/101 (n. 5) OJ L8/3, recital (1).

The aforementioned argument could find its basis in the *US-Gasoline* case where the panel found that reducing air pollution was a policy objective aimed at protecting life or health.[20] Even more pertinently, the Appellate Body in *Brazil-Tyres*, while addressing the climate change issue, recognized that certain environmental problems may be tackled only with a comprehensive policy comprising a multiplicity of interacting measures, and that the result obtained from certain actions—for instance, measures adopted in order to attenuate global warming and climate change, can only be evaluated with the benefit of time.[21] Therefore, it would not be essential to immediately show the contribution the EU measure makes to the objective pursued in order for it to be justified under Article XX(b).

Even though these interpretations have been applied to non-specific environmental damage measures, authors argue that carbon emissions could be treated analogously as the potential damage that may result from increased global temperatures includes, *inter alia*, increased death rates among the young, the old, and sick people; increase in tropical diseases; loss of habitation due to the rising sea level; and adverse effects on biodiversity.[22]

Importantly, since the purported health protection would be achieved through the prevention of carbon leakage generated by foreign countries operators and in foreign countries' airspace and even over the high seas, and because Article XX(b) does not expressly state whether the object of protection needs to be located in the territory of the WTO Member imposing the measure, a jurisdictional issue may not arise, at least not for this subparagraph. However, even where global impact resulting from the generation of carbon emissions may be sufficient, it would still be necessary to demonstrate that the inclusion of aviation in the EU ETS is part of a broader program that aims to combat climate change.

4.1.2 The Necessity Test

The second element in analysing a possible justification of a measure under Article XX(b) is the so-called 'necessity test'. Case law establishes that the term 'necessary' does not mean 'indispensable', but it is stricter than 'making a con-

20 Panel Report, *US-Gasoline* WT/DS32/R (29 January 1996) para. 6.21.

21 Appellate Body Report, *Brazil—Measures Affecting Imports of Retreaded Tyres* (*Brazil-Tyres*) WT/DS332/AB/R (17 December 2007) para. 151.

22 Sikina Jinnah, 'Emission Trading Under the Kyoto Protocol: NAFTA and WTO Concerns' (2003) 15 Geo Int'l Envtl L Rev 709, 733.

tribution to';[23] in other words, a measure providing a 'marginal or insignificant' contribution would not be considered necessary to achieve the stated goal.[24]

As seen from a non-conclusive interpretation, the necessity test has been evolving as a result of dealing with an increased concern for environmental issues. For instance, in GATT case law such as *Tuna/Dolphin II*, panels found that there could be no necessary connection if a policy is only effective where it forced other countries to change their policies.[25] However, in *Brazil-Tyres*, the panel gave a less restrictive interpretation, where 'necessary' includes a balancing of factors and requires a 'genuine relationship of ends and means between the objective pursued and the measure at issue'.[26] The analysis requires a weighting of factors, which can include the importance of the policy goal or interest the measure seeks to achieve and the contribution of the measure to realizing these interests. Thus, as long as the measure makes a serious contribution to its objective, it could be deemed 'necessary' under Article XX(b).[27]

In this regard, it could be argued that the EU measure on aviation will not achieve the outcome of reducing emission as the measure will likely have negative effects such as, for instance, passing the costs on to consumers by increasing ticket prices, or even sectioning flights so as to cover the shortest possible distance going to or departing from the EU territory, a practice which will increase the emission of CO_2.

Moreover, the Appellate Body has stated that in order to find necessity, the test may include weighing and balancing of 'the relevant factors' with an examination of less-restrictive alternatives.[28]

The EU would then have to show that it could not achieve its objective by an alternative measure that is reasonably available and less trade restrictive. Thus, it would be necessary to discuss alternatives such as passenger levy, per-plane taxes, or even the adoption of incentives to reduce fuel consumption by increasing fuel prices, improving air traffic control and developing biofuels.[29] However, it is important to bear in mind that WTO Members have the right to

23 Appellate Body Report, *Korea-Measures Affecting Imports of Fresh, Chilled and Frozen Beef* (*Korea-Beef*), WTO/DS161/AB/R (11 December 2000) para. 161.

24 Appellate Body Report, *Brazil—Tyres*, para. 150–151.

25 Panel Report, *United States—Restrictions on Imports of Tuna* (*Tuna/Dolphin II*), DS/29/R, adopted June 1994, para. 5.39.

26 Appellate Body Report, *Brazil—Tyres* (n. 21) para. 210.

27 Ibid., 151.

28 Ibid., 178.

29 Bartels (n. 14).

set their own standards of protection,[30] and that the use of financial inducements encourages countries to adopt higher environmental standards.[31]

4.2 *Is the EU Measure Related to the Conservation of Exhaustible Natural Resources?*

Article XX(g) allows WTO Members to take measures 'in relation to the conservation of exhaustible natural resources', provided that such measures are 'made effective in conjunction with restrictions on domestic production or consumption'.

4.2.1 Measure Related to the Conservation of Exhaustible Natural Resources

The first question in regard to the EU measure is whether it is related to the conservation of exhaustible natural resources. In *US-Gasoline*, the panel found that clean air is an exhaustible natural resource because, even though it is renewable, it could be depleted.[32] Moreover, the panel in *US-Shrimp* reasoned that 'the term 'exhaustible natural resources' must be read by a treaty interpreter in light of contemporary concerns of the community of nations about the protection and conservation of the environment, and that it is 'not static in its content or reference but is rather "by definition, evolutionary" '.[33]

For the EU measure, the exhaustible natural resource at issue in the climate change context might be the atmosphere remaining at a suitable temperature or a species adversely affected by rising global temperatures. Thus, it seems to be clear that in regard to the EU measure, adopted to mitigate climate change, the atmosphere may be considered to be an exhaustible natural resource.

The second requirement under Article XX(g) 'related to', raises issues which may be ambiguous. WTO case law has interpreted the term 'related to' as a 'substantial relationship' between 'the general structure and the design of the measure... and the policy goal it purports to serve', a situation also characterized as 'a close and genuine relationship of ends and means.'[34]

---

30 Preamble to the Marrakesh Agreement; Appellate Body Report, *European Communities—Measures Affecting Asbestos and Asbestos Containing Products* (*EC-Asbestos*) wt/DS135/AB/R (5 April 2001) para. 174.

31 GATT Secretariat, *Study on Trade and Environment*, GATT Doc. 1529.

32 Panel Report, *US-Gasoline* (n. 20) para. 6.37.

33 Appellate Body Report, *United States—Import Prohibition of Certain Shrimp and Shrimp Products* (*US-Shrimp*) wt/DS58/AB/R (6 November 1998) paras 131–133.

34 Ibid., 136–137.

As mentioned above, the purpose of the EU measure is to offset the effects of carbon leakage. Some commentators have pointed out that the existence of credible studies that question whether leakage would be prevented by such measures may increase the difficulty of showing that an ETS is primarily aimed at preserving the natural resource or resources shown to be at risk.[35] However, as stated by the Appellate Body, the immediate effect of an inconsistent WTO climate change measure may not need to be established in order to successfully invoke Article XX exception.

Finally, the requirement of 'measure made effective in conjunction with similar domestic measure' seems to be satisfied as the EU measure applies indistinctively to both domestic and foreign airlines, besides the fact that the EU has an extensive emission trading scheme aiming at the reduction of CO_2 covering various industrialized sectors.

4.2.2 Jurisdictional Limitations

In dealing with Article XX(g), early GATT jurisprudence was unyielding in denying the application of extraterritorial measures, reasoning that such an approach would permit 'contracting parties to unilaterally determine the conservation policies which other contracting parties could not deviate without jeopardizing their rights under the General Agreement'.[36] More recent WTO case law suggests that Article XX(g) is not limited to purely domestic conservation efforts.[37]

In this regard, it could hardly be argued that the EU Directive has an incentivising effect on other countries without interfering with their domestic policies. Contrary is the ruling of the ECJ where in a preliminary ruling in the Aviation case[38] it was found that the EU Directive neither violates the principle of territoriality nor the sovereignty of third states as the scheme is applicable to the operators only when their aircrafts are physically located in the territory of one of the EU Member States airports. The ECJ highlighted that 'it is only if the operators of such aircraft choose to operate a commercial air route arriving at or departing from an airport situated in the EU that they are subject to the emissions trading scheme'.[39]

---

35 Larry Parker and Jeanne J. Grimmett, 'Climate Change: EU and Proposed U.S. Approaches to Carbon Leakage and WTO Implications' (2009) CRS Report for Congress 7–5700, 56.

36 Panel Report, *United States—Restrictions on Imports of Tuna* (*US-Tuna*), DS21/R (August 1991) para. 5.32.

37 See for instance: ibid. 5.16.; Appellate Body Report, *US-Shrimp* (n. 33) paras 120–121.

38 Case C-366/10 (n. 10).

39 Ibid., preliminary ruling.

Thus far, the ECJ's finding seems reasonable. However, when it comes to the question of how the emission allowances to be surrendered are calculated, the argument faces a loophole. According to the EU Directive, the calculation of the emission allowances to be surrendered is made on the basis of the entire flight, *e.g.* from John F. Kennedy Airport in the US to Frankfurt Airport in Germany. Regarding this issue, the ECJ points out that the EU policy aims at a high level of protection, that the EU is entitled to allow commercial activity to be carried out in its territory only on the condition that operators comply with the criteria established by the EU, and that even the 'effects' doctrine[40] is not relevant enough 'to call into question' these policies.[41]

It seems that the ECJ's argument is not sufficiently strong as the EU measure in fact covers the activity of foreign aviation operators not only in EU territory but also in third countries territory and over the high seas.

As a secondary line of argumentation, if the EU measure were considered to have an extra-jurisdictional implication, it could be argued that the restrictive measure is the outcome of a global concern as demonstrated by the efforts of the international community in reaching an agreement on climate change. Strictly speaking, the substantive jurisdiction of a WTO panel is limited to claims under the WTO covered agreements; however, that does not mean that the applicable law is limited to those rules.[42]

The fact that the EU is party to the Kyoto Protocol may provide a legal nexus for the implementation of the measure as having no territorial connection. Where a country does not have a territorial nexus with the environmental problem, a Multilateral Environmental Agreement (MEA) will provide the legal nexus and thus the evidence that a subject matter is global, if not transnational.[43]

WTO jurisprudence suggests, and some authors support, the idea that trade measures taken pursuant to MEAs would be consistent with GATT if implemented in a non-discriminatory and transparent manner between parties to the MEA.[44] However, the EU measure is also applied to countries which are

40 Some authors argue that extraterritorial jurisdiction can be exercised by the EU based on the 'effects' doctrine, which permits the exercise of jurisdiction over the extraterritorial activities of foreigners that produce effects within their territory.

41 Case C-366/10 (n. 10) preliminary ruling.

42 Joost Pawelyn, *Conflict of Norms in Public International Law: How WTO Law Relates to other Rules of International Law* (Cambridge 2003) 460.

43 Bradly Condon, *Environmental Sovereignty and the WTO: Trade Sanctions and International Law* (Ardsley 2006) 10.

44 Appellate Body Report, *United States—Import Prohibition of Certain Shrimp and Shrimp Products*—Recourse to art. 21.5 of the DSU by Malaysia wt/DS58/AB/RW (21 November 2001).

not parties to the Kyoto Protocol, such as the US, where the use of unilateral trade measures in the international environmental context are even more controversial.

Arguably, measures taken against third parties who are not part of the Kyoto Protocol should not be treated as equivalent. Nevertheless, in cases where the subject matter and degree of global acceptance of the MEA in question permits the problem to be characterized as global, rather than extraterritorial, the measure could be justified under Article XX as one which addresses a global issue.

4.3 *Does the EU Measure Comply with Article's XX Chapeau?*

A measure falling within the scope of an exception is also subject to the so-called '*chapeau*' of Article XX, which requires that any such measure not be 'applied in a manner which would constitute a means of arbitrary or unjustifiable discrimination between countries where the same conditions prevail or a disguised restriction on international trade.'

Cases regarding arbitrary or unjustifiable discrimination require a determination as to whether such discrimination 'has a legitimate cause or rationale in light of the objectives listed in sub-paragraphs of Article XX.'[45]

Following the reasoning of previous cases, for the EU measure to meet the requirements under the *chapeau* of Article XX, it would most likely have to comply with the following elements: (i) serious across-the-border negotiations with the objective of concluding bilateral or multilateral agreements for the reduction of greenhouse gas emissions;[46] and (ii) flexibility in the implementation of the measure allowing that third country's measures are comparable in effectiveness by taking into account countries' dissimilar conditions.[47]

In light of the United Nations Framework Convention on Climate Change (UNFCCC), many countries, including the EU, have committed to engage in a global and comprehensive agreement for a reduction in greenhouse gas emissions, providing an effective, efficient and equitable response on the scale required when facing climate change challenges. Moreover, the Kyoto Protocol requires developed countries to pursue the limitations or reduction of emissions of greenhouse gases from aviation, working through the ICAO.

---

45 Appellate Body Report, *US-Shrimp* (n. 33) paras 158–159.

46 Ibid., 166–172.

47 In Appellate Body Report, *US-Shrimp* (n. 33) para. 144, it was stated that flexibility should be looked at in implementation, and where market access is conditional on an exporting Member adopting a regulatory program that is 'comparable in effectiveness' to that of the importing Member, the exporting Member will have 'sufficient latitude ... with respect to the programme it may adopt to achieve the level of effectiveness required' and may thus adopt a program that is 'suitable to the specific condition prevailing in its territory'.

Despite continued support among the countries working together on the development of measures including market-based instruments, at the sixth meeting of the ICAO Committee it was agreed that an aviation-specific emission trading system was not to be pursued further.

From these facts it could be concluded that the EU has engaged in serious negotiation efforts even if a satisfactory outcome has not been reached. According to the Appellate Body in *US-Shrimps*, actual conclusion of an international agreement is not required, so long as 'serious, good faith efforts' are made to negotiate an accord.[48]

Moreover, the EU measure offers the possibility of exempting airlines from countries that have adopted 'equivalent measures' to tackle carbon emission reduction in aviation; thus, it could be argued that the measure takes into account the different 'conditions prevailing' in different countries. However, it has to be pointed out that the criteria for determining equivalence remain unclear, leaving space for discriminatory treatment at such time as the EU decides which countries will be excluded from the application of the EU Directive and which ones do not comply with the 'equivalent measure' standard. The aforementioned exception provided by the Aviation Directive will possibly lead to a breach of the most favoured national treatment.

Furthermore, the fact that airlines which fail to surrender allowances are subject to a fine of €100 per tone of CO_2 in addition to the cost of making up the shortfall the following year may be problematic; the Appellate Body in *US-Shrimp* found unjustifiable discrimination in the 'intended and actual coercive effect' on foreign government policy decisions for countries lacking not only 'comparable, but rather essential' programs.[49]

A second argument is made on the basis that the EU measure does not, in fact, internalise all carbon emissions produced by airlines, leaving aside flight sectors that do not begin or terminate at EU airports. Thus, discrimination may arise depending on the routes and means of transport chosen by operators.[50]

In regard to the second element of Article's XX *chapeau*, it has been interpreted that the prohibition on creating a 'disguised trade restriction' is aimed

48 Appellate Body Report, *US-Shrimp Article 21.5* (n. 44) para. 134.

49 Appellate Body Report, *US-Shrimp* (n. 33) para. 161.

50 Bartels (n. 14) 14. This argument is exemplified in the following way: 'A flight from Hong Kong to Frankfurt is almost the same as from Guangzhou. However, if the flight from Hong Kong transits in Dubai, it will only have to surrender allowances for the final flight sector from Dubai to Frankfurt. This may amount to discrimination if the Guangzhou flight is not able to land in Dubai (or equivalent), or only with difficulty'.

at avoiding a protectionist effect.[51] Because the EU measure is the outcome of a legitimate objective, which is to combat climate change, and it is applied to all airlines, including national ones, it could hardly be argued that the measure has a protectionist effect to the extent that it benefits a domestic industry to the detriment of foreign ones.

Although GATT practice has evolved to include ever more environmental issues under its exceptions, climate change is a global externality and thus presents a 'wholly novel' issue for Article XX analysis[52] where authors have even suggested that an amendment to the scope and coverage of the GATT exception is needed.[53]

5 Conclusions

The reduction of carbon emissions is a worldwide concern and no workable solution has yet been agreed upon. Due to this lack of agreement, the EU has unilaterally implemented a programme seeking a global solution. The EU-ETS represents the largest and most advanced domestic program addressing climate change. The inclusion of aviation in the EU scheme has raised divergent opinions facing strong resistance.

International law is not entirely clear regarding the legality of unilateral trade measures aimed at changing the domestic law of third countries, and WTO law is no exception. Recent WTO case law suggests that unilateral measures may be viewed as a legitimate exercise of the sovereign right of states with respect to the policy areas covered in Article XX.

Even more, unilateral extraterritorial measures could be provisionally justified under Article XX exceptions. The difficulty lays in the balancing approach involved in assessing the value of the policy objective of such measures.

This chapter concludes that the EU measure is a unilateral extraterritorial measure that will face difficulties in dealing with its justification under GATT rules since: (1) while previous Article XX(b) cases concerned clear and direct health hazards, the relation between Article XX(b) purpose and climate change may not be that clear and direct; (2) it is not entirely certain that atmospheric carbon levels can be characterized as exhaustible or even a resource in terms of Article XX(g); and (3) the contribution that carbon tariffs would make

51 Panel Report, *EC-Asbestos* (n. 30) paras 8.237–8.239.

52 Trebilcock and Howse (n. 15) 523–524.

53 Steve Charnovitz, 'The law of Environmental 'PPMs' in the WTO: Debunking the Myth of Illegality' (2002) 27 YJIL 59, 108.

to climate change mitigation is quite unclear, due to scientific uncertainty in respect to global warming and its effects.

Nevertheless, the EU measure must likely succeed in satisfying one or both of the relevant exceptions when liberally construed. The most important question is thus whether the EU measure would satisfy the *chapeau*, which would largely deal with its implementation.

The foregoing discussion highlights the need for further analysis to define the relationship between specific WTO rules and other rules of international law. Despite the liberalization of WTO jurisprudence in recent years, climate change presents a novel issue in the evolution of the application of Article XX.

In any event, the global debate about the EU's inclusion of the aviation industry in its ETS will continue. Adversely affected countries may choose to bring a case before the WTO adjudicating body, and then the Appellate Body and a ruling of panels will bring clarity to this highly important environmental issue. International actors will be the observers of a continuing trend which started with the GATT *US-Tuna* case followed by the *US-Shrimp* case, or of a new development in global governance favouring legitimate, non-discriminatory environmental policies.

CHAPTER 5

Using Preferential Trade Agreements to Promote Climate Change Mitigation

Rafael Leal-Arcas[1]

1 Introduction

This chapter proposes the introduction of a regional model for promoting climate change mitigation as an alternative to the present structure of the United Nations Framework Convention on Climate Change (UNFCCC)/Kyoto Protocol framework. Given the proliferation of PTAs[2]—especially in the form of bilateral treaties—in the international trading system, this chapter advocates creating PTAs with strong climate change chapters, thus embedding climate goals within bilateral/trilateral/plurilateral trade agreements. Involving major greenhouse gas (GHG) emitters through PTAs which include climate chapters can be an effective avenue towards reducing GHG emissions, and could therefore facilitate the ultimate goal of creating an effective global climate regime. This option may therefore be worth exploring.

The chapter is divided into six sections. After the introduction, Section 2 explains why countries are slowly moving away from multilateralism. Section 3 proposes increasing and improving environmental protection aspects within trade agreements, while Sections 4 and 5 suggest how to do it and which proposed PTAs would be most suitable for the suggested proposition to be successful. The chapter concludes with Section 6.

---

1 I am very grateful to two anonymous commentators for their input, which has enhanced the quality of this contribution. The author can be contacted at: r.leal-arcas@qmul.ac.uk.

2 There are three types of regional trade agreements (RTAs): customs unions (CUs), free-trade agreements (FTAs), and preferential trade arrangements (PTAs). For the purposes of this chapter, they are used interchangeably. Regarding all this international trade terminology, it is interesting to note that Jagdish Bhagwati prefers to use the terminology of PTA instead of RTA 'because the PTAs are not always regional in any meaningful sense. For example, the US-Israel FTA is not regional.' Jagdish Bhagwati, *Termites in the Trading System: How Preferential Agreements Undermine Free Trade* (OUP 2008) xi. I share his views.

 | DOI 10.1163/9789004270190_006

2 Moving Away from Multilateralism

Multilateral trade negotiations and international climate negotiations are similar in one key respect: both have been besieged with institutional difficulties. With the stalemate of the Doha Round and the ineffectiveness of the UNFCCC and its Kyoto Protocol, both domains have been unsuccessful at bringing all parties on board with effective results. In the case of trade, though, countries have found a solution of sorts by circumventing multilateralism altogether. This has resulted in an enormous proliferation of PTAs as countries—increasingly disappointed with the stalemate of multilateralism—turn to smaller fora with the aim of moving their trade agendas forward. As Joy A. Kim points out,

> such a phenomenon is a manifestation that when it comes to contentious global issues, forging a regional consensus first can be instrumental. [...] In addition, regional forums can provide countries with an opportunity to coordinate their positions and reach consensus among themselves before they move to the multilateral arena.[3]

The climate regime, though, is fraught with complications that the trade regime does not face. First, countries generally find it more in their interest to engage in trade agreements than in climate agreements. While taking action towards climate change mitigation is by and large (and rather myopically) seen by many countries as detrimental towards their economic growth, trade only offers economic incentives, and every country in the world is voluntarily a party to some trade agreement or other.

Moreover, it is much more difficult to implement climate-related rules, as opposed to trade rules. As Scott Barrett puts it,

> through rebalancing, punishments for deviating from the trade rules can be targeted to harm the countries that violate the rules without injuring innocent countries. By contrast, for a global public good like climate change mitigation, reciprocity is a very weak tool for enforcement. If countries reduce their own abatement efforts to punish a country for not cooperating, they harm themselves in the process. This limits their incen-

3 Joy A. Kim, 'Harnessing Regional Trade Agreements for the Post-2012 Climate Change Regime' in *Climate and Trade Policies in a Post-2012 World* (UNEP 2009).

> tive to punish; and because the incentive to punish is weak, the ability of an agreement to sustain substantial emission cuts is compromised.[4]

Furthermore, trade sanctions also harm the country that imposes them as well as other trade partners, which explains why they are rarely used. It is in these very differences between the two regimes where a possible answer lies towards pushing the climate regime forward.

3 A Greener Type of Trade

As mentioned above, PTAs have become a necessity because of the stagnation of the development of the multilateral trading system. Since reaching a global climate change agreement is no easy task, this study proposes taking advantage of these mushrooming PTAs by inserting strong climate chapters in them. Already PTAs are no longer just about trade; many include investment chapters. So one could argue the following: if there are PTAs whose scope goes beyond trade (for instance, a PTA that also deals with investment or competition issues), and there is a proliferation of PTAs, why not capitalize on this phenomenon, and insert climate change chapters in these PTAs with a strong commitment to reduce GHG emissions?

The aim would then be to multilateralize all those bilateral and regional trade agreements. By doing so, the international community is achieving two things: first, moving the trade agenda forward through the multilateralization of bilateral and regional trade agreements; second, and at the same time, by having climate chapters in these PTAs, the international community is also multilateralizing the climate agenda. A profusion of such climate-related PTAs would create a network of bilateral/regional trade agreements that would help reduce GHG emissions. Given the rate of PTA proliferation, these mini-climate agreements would hopefully become multilateralized, through a bottom-up, building blocks process.

The ultimate aim, therefore, is to lead up to the creation of a future global climate change agreement, as there is much room for improvement in

4 Scott Barrett, 'Climate Change and International Trade: Lessons on their Linkage from International Environmental Agreements' in *Climate Change, Trade and Competitiveness: Issues for the WTO* (TAIT Conference Background Paper 2010) <http://graduateinstitute.ch/ctei/home/events/TAIT_Climate_Conference/TAIT_Papers.html> accessed 10 August 2013.

this respect.[5] At the moment, the climate regime has one platform, namely the UNFCCC and its Kyoto Protocol. As in the case of the multilateral trading system, the climate change legal platform is going through serious difficulties, with very little and very slow progress. If the approach to climate change were bottom-up via PTAs, perhaps this would prove to be a more efficient system to the extent that PTAs may form a building block towards multilateralism. That way, the international community would have the seeds for a universal, global climate change agreement. In other words, trade may provide a means to 'accidentally' achieve a universal, global climate change agreement.

This idea promises potential success based on the factors mentioned above: every country is interested in pursuing trade, whether bilaterally or regionally, and it is easier to enforce trade rules than climate rules. Overall, though, it is hoped the carrot of trade benefits will prove a greater incentive to comply than the stick of trade restrictions. Certainly trade restrictions provide another plausible means of ensuring compliance, the success of which Barrett has examined very thoroughly in the case of the Montreal Protocol[6]—although they were only potential trade restrictions in that case. For the purposes of this chapter, we shall examine the incentive of jumping on board, even with climate change commitments, thanks to the lure of PTA benefits.

Whatever the approach used, trade mechanisms can doubtlessly be an effective tool for securing environmental objectives.

4 Climate-Related Provisions within Preferential Trade Agreements

Inserting environmental provisions into PTAs is not an entirely new phenomenon. In fact, as stated by Joy Kim, 'RTAs negotiated by most OECD countries include some type of environmental provisions.'[7] However, the present study looks at placing more specific, climate-related provisions within PTAs, and also seeks to advocate the insertion of more strongly worded obligations, backed up by more effective enforcement mechanisms. Ideally these provisions should be designed in a way so that the environment is protected without restricting

5 See Council Decision (EC) on the signing, on behalf of the European Union, and provisional application of the Free Trade Agreement between the European Union and its Member States, of the one part, and the Republic of Korea, of the other part (2010) OJ L 127/6. Art. 13.5.3 states that 'the parties reaffirm their commitment to reaching the ultimate objective of the United Nations Framework Convention on Climate Change and its Kyoto Protocol.'

6 Barrett (n. 4).

7 Kim (n. 3).

trade. Existing 'environmentally friendly' PTAs, with a few exceptions, seem to, by and large, include no more than a cursory nod towards environmental protection, encapsulated in vague agreements to cooperate on green matters. According to Kim,

> while currently only a few RTAs include a direct reference to climate change-related activities, there is much room for such activities to be taken up in both existing and upcoming RTAs in a more concrete manner as many RTAs tend to take an open and flexible approach to environmental cooperation. For example, in the Trans-Pacific Strategic Economic Partnership (TPSEP) and the New Zealand Thailand Closer Economic Partnership (NZTCEP), the scope of environmental cooperation is left open in the agreement and is determined during the implementation phase through discussions among environmental officials.[8]

As can be seen from the box below, much of the environment-related wording within existing PTAs revolves around merely agreeing to cooperate on various matters of environmental protection.

What enforcement mechanisms are in place to ensure this cooperation in fact takes place? How much have parties progressed on environmental matters to cooperate through these agreements? Kim argues that '[a]s of today, there are only a few RTAs whose implementation of environmental provisions has been evaluated; in fact only NAFTA's environmental performance has been properly evaluated at this stage.'[9] Could more tangible points of climate cooperation be inserted without hindering trade objectives?

Moreover, how can we make climate change a somewhat more tangible concern within PTAs? One option would be to use PTAs to stimulate non-Annex I (ie, developing) countries to reduce GHG emissions. The idea is to involve all major GHG emitters through bilateral/trilateral/plurilateral PTAs as avenues to mitigate GHG emissions.[10] This regional approach seems more realistic than aiming for a global climate agreement. Both regional and global approaches share the objective of creating a strong international framework for climate action. However, they differ on how to achieve this goal. The question

---

8 Ibid., 62.

9 Ibid., 63.

10 On this note, the Global Economy and Development team at Brookings Institution hosted a discussion on the possibilities for cooperation between the EU, US, and the business sector for green trade liberalization. The discussion is available at <http://www.brookings.edu/events/2012/0426_green_trade.aspx> accessed 10 August 2013.

EXAMPLES OF COOPERATION IN ONE AREA OF SPECIAL INTEREST TO THE PARTIES

* The Agreement between ASEAN Member States and Korea (2005): Parties commit to "pursue... on a mutually agreed basis: cooperation in environmental technologies and policies, such as compressed natural gas technology and policy."[14]

* The Japan-Thailand Agreement (2007): Parties have agreed to "promote cooperation between the governments of the Parties... such as in the fields of 'agriculture, forestry and fisheries' and 'science, technology, energy and environment.' "[15]

* The Environment Cooperation Agreement between New Zealand and China (2008): "Cooperative activities may be in areas including but not limited to: environmental management, environmental remediation, nature conservation, and technologies for environmental benefit. Examples could include: a) management of water environment; b) coastal ecological conservation and pollution control; c) air pollution control and monitoring; d) improvement of environmental awareness, including environmental education and public participation; e) management and disposal of waste including hazardous waste; f) environmental management of chemicals; g) environment and trade; h) biodiversity and conservation."[16]

* Agreement between Japan and Mexico for the Strenghtening of the Economic Partnership (2004): "Cooperative activities under this article may include... b) promotion of capacity and institutional building to foster activities related with the CDM under the Kyoto Protocol to the UNFCCC, as may be amended, by means of workshops and dispatch of experts, and exploration of appropriate ways to encourage the implementation of the CDM projects; c) encouragement of trade and dissemination of environmentally sound goods and services."[17]

Source: Climate and Trade Policies in a Post-2012 World/United Nations Environment Programme, 2009

therefore is how to persuade countries to be parties to PTAs which contain climate-related provisions and find ways to make trade regionalization greener by inserting climate-related provisions in future PTAs.[11]

11 See Habib Ghérari, 'The Adaptation of International Economic Law to Environmental Issues: Regional Trade Agreements and Environmental Protection' in Y. Kerbrat and S. Maljean-Dubois (eds), *The Transformation of International Environmental Law* (Hart 2011).

Current and future PTAs could be used not only as discussion platforms of climate-related trade issues, but also as platforms to agree upon tangible climate results, using trade objectives as a way to guarantee success. For example, countries should include climate-protection chapters in their bilateral/plurilateral/regional trade agreements (making sure that they are WTO-compliant) and support GHG-reducing activities in third countries. This could mean commitments in solar energy or the reduction of tariffs in the energy sector. Such PTAs could be broad in scope so as to cover, for instance, investment and environmental technology transfer. By doing so, issues such as climate change and other environment-related issues do not necessarily have to be the least relevant policy priority in situations of macroeconomic crisis because they can actually contribute towards job creation. For instance, given the need for further research in climate matters, the environmental industry can generate jobs through research and development (R&D) in this sector. In other words, regional arrangements could be designed to provide for an attractive package to settle trade-offs and conflicts of interest as well as facilitate the ultimate goal of creating an effective global climate regime.[12]

Moreover, joint ventures could take place between developed countries (Canada, Japan, the US and EU countries) focusing on emerging markets such as China and India as their target market. This would create business opportunities for all parties involved.

As Trevor Houser argues, 'the climate doesn't have time for a Doha-like approach,'[13] referring to the extremely slow progress of the ongoing multilateral trade negotiations within the WTO context. An extra burden to multilateral trade negotiations such as a proposal to include the climate agenda does not seem feasible or realistic. So this is how trade and climate change get to cooperate: based on the premise that PTAs can be used as building blocks to multilateralize regionalism, one could envisage a global climate change agreement based on climate-related PTAs, especially large PTAs such as the Trans-Pacific Partnership (TPP). The results of this Trans-Pacific agreement could then be placed within the enforceable framework of the WTO.

---

12 N. Fujiwara and C. Egenhofer, 'Do Regional Integration Approaches Hold Lessons for Climate Change Regime Formation? The Case of Differentiated Integration in Europe' in C. Carraro and C. Egenhofer (eds), *Climate and Trade Policy: Bottom-Up Approaches Towards Global Agreement* (Edward Elgar 2007).

13 Trevor Houser, 'Copenhagen, the Accord, and the Way Forward' (2010) Peterson Institute for International Economics Policy Brief PB10-5.

5 Proposed Preferential Trade Agreements for Climate Purposes

Given that the major GHG emitters are large economies, the most effective climate-related PTAs would be large PTAs such as the TPP or the currently being negotiated Trans-Atlantic Trade and Investment Partnership (TTIP). Indeed, given how proactive developing countries are in the conclusion of PTAs, the option of climate-related PTAs would be an effective way towards a future global climate change agreement, especially since the Kyoto Protocol imposes no concrete obligation on developing countries. In this sense, climate-related PTAs can be used as a legal mechanism to further the multilateral climate change agenda, thereby including also major developing countries.[14]

5.1 *The Trans-Pacific Partnership*

The Trans-Pacific Partnership (TPP) is an Asia-Pacific regional trade agreement being negotiated among the United States and 11 other partners as of January 2014. The United States' TPP negotiating partners are Australia, Brunei, Canada, Chile, Japan, Malaysia, Mexico, New Zealand, Peru, Singapore and Vietnam.[15] China is not yet a party to the TPP, which diminishes the effectiveness and value of a potential large PTA with a strong climate chapter. To make the TPP an effective avenue, having China on board would be a necessary condition as China is responsible for over 20 per cent of the total GHG emissions. It is the aim of the TPP negotiators to eventually expand the agreement to include all 21 Asia-Pacific Economic Cooperation (APEC) economies, which includes China. The decision to join the TPP is up to China.[16]

---

14 Some scholars have compared developments in the trade policy area with the building-block approach to climate change governance. See Daniel Bodansky and Elliot Diringer, 'Towards an Integrated Multi-Track Climate Framework' (Pew Center on Global Climate Change 2007) <http://www.pewclimate.org/docUploads/Multi-Track-Report.pdf> accessed 10 August 2013; William Antholis, '"Five 'Gs": Lessons from World Trade for Governing Global Climate Change' in L Brainard and I Sorkin (eds), *Climate Change, Trade, and Competitiveness: Is a Collision Inevitable?* (Brookings Institution Press 2009).

15 For an outline of the TPP Agreement, see <http://www.ustr.gov/about-us/press-office/fact-sheets/2011/november/outlines-trans-pacific-partnership-agreement> accessed 10 August 2013. For an analysis of the TPP, see Meredith Kolsky Lewis, 'The Trans-Pacific Partnership: New Paradigm or Wolf in Sheep's Clothing?' (2011) 34 B C Int'l & Comp L Rev 27.

16 Special Report, 'Kirk Hopes for TPP Progress by June, Highlights Ultimate Expansion' (*Inside U.S. Trade*, 2012) <http://wtonewsstand.com/> accessed 10 August 2013.

Regarding the TPP, a meaningful outcome on environmental issues will ensure that the agreement appropriately addresses the link between trade and climate change, and enhances the mutual supportiveness between these two fields.[17] The TPP countries are in agreement that there should be effective provisions in the TPP on trade-related climate change issues that would help reinforce environmental protection.[18] In this sense, New Zealand and Peru have pushed the agenda to have climate change on the TPP. In the case of New Zealand, by trying to set up an Asia-Pacific market for trading carbon emissions, which has not been welcome by several environmental groups on the grounds that such a proposal would undermine global climate change negotiations.[19] Discussions are also taking place to create an effective institutional arrangement to administer the implementation of the TPP and a cooperation framework to address capacity-building needs.[20] Other environment-related issues under discussion are marine fisheries, biodiversity, and environmental goods and services.[21]

Despite the US desire to make environmental commitments fully enforceable under the same dispute settlement mechanisms as commercial obligations, strong opposition has taken place from some countries in the TPP negotiations such as Chile and Australia. They argue that they already have

17 However, there has been criticism regarding the lack of transparency in TPP negotiations. A group of law professor wrote a letter to USTR Ambassador Kirk in May 2012, in which, among other things, the following was argued: 'Our concerns flow from the now-established observation that 'trade' agreements no longer focus exclusively, or perhaps even predominantly, on the regulation of trade. Rather, the agreements increasingly propose international law standards that bind the legislative branch to change, or lock in place, domestic regulatory decisions. Democratic values demand that, at minimum, the promulgation of such restrictions on domestic law making processes afford the full range of participatory inputs as similar initiatives at the domestic level.' The letter can be read at <http://infojustice.org/wp-content/uploads/2012/05/Transparencyletter-5-9-pdf.pdf> accessed 10 August 2013. The response to the letter by Ambassador Kirk can be read at <http://infojustice.org/archives/21385> accessed 10 August 2013.

18 See USTR, Outlines of the Trans-Pacific Agreement, <http://www.ustr.gov/about-us/press-office/fact-sheets/2011/november/outlines-trans-pacific-partnership-agreement> accessed 10 Augusto 2013. See also M.J. Manton and others, 'Climate in Asia and the Pacific: A Synthesis of APN Activities' (Asia Pacific Network for Global Change Research 2011).

19 Special Report, 'The TPP Negotiations' (*Inside U.S. Trade*, 31 August 2012) <http://wtonewsstand.com/> accessed 10 August 2013.

20 See (n. 18).

21 Ibid.

legally binding environment chapters in existing PTAs with the US.[22] What the US proposes is for TPP countries to have the obligation to enforce their environmental laws and to ensure that their laws fulfill their obligations under any of the multilateral environmental agreements to which they are parties.[23] Past US PTA negotiations, aimed at convincing US trade partners that environmental obligations should be treated in the same way as commercial commitments for purposes of dispute settlement, have received the same reticence from US trading partners, but in the end the Americans have succeeded at full enforceability for environmental commitments.[24]

All this said, environmental matters—among others—are not yet a priority in the TPP negotiations,[25] on the grounds that other political issues on the agenda are more pressing for countries such as the US[26] Nevertheless, leaders of APEC agreed in September 2012 to liberalize over 50 environmental goods by 2015, including solar panels and wind turbines.[27] The agreement was that applied tariff rates would be cut to five per cent or less by 2015.

5.2 *The Trans-Atlantic Trade and Investment Partnership*

The trans-Atlantic economic relationship is the world's largest economic relationship, encompassing almost 50 per cent of global trade.[28] It has dominated the world economy since the beginning of the 20th century. In fact, major global economic institutions are based upon American and European values and interests. In June 2012, both sides of the Atlantic showed an interest to start negotiations for an FTA because both parties have much to gain economically if non-tariff measures were to be removed.[29] EU trade commissioner

---

22 'US Faces Opposition on Enforceability of TPP Environmental Chapter' (*Inside U.S. Trade*, 25 May 2012) <http://wtonewsstand.com/> accessed 10 August 2013.

23 'USTR Acknowledges Objections on Enforceability in TPP Environment Talks' (*Inside U.S. Trade*, 29 June 2012) <http://wtonewsstand.com/> accessed 10 August 2013.

24 Ibid.

25 'TPP Countries Aim to Close Multiple Chapters, but May Leave Key Issues' (*Inside U.S. Trade*, 6 July 2012) <http://wtonewsstand.com/> accessed 10 August 2013.

26 'US, TPP Partners Not Likely to Tackle Tough Issues Prior to US Elections' (*Inside U.S. Trade*, 6 July 2012) <http://wtonewsstand.com/> accessed 10 August 2013.

27 For a list of the environmental goods, see <http://www.apec.org/Meeting-Papers/Leaders-Declarations/2012/2012_aelm/2012_aelm_annexC.aspx> accessed 10 August 2013.

28 See <http://ec.europa.eu/trade/creating-opportunities/bilateral-relations/countries/united-states> accessed 10 August 2013.

29 Koen G. Berden and others, *Non-Tariff Measures in EU-US Trade and Investment—An Economic Analysis* (Ecorys 2009).

Karel De Gucht made a statement in June 2012 on the interim report[30] on the trans-Atlantic trade relationship in the following manner:

> The announcement of Presidents Barroso and Obama welcoming the publication of the interim report on how to deepen the transatlantic trade relationship is extremely encouraging. We are now entering the last leg of mapping out how we should tackle any eventual negotiation to boost growth and jobs through our trade partnership. I look forward to continue working with my US counterpart to complete the final stage allowing us to present both leaders with the final report as quickly as possible.[31]

From the perspective of climate change, in addition to the typical provisions on trade, investment, government procurement and intellectual property rights—among others—inserting a chapter on climate change mitigation in such an FTA would be a meaningful and effective way to reduce GHG emissions, since the US and the EU are the second and third largest emitters of GHG, respectively.

5.3 *Plurilaterals within Major Economies*

The Major Economies Forum on Energy and Climate (MEF)[32] and other international and regional clubs of major countries (e.g. G-8, G-8+5, G-20, APEC) as well as potential PTAS, such as an East Asia PTA or the kind of mega-bloc PTAS under consideration such as the Association of Southeast Asian Nations (ASEAN) + 3[33] and ASEAN + 6 (also known as the Regional Comprehensive Economic Partnership),[34] could serve as a platform to conclude these PTAS in green energy technologies. Such measures are reciprocal in character, easing competitiveness concerns. International organizations as well as global and regional clubs of major jurisdictions can play key bottom-up roles by generating specific initiatives and supporting initiatives by other governmental and

30 See <http://trade.ec.europa.eu/doclib/docs/2012/june/tradoc_149557.pdf> accessed 10 August 2013.

31 See <http://trade.ec.europa.eu/doclib/press/index.cfm?id=807> accessed 10 August 2013.

32 See Major Economies Forum on Energy and Climate, available at <http://www.majoreconomiesforum.org/about/descriptionpurpose.html> accessed 10 August 2013.

33 ASEAN + 3 comprises ASEAN plus China, Japan, and South Korea.

34 ASEAN + 6 comprises ASEAN plus China, Japan, South Korea, India, New Zealand, and Australia.

non-governmental actors.[35] To prevent further erosion of the WTO *acquis* due to PTA proliferation, these plurilateral agreements should ideally be arranged within the WTO to secure most-favored nation (MFN) treatment, rather than outside of the WTO, as PTAs proliferation implies the erosion of the WTO law principle of non-discrimination. Plurilateral agreements within the WTO are governed by the WTO's dispute settlement process,[36] albeit to use the WTO's dispute settlement system, countries needed a decision by the WTO Dispute Settlement Body,[37] and remain open for other WTO Members to accede to them if they find them useful for their offensive and defensive interests. It is therefore crucial to avoid plurilaterals outside of the WTO context.

6 Concluding Remarks

Admittedly, the approach of using climate-related PTAs as building blocks for multilateralism may lead to regulatory fragmentation as well as lack of coordination and confusion, known as the spaghetti-bowl effect,[38] legal conflict, and uncertainty[39] until all these PTAs are multilateralized. On the other hand, a global climate change agreement would serve as a more coherent and unified international framework for regulating climate change.[40] Moreover, since the building-blocks approach does not require universal participation, it may reduce the urgency of global cooperation.[41] Therefore, even if climate change

35 Richard Stewart and others, 'Strategic Analytics for Building a Global Climate Regime Bottom-Up' pp. 20–21, paper presented at the conference 'Reaching International Cooperation on Climate Change Mitigation,' December 21–23, 2011 (unpublished paper; on file with author).

36 See for instance art. XXII of the Agreement on Government Procurement of the WTO.

37 Notification under Appendix 1 of the Dispute Settlement Understanding—Communication from the Chairman of the Committee on Government Procurement WT/DSB/7 (July 1996).

38 T. Sugiyama and J. Sinton, 'Orchestra of Treaties: A Future Climate Regime Scenario with Multiple Treaties among Like-minded Countries' (2005) 5(1) International Environmental Agreements 65, 65.

39 See for instance Richard Stewart, 'Environmental Regulatory Decision Making Under Uncertainty' in R.O. Zerbe and T. Swanson (eds), *An Introduction to the Law and Economics of Environmental Policy: Issues in Institutional Design* (Elsevier 2002).

40 See generally F. Biermann and others, 'The Fragmentation of Global Governance Architectures: A Framework for Analysis' (2009) 9 Glob Environ Polit 14, 14.

41 Ibid., 26.

policy does become increasingly bilateral,[42] these agreements would ultimately have to lead to a global climate treaty with common rules and common procedures. Nonetheless, overall there is much within the trade experience that can be inspirational for the case of climate change.

Existing PTAs (such as NAFTA) which do not include climate change mitigation chapters should be re-negotiated in order to insert such provisions. One potential negative aspect of using PTAs to promote climate change mitigation is that to get to the conclusion of the proposed large PTAs (the TTIP and the TPP) may take very long, which is precisely what the climate change agenda needs to avoid. Furthermore, even if economically and legally feasible, it is politically less easy to have PTAs with strong climate change chapters.

42 Indeed, as a result of the outcome of the COP-17 in Durban, countries are planning bilateral and plurilateral negotiations to create emissions trading markets.

PART THREE

Considering Human Rights and Development Objectives

CHAPTER 6

Guaranteeing Socio-Economic Rights through Public-Private Partnerships between Host State and Foreign Investor—The Example of Ghana's Public Housing Project

Lars Schönwald[1]

1 Introduction

The right to housing belongs to the so-called second generation of human rights.[2] Deriving from the right to an adequate standard of living, the right to housing is of central importance for the enjoyment of all economic, social and cultural rights.[3] It has been recognized in numerous texts at both the

1 This chapter is a revised version of a paper presented at the '1st Conference of the Postgraduate and Early Professionals/Academics of the Society of International Economic Law (PEPA/SIEL)', held at Hamburg on 27 and 28 January 2012. Many thanks for valuable comments on this chapter go especially to Gabrielle Marceau, Anne Trebilcock and Freya Baetens as well as to Anthony Frazer. E-mail: lars.schoenwald@uni-passau.de.

2 The division of human rights into three generations was initially proposed by Karel Vasak, 'Human Rights: A Thirty-Year Struggle: the Sustained Efforts to Give Force of Law to the Universal Declaration of Human Rights' in United Nations Educational, Scientific, and Cultural Organization (UNESCO) (ed.), *UNESCO Courier 30:11* (UNESCO 1977). First generation human rights contain civil and political rights, and serve negatively to protect the individual from excesses of the State (just see Christian Tomuschat, *Human Rights, Between Idealism and Realism* (2nd edn, OUP 2008) 26–8). The second generation of human rights is composed of economic, social and cultural rights (just see Tomuschat, 27–8). Collective human rights such as the right of self-determination are part of the third generation of human rights (just see Tomuschat, 48–52). For the general division of human rights into generations see also Javaid Rehman, *International Human Rights Law* (Pearson Education Limited, 2010) 9–10 and Joseph Wronka, *Human Rights and Social Policy in the 21st Century, A History of the Idea of Human Rights and Comparison of the United Nations Universal Declaration of Human Rights with United States Federal and State Constitutions* (University Press of America, 1992) 25–8.

3 Committee on Economic, Social and Cultural Rights, *General Comment No 4 on the Right to Adequate Housing*, UN Doc E/1992/23, adopted on 13 December 1991.

 | DOI 10.1163/9789004270190_007

international and the regional level,[4] and also at the national level.[5] At the international level, the two most important texts are the (non-binding) 1948 Universal Declaration of Human Rights (UDHR)[6] and the 1966 International Covenant on Economic, Social and Cultural Rights (ICESCR).[7] At the regional level, the most important texts are the 1961 European Social Charter (ESC)[8] and various African instruments, such as the 1990 African Charter of Human and Peoples' Rights (ACHPR).[9]

Whereas so-called first generation human rights are considered to be inherent to each individual, so-called second generation human rights, such as the right to housing, have to be realized by the respective State.[10] Despite the willingness of most States to provide socio-economic rights,[11] several States

---

4 Just see Scott Leckie, *From Housing Needs to Housing Rights: An Analysis of the Right to Adequate Housing Under International Human Rights Law* (International Institute for the Environment and Development 1992).

5 Just see Scott Leckie, 'The UN Committee on Economic, Social and Cultural Rights and the Right to Adequate Housing: Towards an Appropriate Approach' (1989) 11 Hum. R. Q. 522, 522–4.

6 Adopted on 10 December 1948 by GA Res. 217A (III) of 10 December 1948, UN Doc A/810 at 71 (1948).

7 Adopted on 16 December 1966 by United Nations General Assembly Resolution 2200A (XXI), 21 U.N. GAOR Supp (No 16) at 49, UN Doc A/6316 (1966), 993 UNTS 3, entered into force on 3 January 1976. Besides that, housing rights have also been extensively recognized in the framework of a wide range of (mostly non-binding) international declarations on related fields. References to housing rights have been included within the Habitat Agenda (adopted at the Second United Nations Conference on Human Settlements (Habitat II) 1996, endorsed by GA Res. 51/177 of 16 December 1996, UN Doc A/CONF.165/14), the Agenda 21 (adopted at the United Nations Conference on Environment and Development 1992, endorsed by GA Res. 47/179 of 22 December 1992, UN Doc A/CONF.151/26/REV1 (Vol. I)), the Vancouver Declaration on Human Settlement (adopted at Habitat: United Nations Conference on Human Settlements 1976; United Nations Publications, Sales No E.76.IV7 and corrigendum), the Global Strategy for Shelter (GSS; adopted by GA Res. 43/181 on 20 December 1988), and other texts. For further information about these texts see United Nations Human Settlements Programme (UN-HABITAT) and Office of the High Commissioner for Human Rights (OHCHR) (eds), *Housing Rights Legislation: Review of International and National Legal Instruments* (UN-HABITAT 2002) 8 et seq.

8 Adopted on 18 October 1961, 529 UNTS 89, entered into force on 26 February 1965; revised on 3 May 1996, ETS No 163 (1996), entered into force on 1 July 1999.

9 Adopted on 27 June 1981, OAU Doc. CAB/LEG/67/3 rev5, 21 ILM 58 (1982), entered into force on 21 October 1986.

10 See Tomuschat (n. 2) 110.

11 Just see Modibo Ocran, 'Socioeconomic Rights in the African Context: Problems with Concept and Enforcement' (2008) 5 Loy U Chi Int'l L Rev 1.

lack of sufficient funds in order to do so.[12] Therefore, a few States have already concluded public-private partnerships (PPPs)[13] aiming at guaranteeing socio-economic rights.[14] Other States are observing the progress of these PPPs quite carefully and analyze whether these PPPs can foster the development of the respective State and stimulate economic growth,[15] as they are also planning to conclude such agreements.[16]

One of the first PPPs with regard to the right to housing was the so-called Ghanaian Housing Project. This project, agreed upon the Republic of Ghana (hereafter Ghana) and the Korean-based corporation STX Engineering and Construction, Ghana Ltd., was inaugurated on 27 January 2011.[17] It aimed at providing mainly members of the security forces with affordable and adequate housings, thus was aiming at guaranteeing the right to housing at least of one

---

12 See ibid. See also Henry J. Steiner, Philip Alston and Ryan Goodmann, *International Human Rights in Context—Law Politics Morals* (OUP, 2007) 275 who argues that especially developing countries are confronted with an impossible challenge as the nature of the obligations under the ICESCR is so onerous that most States will not be able to comply; similarly in this regard Office of the High Commissioner for Human Rights, *General Comment No 4 on the Right to Adequate Housing (art. 11 (1) of the Covenant)*, UN Doc E/1992/23, adopted on 13 December 1991.

13 There is no accepted definition of PPPs (see Guy Peters, '"With a Little Help From Our Friends": Public-Private Partnerships as Institutions and Instruments', in J. Pierre (ed.), *Partnerships in Urban Governance, European and American Experience* (Macmillan Press 1997) 11–33, 11.). PPPs are generally characterized by the cooperative partnership of government and one or more private sector companies aiming at delivering societal goods in a more efficient way (see ibid).

14 Just see with regard to the Federal Republic of Nigeria Israel A. Ademiluyi, 'Public Housing Delivery Strategies in Nigeria: A Historical Perspective of Policies and Programmes' 12 Journal of Sustainable Development in Africa (2010) 153.

15 More critical in this regard Richard H. Adams, Jr., Alfredo Cuecuecha and John Page, 'Remittances, Consumption and Investment in Ghana', World Bank Policy Research Working Paper Series No 4515, Washington D.C. 2008, who show that households receiving remittances in Ghana do not spend more at the margin on food, education and housing than households with similar income levels and characteristics that do not receive remittances.

16 Just see for example the Republic of Kenya and its plan to guarantee the right to housing through PPPs, <http://www.housing.go.ke/?p=451> accessed 27 August 2013.

17 Ghana Government, 'Brief on the Ghana National Housing Project to be executed by STX Engineering and Construction, Ghana Ltd' <http://www.ghana.govgh/index.php/information/speeches/5739-brief-on-the-ghana-national-housing-project-to-be-executed-by-stx-engineering-and-construction-ghana-ltd> accessed 27 August 2013.

group of individuals.[18] Ghana ratified the ICESCR on 7 September 2000 without reservation.[19] In addition, Ghana ratified the ACHPR on 24 January 1989 without reservations relating to the right to housing.[20] Although Ghana does not belong to the group of so-called Least-Developed Countries (LDCs) as determined by the United Nations Office of the High Representative for Least Developed Countries, Landlocked Developing Countries and Small Island Developing States (OHRLLS),[21] it still belongs to the group of Heavily Indebted Poor Countries (HIPC) as determined by the World Bank.[22] As a result of limited financial resources, Ghana regularly lacks sufficient funds in order to comply with its obligations arising out of the ICESCR, the ACHPR and other international treaties.[23]

By ratifying the ICESCR and the ACHPR, Ghana has committed itself to guarantee the socio-economic rights contained within the respective treaty. However, neither the two treaties nor human rights law in general require that States have to guarantee the respective rights directly. Instead, the treaties and human rights law in general leaves it to the discretion of the respective State how it guarantees socio-economic rights, as long as the rights are guaranteed effectively at all.[24] By analyzing the various obligations for States arising out of international human rights law and by examining whether and to

18 Ibid. Due to various difficulties and disputes, the government of Ghana has meanwhile exited from the project and withdrew its sovereign guarantee on the project in July 2012; just see Della Russel Ocloo, 'Govt Withdraws Sovereign Guarantee on STX Housing Project' <http://www.modernghana.com/news/405867/1/govt-withdraws-sovreign-guarantee-on-stx-housing-phtml> accessed 27 August 2013.

19 United Nations, 'United Nations Treaty Collection' <http://treaties.un.org/Pages/ViewDetails.aspx?chapter=4&lang=en&mtdsg_no=IV-3&src=TREATY> accessed 27 August 2013.

20 See African Union, 'List of Countries Which Have Signed, Ratified/Acceded to the African Charter on Human and Peoples' Rights' <http://www.africa-union.org/root/au/Documents/Treaties/List/African%20Charter%20on%20Human%20and%20Peoples%20Rights.pdf> accessed 27 August 2013.

21 See Commission of the European Communities, 'Proposal for a Council Decision concluding the stepping stone Economic Partnership Agreement between the European Community and its Member States, of the one part, and Ghana, on the other part', COM(2008) 441 final; 2008/0137 (AVC).

22 Just see The World Bank, 'Heavily Indebted Poor Countries (40 countries)' <http://go.worldbank.org/ 4IMVXTQ090> accessed 27 August 2013.

23 Philip Alston, 'Ships Passing in the Night: The Current State of the Human Rights and Development Debate seen through the Lens of the Millennium Development Goals' (2005) 27 HRQ 755.

24 Tomuschat (n. 2) 97–8.

what extent these obligations promote or exclude the possibility to guarantee socio-economic rights through PPPs, it will be analyzed to what extent socio-economic rights can be guaranteed through PPPs and it will be examined whether the Ghanaian Public Housing Project would have been in accordance with international law. In order to do so, the compliance of PPPs aiming at guaranteeing socio-economic rights with specific ICESCR and ACHPR provisions relating to the right to housing will be assessed in the first part, followed by an examination of the more general ICESCR and ACHPR provisions and their limitations on the possibility to guarantee socio-economic rights through PPPs in the second part.

2 Compliance with Specific ICESCR and ACHPR Provisions Relating to the Right to Housing

Both, the ICESCR and the ACHPR contain specific provisions relating to the right to housing. Whereas the right to housing is explicitly mentioned in Article 11 of the ICESCR, Articles 14 (right to property), 16 (right to health), 18(1) (right to family life) and 24 (right of peoples to a general satisfactory environment) of the ACHPR can be interpreted as to comprise the right to housing as well.[25]

2.1 *Compliance with Article 11 of the ICESCR*

Pursuant to Article 11 of the ICESCR, Member States to the ICESCR such as Ghana are obliged to take all necessary measures to realize

> the right of everyone to an adequate standard of living for himself and his family, including ... to the continuous improvement of living conditions. The States Parties will take appropriate steps to ensure the realization of this right, recognizing to this effect the essential importance of international co-operation based on free consent.

25 See African Commission on Human and Peoples' Rights, 'The Social and Economic Rights Action Center and the Center for Economic and Social Rights v Nigeria', ACHRP Commn No 55/96, para. 60. See also Chidi Anselm Odinkalu, 'Implementing Economic, Social and Cultural Rights Under the African Charter on Human and Peoples' Rights' in Malcolm D. Evans and Rachel Murray, *The African Charter on Human and Peoples' Rights, The System in Practice, 1986–2000* (CUP 2002) 192. See also Anselm Chidi Odinkalu, 'Analysis of Paralysis or Paralysis by Analysis? Implementing Economic, Social, and Cultural Rights Under the African Charter on Human and Peoples' Rights' (2001) 23 HRQ 327.

Regardless of the reference to 'himself and his family', the right to adequate housing applies to everyone.[26] It is also noteworthy that Article 11(1) of the ICESCR is considered to provide more than just a roof over one's head, but that adequacy is of great importance.[27] Both, the Commission on Human Settlements and the Global Strategy for Shelter to the Year 2000 have stated that adequate shelter refers to an adequate privacy, space, security, lighting and ventilation, basic infrastructure and location with regard to work and basic facilities and all at a reasonable cost.[28]

With regard to the Ghanaian Public Housing Project, it could be argued that the housing units which should have been built under that scheme were only designated to members of Ghana's security forces, and therefore, the Ghanaian Public Housing Project was in violation of Article 11(1) of the ICESCR as it did not provide the right to housing for everyone. However, Article 11(1) of the ICESCR does not require that every public housing project has to be designed to provide shelter for everyone as long as in total everyone has the right to housing.

Ghana was and still is facing a severe housing deficit. In its overview of the current housing rights situation and related activities in Ghana, the United Nations Human Settlements Programme (UN-HABITAT) points out that the housing deficit is in excess of 500,000 units whilst supply figures vary between 25,000 and 40,000 units per annum as against annual requirement of 70,000 to 100,000 units leading to a national annual housing demand supply ratio of about 35%.[29] The average ratio worldwide is about 40%.[30]

Although the Ghanaian Public Housing Project was considered to be the first public housing project in Ghana, and despite its failure, the government of the West-African State is currently planning similar projects which have the overall aim to provide housing units for poor as well as low- and

---

26 Office of the High Commissioner for Human Rights (n. 12) para. 6.

27 Ibid., 7.

28 See UN Commission on Human Settlements (UN-HABITAT), 'First report of the Commission on Human Settlements on the implementation of the Global Strategy for Shelter to the year 2000', UN Doc A/43/8/Add.1, § 2. For the Global Strategy for Shelter just see UN Doc A/RES/43/181.

29 UN-HABITAT, Housing and Urban Development in Ghana: with Special Reference to Low-Income Housing (Nairobi 2004); see also UN-HABITAT, Ghana Housing Profile (Nairobi 2011) 58–68.

30 See United Nations Department of Economic and Social Affairs (UNDESA)—Population Division, *Population Distribution, Urbanization, Internal Migration and Development: An International Perspective* (DESA, New York 2011) 1–2.

middle-income citizens.[31] Therefore, the Ghanaian Public Housing Project was only a part of an overall policy aiming at guaranteeing everyone the right to housing as prescribed by Article 11(1) of the ICESCR.

The simple availability of housing units does not, however, suffice in order to fulfill the obligation arising out of Article 11(1) of the ICESCR. Instead, Article 11(1) of the ICESCR requires that all persons shall possess a certain degree of security of tenure which guarantees legal protection against forced eviction, harassment and other threats.[32] Article 11(1) of the ICESCR does not prohibit evictions at all. However, a State party to the ICESCR is obliged to take immediate measures aiming at conferring legal security of tenure[33] by, for example, adopting laws regulating evictions which also ensure that that evictions are only carried out as a last resort after all alternatives to eviction have been provided and that all evictions comply with international standards.[34] A recent statement by the international non-governmental organization *Amnesty International* concluded that Ghana's laws do not provide adequate protection against forced evictions.[35] In fact, neither does the constitution of Ghana contain any provision on the right to housing, nor does an explicit provision exists within the Ghanaian legal system which outlaws forced evictions which are not carried out as a last resort and which do not comply with international standards.[36] The case *Old Fadama*[37] illustrates that there is no legal protection against forced evictions available in Ghana.

---

31 Just see the 2005 State of the Nation Address of then President J. A. Kuffour which highlights are available at <http://www.ghanaweb.com/GhanaHomePage/NewsArchive/artikel.php?ID=74665> accessed 13 December 2013; see also Republic of Ghana, *The Coordinated Programme of Economic and Social Development Policies, 2010–2016—An Agenda for Shared Growth and Accelerated Development for a Better Ghana* (Accra 2010) 58–60.

32 Office of the High Commissioner for Human Rights (n. 12) para. 8.

33 Ibid.

34 See also African Commission on Human and Peoples' Rights (ACommHPR), 'Resolution 231: Resolution on the Right to Adequate Housing and Protection from Forced Evictions', adopted at the 52nd Ordinary Session of the African Commission on Human and Peoples' Rights held in Yamoussoukro, Côte d'Ivoire, from 9 to 22 October 2012.

35 Amnesty International, 'Amnesty International statement to the African Commission on Human and Peoples' Rights: State of housing rights and forced evictions in Africa' (IOR 63/004/2011, 7 November 2011) available at <http://www.unhcr.org/refworld/docid/4eba7e912.html> accessed 27 August 2013.

36 See ibid.

37 Just see Afia Afenah, 'Conceptualizing the Effects of Neoliberal Urban Policies on Housing Rights: An Analysis of the Attempted Unlawful Forced Eviction of an Informal Settlement in Accra, Ghana' (Development Planning Unit, London 2009) available at <http://www.

In addition, Article 11(1) of the ICESCR requires that the housing units must contain certain facilities essential for health, security, comfort and nutrition.[38] This includes the right to sustainable access to safe drinking water for example.[39] In 2008, Ghana launched the 'National Water Policy' which aims at introducing a comprehensive sector policy and at reducing the various challenges the drinking water supply is facing in Ghana.[40] Despite these efforts, the sustainable supply with safe drinking water remains rather problematic in most parts of Ghana.[41] Especially in rural areas, but also in urban areas, the access to safe water supply is very limited.[42] Furthermore, Article 11(1) of the ICESCR determines that the adequate housing must be accessible to those entitled to it.[43] States are obliged to give priority to those social groups living in unfavorable conditions by giving them particular consideration.[44] This includes such disadvantaged groups as the elderly, children, the physically disabled, the terminally ill, HIV-positive individuals, persons with persistent medical problems, the mentally ill, victims of natural disasters, people living in disaster-prone areas and similar groups.[45] Although the Ghanaian Public Housing Project was intended to be only a part of an overall housing program, the housing units which should have been built under this PPP were designated for members of Ghana's security forces.[46] As a result, although Ghana is one out of only three States in West Africa which has a female police association and gender policies within the police and security forces,[47] and thus it

---

bartlett.ucl.ac.uk/dpu/latest/publications/dpu-working-papers/WP139_Afia_Afenah_Internet_copy.pdf> accessed 27 August 2013 for more information on the evictions.

38 Office of the High Commissioner for Human Rights (n. 12).

39 Ibid.

40 Ghanaian Water Resources Commission, 'National Water Policy' <http://www.wrc-gh.org/nationalwaterpoli cy.html> accessed 27 August 2013.

41 Just see Water and Sanitation Monitoring Platform (WSMP), 'Status of Ghana's Drinking Water and Sanitation Sector' (WSMP, Accra 2009) available <http://www.wsmporg/downloads/country-summary-sheet-09.pdf> accessed 27 August 2013.

42 See World Health Organization (WHO) and United Nations International Children's Emergency Fund (UNICEF), 'Joint Monitoring Program for Water Supply and Sanitation (JMP)' <http://www.wssinfo.org/> accessed 27 August 2013.

43 Office of the High Commissioner for Human Rights (n. 12) para. 8.

44 Ibid., 11.

45 Ibid., 8.

46 See (n. 3).

47 The North-South Institute, 'Policy Brief: Freedom through Association: Realizing the Potential of West Africa's Female Police Staff Associations' (Spring 2012) <http://www.nsi-ins.ca/images/documents/freedom_through_association_brief_finalrev.pdf> accessed 27 August 2013.

seems to increase the likelihood that no discrimination will take place against women, priority was not given to disadvantaged societal groups.

Finally, pursuant to Article 11(1) of the ICESCR, adequate housing must be in a location which allows access to employment options, health-care services, schools, child-care centers and other social facilities.[48] The 30,000 housing units which should have been built under the Ghanaian Public Housing Project were to be spread throughout the country.[49] Especially in rural areas in Ghana, social facilities are scarce.

2.2 *Compliance with Articles 14, 16, 18(1) and 24 of the ACHPR*

Articles 14, 16, 18(1) and 24 of the ACHPR are interpreted as providing the right to adequate housing.[50] This right includes among other issues the affordability of housing through housing subsidies or even public housing projects.[51] In addition, the right to housing implicitly guaranteed by Articles 14, 16, 18(1) and 24 of the ACHPR is considered to oblige States parties to the ACHPR to, among other issues, guarantee to all persons a certain degree of security of tenure, ensure that every individual enjoys access to adequate housing which includes access to natural and common resources, safe drinking water and sanitation, and ensure that housing developments are in areas which allow access to employment, health care services, schools, child-care centers and other social facilities.[52] Hence, the ACHPR contains with regard to the right to housing at least the same guarantees as Article 11(1) of the ICESCR. As a result, the findings with regard to the compliance of the Ghanaian Public Housing Project with Article 11(1) of the ICESCR also apply to the compliance of the project with the right to housing implicitly provided by the ACHPR.

---

48 Office of the High Commissioner for Human Rights (n. 12) para. 8.

49 Ibid., 3.

50 Ibid., 5.

51 See UN Commission on Human Settlements (UN-HABITAT) (n. 29). For the Global Strategy for Shelter just see UN Doc A/RES/43/181. See also the Report of the Special Rapporteur on Adequate Housing, Miloon Kothari, UN Doc E/CN.4/2006/41, para. 29 and Walter Kälin and Jörg Künzli, *Universeller Menschenrechtsschutz* (Helbing Lichtenhahn Verlag 2008) 352. For a general definition of affordable housing just see Basudeh Bhatta, *Analysis of Urban Growth and Sprawl from Remote Sensing Data* (Springer 2010) 23.

52 African Commission on Human and Peoples' Rights, 'Draft Principles and Guidelines on Economic, Social and Cultural Rights' in African Commission on Human and Peoples' Rights (ed.), *Second Annual Activity Report of the African Commission on Human and Peoples' Rights 1988–1989*, ACHPR/RPT/2nd, Annex XII, para. 64 <http://www.achpr.org/files/instruments/economic-social-cultural/achpr_instr_guide_draft_esc_rights_eng.pdf> accessed 13 December 2013.

Furthermore, States parties to the ACHPR are also obliged to, among other issues, legislate against forced evictions and should ensure that adequate and effective legal or other appropriate remedies are available to any persons who are threatened with, undergo, remain vulnerable to, or defend against forced evictions.[53] As pointed out above,[54] there is no legislation against forced evictions in Ghana. Because of the lacking legislation against forced evictions, there are no legal remedies available.[55]

3 Compliance with More General ICESCR and ACHPR Provisions

Besides the specific ICESCR and ACHPR provisions providing a right to housing, States have to comply of course with the more general provisions of the human rights treaties as well. Consequently, the Ghanaian Public Housing Project must also fulfill the criteria established by these general provisions.

3.1 *Compliance with More General ICESCR Provisions*

Part II of the ICESCR contains a number of general provisions relevant for the application and execution of the various more specific provisions of this treaty. With regard to the present question, the most pertinent provisions of Part II of the ICESCR are Articles 2(1), 2(2) and 3 of the ICESCR.

3.1.1 Obligations Arising Out Article 2(1) of the ICESCR

Basically, it is up to the State to decide how it complies with its obligations arising out of international human rights treaties such as the ICESCR or the ACHPR.[56] It is obvious that States cannot immediately fulfill these obligations upon ratifying the treaty. However, as human rights, the right to housing and other second generation human rights are not political options that governments can choose to adopt or not.[57] It is for these and other important reasons that the ICESCR for example uses a very careful combination of terms to describe the nature and scope of legal obligations possessed by each State

53 Ibid.

54 Ibid., 8–9.

55 Ibid.

56 See Thomas Buergenthal, 'Modern Constitutions and Human Rights Treaties' (1998) 36 Colum. J. Transnat'l L. 211.

57 Ibid., 211ff.

Party to the Covenant.[58] Article 2(1) of the ICESCR asserts that States have to use all appropriate means to the maximum of their available resources in order to progressively realize the rights recognized in the ICESCR to their full extent. This might even require international technical and economic assistance and co-operation.

(a) *Obligation to 'Progressively Realize' Socio-Economic Rights*

Article 2(1) of the ICESCR is seen as the cornerstone of the entire Covenant.[59] Therefore, a proper understanding of the idea of the progressive realization of socio-economic rights is fundamental for the understanding of housing rights.[60] It has to be noted that the 'progressive realization' component of the ICESCR does not imply that only once a State reaches a certain level of economic development, the rights established under the ICESCR must be realized. Rather, States parties to the ICESCR are obliged 'to move immediately and as quickly as possible towards the realization of economic, social and cultural rights'.[61] Certainly, certain rights may be more apt to be implemented in terms of the 'progressive obligation' rule. This applies

> especially to non-discrimination provisions and to the obligations of States parties to refrain from actively violating economic, social and cultural rights or withdrawing legal and other protection relating to these rights.[62]

In addition, States parties to the ICESCR are obliged to devote all existing resources in the most effective way possible to the realization of the rights enshrined in the ICESCR.[63]

58 United Nations Human Settlements Programme (UN-HABITAT) and Office of the High Commissioner for Human Rights (OHCHR) (eds) (n. 7) 13.

59 See Committee on Economic, Social and Cultural Rights, *General Comment No 3 on the nature of States parties obligations (art. 2, para. 1 of the Covenant)*, UN Doc E/1991/23, adopted on 14 December 1990.

60 United Nations Human Settlements Programme (UN-HABITAT) and Office of the High Commissioner for Human Rights (OHCHR) (eds) (n. 7) 13.

61 United Nations Centre for Human Rights (ed.), 'Fact Sheet No 16 (Rev 1), The Committee on Economic, Social and Cultural Rights' (OHCHR 1996) <http://www.ohchr.org/Documents/Publications/FactSheet16rev1en.pdf> accessed 27 August 2013.

62 Ibid.

63 Ibid.

These points are largely based on the General Comment No. 3[64] and the so-called Limburg Principles.[65] Ultimately, 'progressive realization' means that States are obliged to continuously strive to strengthen socio-economic rights such as the right to housing.[66] The 'progressive realization' clause imposes an obligation on States to move as expeditiously and effectively as possible towards realizing fully the right to housing.[67]

However, this does not imply that the State is required to build housing units for the entire population by itself.[68] Instead, States have the primary duty to create conditions so that all residents may benefit from and enjoy in full the entitlements implied in the right to housing, within the shortest possible timeframe.[69] General Comment No. 4 reiterates this perspective, attesting that

> [m]easures designed to satisfy a State party's obligations in respect of the right to adequate housing may reflect whatever mix of public and private sector measures considered appropriate. While in some States public financing of housing might most usefully be spent on direct construction of new housing, in most cases, experience has shown the inability of Governments to fully satisfy housing deficits with publicly built housing.[70]

Consequently, it is at least in general possible for States to guarantee socio-economic rights such as the right to housing through PPPs, as long as the other obligations under the ICESCR are fulfilled,[71] and as long as the State ensures that access to the housing units provided under the PPP is granted in a non-discriminatory way pursuant to Articles 2(2) and 3 of the ICESCR.

---

64 Committee on Economic, Social and Cultural Rights (n. 59).

65 United Nations Commission on Human Rights, Note verbale dated 86/12/05 from the Permanent Mission of the Netherlands to the United Nations Office at Geneva addressed to the Centre for Human Rights ('Limburg Principles'), UN Doc E/CN.4/1987/17, 8 January 1987.

66 United Nations Human Settlements Programme (UN-HABITAT) and Office of the High Commissioner for Human Rights (OHCHR) (eds) (n. 7) 14.

67 Ibid.

68 United Nations, 'The right to adequate housing', Final Report submitted by Mr. Sachar Ravindar, Special Rapporteur, UN Doc E/CN.4/Sub.2/1995/12, paras 4–5.

69 United Nations Human Settlements Programme (UN-HABITAT) and Office of the High Commissioner for Human Rights (OHCHR) (eds) (n. 7) 19.

70 Office of the High Commissioner for Human Rights (OHCHR), *General Comment No. 4 on the right to adequate housing*, UN Doc E/1992/23, para. 14.

71 For an overview over the various obligations under the ICESCR, just see United Nations Centre for Human Rights (ed.) (n. 61).

(b) *Obligation to Co-operate and Assist Internationally Regarding the Realization of Socio-Economic Rights*

The wording of Article 2(1) of the ICESCR, which even creates the obligation of international co-operation and assistance with regard to the realization of socio-economic rights, emphasizes this finding. If the poorest countries have the obligation to appeal to international co-operation in order to realize socio-economic rights, rich countries have the obligation to respond. They have committed themselves to this by ratifying the ICESCR, which obliges governments to act, both through their own efforts and through international co-operation and assistance, to the full extent of available resources in order to realize socio-economic rights.[72]

In its General Comment No. 4, the Committee on Economic, Social and Cultural Rights has stated that, with regard to international assistance, the funding provided 'does little to address the housing needs of disadvantaged groups'.[73] Therefore, 'State Parties should, when contemplating international financial cooperation, seek to indicate areas relevant to the right to adequate housing where external financing would have the most effect'.[74] As a result, the obligation of international co-operation and assistance enables States to guarantee human rights through PPPs. International financial institutions such as the International Finance Corporation (IFC) encourage States and foreign investors alike to undertake PPPs aiming at guaranteeing socio-economic rights.[75]

(c) *Obligation to Implement Socio-economic Rights*

Pursuant to Article 2(1) of the ICESCR, States are obliged to implement the right to housing.[76] This obligation requires governments to adopt necessary legislative measures to design a strategy and an action plan for housing at the national level, and to guarantee that housing will be adequate, available, accessible, and affordable to everybody, including in rural areas and the most vulnerable urban areas.[77] The fact that economic, social and cultural rights

---

72 See art. 2(1) of the ICESCR and art. 2 of the ACHPR.

73 Committee on Economic, Social and Cultural Rights (n. 3).

74 Ibid.

75 See International Finance Corporation, 'IFC's Vision, Values & Purpose' <http://www1.ifc./org/wps/wcm/connect/corp_ext_content/ifc_external_corporate_site/about+ifc/vision> accessed 27 August 2013.

76 See Committee on Economic, Social and Cultural Rights (n. 59).

77 See Robert E. Robertson, 'Measuring State Compliance with the Obligation to Devote the 'Maximum Available Resources' to Realize Economic, Social, and Cultural Rights' (1994) 16 HRQ 693.

must be guaranteed also in rural areas and most vulnerable urban areas, is a common problem with PPP projects aiming at guaranteeing human rights.[78] Private corporations will regularly only agree to a PPP contract if it appears profitable. If there is just one bidder for a PPP, the imbalance between providing everyone with an adequate and affordable shelter, and the profit for the private corporation might be even bigger. However, States must be aware during the negotiating phase of the PPP that they deal with a right of their citizens. Providing housing is naturally more lucrative in urban than in rural areas, as certain infrastructure, especially water supply and sanitation, will be already present in urban areas whereas it has to be constructed in rural areas first.[79] However, it is required under the principle of the right to housing for everyone that basic housing must be provided in remote areas as well.[80] Therefore, a purely economic calculation cannot be applied to the question of increasing access to housing. Given that private corporations will, however, apply an economic calculation, the affordability of the housing units built under the PPP might be debatable.[81]

Affordability means that the personal or household financial costs associated with housing should be at such a level that the attainment and satisfication of other basic needs are not threatened or compromised.[82] This includes the requirement of providing subsidies and tax incentives and to expand housing construction to meet the needs of all categories of the population, particularly low-income families.[83]

78 See Stephen C. McCaffrey, 'A Human Right to Water: Domestic and International Implications' (1992–1993) 5 GIELR 1.

79 See Philip Amis, 'Introduction: Key themes in contemporary African urbanisation' in P. Amis and P. Lloyd (eds), *Housing Africa's Urban Poor* (Manchester University Press 1990) 1, 24ff.

80 See—with regard to the right to water—Pierre Thielbörger, 'The Human Right to Water Versus Investor Rights: Double-Dilemma or Pseudo-Conflict?', in P.-M. Dupuy, F. Francioni and E.-U. Petersmann (eds), *Human Rights in International Investment Law and Arbitration* (OUP 2009) 487, 504.

81 For a general definition of affordable housing just see Basudeh Bhatta, *Analysis of Urban Growth and Sprawl from Remote Sensing Data* (Springer 2010) 23. See also UN Commission on Human Settlements (UN-HABITAT), 'First report of the Commission on Human Settlements on the implementation of the Global Strategy for Shelter to the year 2000', UN Doc A/43/8/Add.1, § 2; for the Global Strategy for Shelter just see UN Doc A/RES/43/181. See also the Report of the Special Rapporteur on Adequate Housing, Miloon Kothari, UN Doc E/CN.4/2006/41, para. 29, and Walter Kälin and Jörg Künzli, *Universeller Menschenrechtsschutz* (Helbing Lichtenhahn Verlag 2008) 352.

82 Office of the High Commissioner for Human Rights (n. 12) para. 8.

83 African Commission on Human and Peoples' Rights (n. 52) para. 64.

Although the Ghanaian Public Housing Project itself does not meet these requirements in total, as the housing units—despite the original intent—should have been built mainly in urban areas, Ghana was and still is striving for an overall public housing policy which would also include subsidies and tax incentives.

As seen, the obligation to implement the right to housing imposes certain legal restraints which States have to observe in order to comply with international human rights law. Although the Ghanaian Public Housing Project itself does not meet these requirements, the overall Ghanaian public housing policy arguably complies with these requirements.

3.1.2 Obligations Arising Out of Articles 2(2) and 3 of the ICESCR

According to Articles 2(2) and 3 of the ICESCR, States are obliged to provide the rights guaranteed in the Covenant in a non-discriminatory way. With regard to the Ghanaian Public Housing Project, the housing units which will be built under this scheme are primarily designed to accommodate Ghanaians working for the police and other forms of security force.[84] Therefore, it has to be determined whether this constitutes 'discrimination' within the meaning of Articles 2(2) and 3 of the ICESCR. In order to do so, the notion of 'discrimination' under these Articles has to be defined first, followed by an analysis of whether the Ghanaian Public Housing Project is discriminatory.

(a) *Discrimination in the Meaning of Articles 2(2) and 3 of the ICESCR*

Article 2(2) of the ICESCR prohibits any discrimination based on race, colour, sex, language, religion, political or other opinion, national or social origin, property, birth or other status. In addition, Article 3 of the ICESCR obliges States to 'undertake to ensure the equal right of men and women to the enjoyment of all economic, social and cultural rights'. As Ghana is (still) considered to be a developing country,[85] the exception in Article 2(3) ICESCR is applicable. This provision allows developing countries to discriminate against non-nationals to some extent. However, Article 2(3) of the ICESCR does only allow some kind of discrimination with regard to national origin; it does not allow any other kind of discrimination.[86]

84 Ghana Government (n. 17).

85 Ibid., 4.

86 See Committee on Economic, Social and Cultural Rights, General Comment No. 16 on the equal right of men and women to the enjoyment of all economic, social and cultural rights (art. 3 of the International Covenant on Economic, Social and Cultural Rights) para. 16, UN Doc E/C.12/2005/4, adopted on 11 August 2005.

The Committee on Economic, Social and Cultural Rights asserts in its General Comment No. 20[87] that the provision on non-discrimination is one of the most fundamental obligations of States in the ICESCR.[88] Discrimination is understood to constitute 'any distinction, exclusion, restriction or preference or other differential treatment that is directly or indirectly based on the prohibited grounds of discrimination'.[89] Similarly, discrimination against women is considered to be

> any distinction, exclusion or restriction made on the basis of sex which has the effect or purpose of impairing or nullifying the recognition, enjoyment or exercise by women, irrespective of their marital status, on a basis of equality of men and women, of human rights and fundamental freedoms in the political, economic, social, cultural, civil or any other field.[90]

Basically, Member States to the ICESCR are primarily obliged pursuant to Article 2(2) and 3 of the ICESCR alike to adopt legislative measures in order to ensure that the prohibition of discrimination is recognized at the national level.[91] Although the 1992 Constitution of Ghana prohibits all forms of discrimination on the basis of race, gender, disability, language, or social status,[92] the 2011 Country Report on Human Rights Practices in Ghana concludes that enforcement of this prohibition was generally inadequate.[93] The report found that '[d]iscrimination against persons with HIV/AIDS was a problem. [...]

87 Committee on Economic, Social and Cultural Rights, General Comment No 20 on Non-discrimination in economic, social and cultural rights (art. 2, para. 2, of the International Covenant on Economic, Social and Cultural Rights), UN Doc E/C.12/GC/20, adopted on 2 July 2009.

88 Ibid., 7.

89 Ibid.

90 See the definition in art. 1 of the 1980 Convention on the Elimination of All Forms of Discrimination against Women (CEDAW) which is also considered to be applicable with regard to art. 3 ICESCR, see Committee on Economic, Social and Cultural Rights (n. 86), para. 10.

91 See Committee on Economic, Social and Cultural Rights (n. 87), para. 37, Committee on Economic, Social and Cultural Rights (n. 86), para. 21 respectively.

92 Art. 17(2) of the 1992 Ghanaian Constitution.

93 United States Department of State, 2011 Country Reports on Human Rights Practices—Ghana (24 May 2012), available at <http://www.unhcr.org/refworld/docid/4fc75a9bc.html> accessed 27 August 2013.

Instances where HIV-positive people were forced to leave their jobs or houses were common'.[94] In addition, the report revealed that

> women continued to experience discrimination in access to employment. [...] Traditional practices and social norms often denied women their statutory entitlements to inheritance and property, a legally registered marriage with the associated legal rights, and the maintenance and custody of children.[95]

Ghana is one out of only three States in West Africa which has a female police association and gender policies within the police and security forces.[96] This seems to increase the likelihood that no discrimination will take place. As there are no reports available stating whether people with HIV/AIDS are excluded from Ghana's security force, no statement can be made whether people with HIV/AIDS are discriminated against in Ghana.

However, at least in theory, it is thinkable that discrimination takes place. Discrimination can occur on the one hand by the State itself, and on the other hand by the foreign investor. In order to determine whether the possibility to guarantee socio-economic rights through PPPs is in accordance with international human rights law, it has to be examined how the individual and/or the State can—or even has to—respond to any discrimination.

(b) *Response to Discrimination by the Host State*

Any discrimination within the meaning of Articles 2(2) and 3 of the ICESCR by the host State would constitute a breach of the State's obligations arising out of this treaty. The Optional Protocol to the ICESCR has been adopted recently, but has not been ratified by most States, and thus is not yet in force.[97] Thus a violation of the right to housing contained in the ICESCR cannot be brought to the attention of the Committee on Economic, Social and Cultural Rights by an individual. Therefore, individual complaints at the international level are not available.

Another possibility would be a State-to-State complaint. The ICESCR does not contain a specific State-to-State complaint procedure like the 1966 International Covenant on Civil and Political Rights (ICCPR). However, the ratification of the ICESCR imposes several *erga omnes*-obligations upon

94 Ibid.
95 Ibid.
96 The North-South Institute (n. 47).
97 See Thielbörger (n. 80) 507.

the various Member States.[98] If a State is in breach of its *erga omnes*-obligations, every other State might bring the case to the attention of the International Court of Justice (ICJ) pursuant to Article 48 of the International Law Commission Draft articles on Responsibility of States for Internationally Wrongful Acts (ILC Articles).[99] In practice, only a few States have at all referred to an infringement of an *erga omnes*-obligation and the ICJ denied in these cases the justiciability of the alleged infringements, although it affirmed the concept of *erga omnes*-obligations.[100] Reasons for the limited number of cases might be that the ICJ is not considered to be a human rights court. Its main function is to solve disputes between States which normally do not arise in the field of human rights law. In addition, disputes involving human rights normally arise between individuals and the respective State. Bringing a claim to the ICJ against another State for the violation of human rights might even be considered as an intervention into the domestic affairs of the other State, and thus would constitute a breach of one of the most fundamental principles of public international law itself.

Since 1970, the former Sub-Commission on the Promotion and Protection of Human Rights could consider individual communications, under a procedure known as the '1503-Procedure'.[101] The '1503-Procedure' was limited in its scope. It enabled two United Nations bodies, the former Sub-Commission on the Promotion and Protection of Human Rights[102] and the former Commission on Human Rights[103] to investigate specific types of complaints—those which appear to show consistent or widespread patterns of gross and reliably attested human rights abuses. However, neither the Sub-Commission on the Promotion

98 The concept of *erga omnes* obligations was mentioned for the first time in the so-called Barcelona Traction Case (ICJ, *Case Concerning the Barcelona Traction, Light and Power Company, Limited* (*Belgium v Spain*), ICJ Rep 1970, 3, 32). For more information about this concept just see Malcolm N. Shaw, *International Law* (CUP 2008) 124–5, 260.

99 Annex of UNGA Res. 56/83 of 12 December 2001.

100 Just see for example ICJ, *East Timor Case* (*Portugal v Australia*), ICJ Rep 1995, 90, especially at 102, para. 29, and ICJ, *Armed Activities on the Territory of the Congo* (*New Application: 2002*) (*Democratic Republic of Congo v Rwanda*), Provisional Measures, ICJ Rep 2002, 219, especially at 245, para. 71.

101 This procedure is named after ECOSOC Res. 1503 (XLVIII), adopted on 27 May 1970 and revised by ECOSOC Res. 2000/3, adopted on 19 June 2000.

102 The Sub-Commission on the Promotion and Protection of Human Rights has ceased to exist; see UNGA Res. 60/251 of 15 March 2006. Its work is now carried out by the Human Rights Council Advisory Committee pursuant to HRC Res. 6/102, adopted on 27 September 2007.

103 The Commission on Human Rights was replaced by the Human Rights Council in 2006 by GA Res. 60/251 of 15 March 2006.

and Protection of Human Rights, nor the Commission on Human Rights were able to actually force States to terminate any violation of human rights. Therefore, enforcement of socio-economic rights on the international level was rather weak.[104]

Also based on this criticism, both organs were replaced by the Human Rights Council (HRC) and the Human Rights Council Advisory Committee in 2006 and 2007 respectively. In addition, the '1503-Procedure' was revised and, subsequently, replaced by the procedure contained in HRC Resolution 5/1 which was adopted on 18 June 2007. Whereas reviewing the complaint procedure led to some improvements, it is generally considered to be a 'lost opportunity'.[105] Given that the HRC is equally unable to force States to terminate human rights violations, the enforcement of socio-economic rights on the international level is still weak.

Whether the individual can bring a complaint about discrimination at the national level depends entirely on the national legal system. Article 2(1) of the 1992 Constitution of Ghana for example allows individual complaints about the infringement of constitutional provisions to the Supreme Court. Therefore, Ghanaians have the possibility to bring a complaint about discrimination by Ghana's authorities. Thus, the level of protection is rather high.

(c) *Response to Discrimination by the Foreign Investor*

Also foreign investors might discriminate against women, people with HIV/AIDS, or other societal groups. This gives rise to the question whether and if so how the host State can and should react in order to enforce respect for the right in question. It is obvious that States cannot dispose of their obligations arising out of international human rights treaties such as the ICESCR by simply agreeing to a PPP. They remain the bearer of the obligation to respect and to protect socio-economic rights.[106]

The obligation to respect the right to housing primarily implies that governments must refrain from any measure that would impede the exercise of this right.[107] This is a negative commitment prohibiting governments from doing anything that would compromise already acquired access to housing. This

104 See Michael J. Dennis and David P. Stewart, 'Justiciability of Economic, Social, and Cultural Rights' (2004) 98 Am J Int L 462, 514.

105 Megnah Abraham, 'Building the New Human Rights Council—Outcome and Analysis of the Institution-Building Year' in Friedrich Ebert Stiftung (ed.), *Dialogue on Globalization—Occassional Papers* (Friedrich Ebert Stifung 2007) 23.

106 See United Nations Centre for Human Rights (n. 61).

107 See Robertson (n. 77) 693ff.

obligation corresponds with the obligation to enforce respect of the right to housing as defined in the ICESCR. This means that governments are obliged to use all 'appropriate means' pursuant to Article 2(1) of the ICESCR, including the adoption of legislative measures,[108] to promote all the rights protected under the ICESCR not only from interferences by the respective State, but also from interferences by private actors, such as foreign investors.[109] Consequently, Member States to the ICESCR are obliged to provide their population a high level of protection of the right to housing within its legal system.

With regard to Ghana, it has to be noted that the right to housing is only dealt with marginally in various laws.[110] None of these laws actually contain an explicit right to housing. As Ghana is a dualist State,[111] resulting in the requirement to transform public international law into domestic law in order to render it applicable,[112] the foremost duty for the Ghanaian government would have been to incorporate the right to housing into its national legislation. Without this, it is mostly impossible to effectively protect the population's right to housing, especially against interferences by foreign investors.

Besides enacting a law providing the right to housing, it would be possible to include the requirement of non-discrimination in the concession or PPP agreement. If a foreign investor then discriminates against certain societal groups, it breaches its obligations under the concession or PPP agreement and can be at least sanctioned by the host State. As the agreement between Ghana and STX Engineering and Construction, Ghana Ltd. is confidential, a statement cannot be made whether this PPP agreement contained such a provision.

---

108 In this regard, the *Loi Besson* (loi n°90–449 du 31 mai 1990 visant à la mise en oeuvre du droit au logement, JORF n° 127 du 2 juin 1990 page 6551) is considered to be best practice with regard to the right to adequate housing. For more information about this French law and the equivalent law in the United Kingdom of Great Britain and Northern Ireland, see Suzanne Fitzpatrick, 'Homeless in the EU' in M. Kleinman, W. Matznetter and M. Stephens (eds), *European Integration and Housing Policy* (Routledge 1998) 197, 211.

109 See Committee on Economic, Social and Cultural Rights, *General Comment No. 7 on the Right to Adequate Housing: Forced Evictions*, UN Doc E/1998/22, adopted on 20 May 1997.

110 Just see the 1963 Rent Act (ACT 220) for example. For more information see also Franklin Obeng-Odoom and Laurence Amedzro, 'Inadequate housing in Ghana' (2011) 22 Urbani izziv 127.

111 Open Society Initiative for West Africa (ed.), *Ghana, Justice Sector and the Rule of Law* (Open Society Initiative for West Africa 2007) 21.

112 Just see Ignaz Seidl-Hohenveldern, 'Transformation or Adoption of International Law into Municipal Law' (1963) 12 ICLQ 88.

Direct Horizontal Effect of Human Rights in Private Relations

Even if Ghana would have recognized the right to housing explicitly at the national level—either within the constitution or within a domestic law—, the State would still be the addressee of the human rights obligations.[113] From the discriminated person's perspective, there is however no big difference between being discriminated by the State itself or by a foreign investor who is fulfilling some of the State's obligations, especially if there is no alternative available as is the case with regard to most PPPs aiming at guaranteeing socio-economic rights.[114] Therefore, it has been suggested to extend the scope of human rights addressees to some private parties, especially to internationally operating corporations.[115]

As some poorer countries have sometimes lower socio-economic and environmental standards than richer countries,[116] it is suggested that these shortcomings could be compensated by offering direct redress against private actors.[117] However, this is linked to the basic problem of establishing direct human rights obligations between private actors, as human rights are generally considered as a defense of an individual against a State who is obliged to protect human rights holders by national legislation and administration[118] which prohibit third parties from preventing the enjoyment of human rights in any way.[119]

---

113 See Tomuschat (n. 2) 97.

114 See Thielbörger (n. 80) 504.

115 See with regard to the right to water Stephen Tully, 'A Human Right to Access Water? A Critique of General Comment No. 15' (2005) 23 NQHR 35, 51ff; see also Danwood Mzikenge Chirwa, 'The right to health in international law: its implications for the obligations of state and non-state actors in ensuring access to essential medicine' (2003) 19 SAJHR 541, 561ff, who assumes the already existence of some direct human rights obligations of private actors. Such direct human rights obligations of private actors are also assumed with regard to some human rights provided in the German Constitution (the *Grundgesetz*; just see Elke Gurlit, 'Grundrechtsbindung von Unternehmen' (2012) NZG 249), and at least assumed by some commentators with regard to provisions of the Treaty of the Functioning of the European Union (TFEU) and the European Convention on Human Rights (ECHR), just see Eric Engle, 'Third Party Effect of Fundamental Rights (Drittwirkung)' (2009) 5 HLR 165.

116 See Joshua P. Eaton, 'The Nigerian Tragedy, Environmental Regulation of Transnational Corporations, and the Human Right to a Healthy Environment' (1997) 15 BU ILJ 261, 274.

117 Knut Bourquain, *Freshwater Access from a Human Rights Perspective: A Challenge to International Water and Human Rights Law* (Martinus Nijhoff Publishers 2008) 107.

118 See United Nations Centre for Human Rights (n. 61).

119 See Odinkalu (n. 25) 197.

Due to the monopoly of power States have, an individual has to rely on the State's judicial system in order to seel redress for human rights violations by foreign investors. If an individual cannot seek judicial remedies for human rights violations by foreign investors because States failed to establish efficient protective mechanisms in the national context,[120] direct human rights obligations on the horizontal level become rather useless.[121]

Indirect Horizontal Effect of Human Rights in Private Relations

If a foreign investor discriminates against a specific societal group by interfering with the right to housing, the discriminated members of this group might seek judicial redress before domestic courts. When deciding such a case between private parties, the court has to take into account human rights.[122] While applying a statute, the civil court must consider the importance of the pertinent human right and must protect the citizen from human rights infringements by non-State actors. This concept, which is called the theory of indirect third-party effect, is based on the notion that human rights permeate the whole legal system as objective values that influence the interpretation and application of all statutes.[123] The gateway for a human rights-orientated interpretation of private law will usually be the general provisions within private law because they provide the court with a margin of appreciation.[124] In the absence of such a general provision, courts can hardly give effect to human rights as they are bound by the law and regularly are foreclosed from interpreting a statute *contra legem*.[125]

Consequently, if a foreign investor discriminates against societal groups with regard to the right to housing or other socio-economic rights, a domestic court might establish the unlawfulness of this discrimination based on the theory of third-party effect of the particular human right, and thus force the investor to provide the discriminated person(s) with the right to housing or any other

120 Bourquain (n. 117) 108.

121 Ibid.

122 See Ralf Brinktrine, 'The Horizontal Effect of Human Rights in German Constitutional Law: the British Debate on Horizontality and the Possible Model of the German Doctrine of "mittelbare Drittwirkung der Grundrechte"' (2001) HRLR 421, 424.

123 See in this respect the judgment of the German Constitutional Court (*Bundesverfassungsgericht*) with regard to the freedom of opinion (BVerfGE 7, 198, 205).

124 Bourquain (n. 117) 108.

125 Just see Joanna Jemielniak and Przemysław Mikłaszewicz, 'Capturing the Change: Universalising Tendencies in Legal Interpretation' in J. Jemielniak and P. Mikłaszewicz (eds), *Interpretation of Law in the Global World: From Particularism to a Universal Approach* (Springer 2010) 1–27.

particular socio-economic right in a non-discriminatory way. Such a court order would generally not collide with the law on foreign investments As such a judgment would neither constitute an expropriation, nor would it violate the legitimate expectations of the investor. Throughout the investment project, the investor is subject to the laws and the jurisdiction of the host State.[126]

Most bilateral investment treaties (BITS) require that the investment has to be in accordance with the law of the host State. This clause does not only render all statutes applicable to the foreign investor, but also the interpretation of these statutes, including the theory of third-party effect of human rights. Although the accordance-with-the-law-clause generally provides that the investment has to be in accordance with the law of the host State upon establishment, the whole conduct of a foreign investor is governed at least to some extent by the law of the host State.[127] Some commentators argue that a stabilization clause in the concession agreement between investor and host State would disallow the host State to adopt new laws which have a negative impact on the investment.[128] Even if such a clause is not contained in the concession agreement, it is argued that the adoption of new laws having a negative impact on the investment would violate the investor's legitimate expectations as part of the principle of fair and equitable treatment.[129] If this would be the case, host State's would be disentitled from adopting new legislation aiming at providing socio-economic rights for example.

However, neither does any stabilization clause, nor the notion of legitimate expectations render a legal system completely static. In fact, the basis of the stabilization clause was that the host State was bound by the agreement contained in the clause not to apply any later changes to its laws to the particular contract or to alter the terms of the contract directly by legislation.[130] The State must act in the public good as it perceives it to be at any given time. Consequently, at least a clause which is unlimited in time will be void.[131] As

---

126 See Muthucumaraswamy Sornarajah, *The International Law on Foreign Investment* (Cambridge 2010) 88–143.

127 See Campbell McLachlan Q.C., Laurence Shore and Matthew Weiniger, *International Investment Arbitration—Substantive Principles* (OUP 2007) 236.

128 Just see Evaristu Oshionebo, 'Stabilization Clauses in Natural Resource Extraction Contracts: Legal, Economic and Social Implications for Developing Countries' (2010) 10 Asper Rev Int'l Bus & Trade L 1, 1–2.

129 Just see McLachlan Q.C., Shore and Weiniger (n. 127) 237; see also LCIA, *Occidental Exploration and Production Company v The Republic of Ecuador*, LCIA Case No UN3467, Award, para. 191 (1 July 2004).

130 Sornarajah (n. 126) 281–2.

131 See *Ad hoc* Arbitral Tribunal, *Kuwait v Aminoil* (1982) 21 ILM 976.

a legislator is generally not bound by its own legislation and has the power to change it, a provision in a contract cannot bind the State.[132] Consequently, a stabilization clause is nothing more 'than a comforter to the foreign investor, who may derive some security from the belief that there is a promise secured from the State not to apply its future legislation to the contract'.[133]

Similarly, the notion of legitimate expectations of investors does not imply that an investor can rely on the legal system of the home State being unchanged. Instead, investors have to perform a diligent inquiry into the legal framework of the home State.[134] In fact, 'legitimate expectations cannot be solely the subjective expectations of the investor'.[135] Instead, investors are only entitled to rely on specific representations or assurances made directly to them by the host State and upon which they were induced to invest.[136] It is rather unlikely that a host State will assure that it will not adopt new human rights legislation. The mere fact of an amendment of the laws does not violate the legitimate expectations of the investor.[137]

Discrimination with regard to the right to housing by foreign investors might not be preventable in general as some investors might violate the law occasionally. These violations can be sanctioned by the host State. In such an event, the State would fulfill its obligation to enforce respect for the right to housing. Thus, the right to housing can be guaranteed through PPPs, provided

132 Sornarajah (n. 126) 282.

133 Ibid.

134 Michele Potesta, 'The Doctrine of Legitimate Expectations in Investment Treaty Law' (9 July 2012, Society of International Economic Law (SIEL), 3rd Biennial Global Conference) <http://www.ssrn.com /abstract=2102771> accessed 27 August 2013.

135 ICSID, *EDF (Services) Limited v Romania*, ICSID Case No ARB/05/13, Award, para. 219 (8 October 2009).

136 McLachlan Q.C., Shore and Weiniger (n. 127) 237.

137 See the awards in the cases ICSID, Parkerings-Compagniet AS v Republic of Lithuania, ICSID Case No ARB/05/8, Award, paras 333–7 (11 September 2007); ICSID, Plama Consortium Limited v Republic of Bulgaria, ICSID Case No ARB/03/24, Award, para. 267 (27 August 2008), ICSID, ADF Group Inc v United States of America, ICSID Case No ARB(AF)/00/1, Award, para. 189 (9 January 2003), ICSID, Biwater Gauff (Tanzania) Ltd. v United Republic of Tanzania, ICSID Case No ARB/05/22, Award, paras 635–40 (24 July 2008); ICSID, Continental Casualty Company v Argentine Republic, ICSID Case No ARB/03/9, Award, para. 260 (5 September 2008); ICSID, Jan de Nul NV and Dredgig International NV v Arab Republic of Egypt, ICSID Case No ARB/04/13, Award, para. 263 (6 November 2008); SCC, William Nagel v The Czech Republic, SCC Case No 049/2002, Final Award, paras 158–64 (9 September 2003); see also Kenneth J. Vandevelde, 'A Unified Theory of Fair and Equitable Treatment' (2010–11) 43 New York Univ J Intl L& Pol 43, 71–9.

that the right is recognized at the national level. As mentioned above, this is not the case in Ghana.

Third-Party Effect of International Human Rights

As Ghana has not recognized the right to housing at the national level, but has ratified the ICESCR, the question arises whether citizens, who are discriminated against by the foreign investor with regard to the right to housing, can directly rely upon the provisions of the ICESCR. In other words, do ICESCR provisions have third-party effect?

Obligations under international human rights treaties are addressed to the State parties only.[138] While responsibility of non-State actors with regard to some selected human rights has been discussed,[139] States remain the only entities with all-embracing responsibility for human rights protection.[140] The wording of Article 2(1) of the ICESCR makes it rather difficult to impose direct binding obligations upon individuals or legal persons.[141]

As disputes between foreign investors and discriminated citizens would be settled before domestic courts which apply domestic law, and as international human rights are neither directly nor indirectly applicable between non-State actors, there is no need to discuss whether international human rights have at all indirect horizontal effect. As a result, if a foreign investor discriminates against certain citizens of a State with regard to the right to housing, the citizen cannot refer to the provisions in the ICESCR or any other international or regional human right treaty such as the ACHPR.

Corporate Social Responsibility

As some transnational corporations bear a heavy moral responsibility because of their economic power which may even exceed that of the host State, some

---

138 See for example the wording of art. 2(1) ICESCR, which exclusively speaks of 'State Party to the present Covenant'. Nevertheless, human rights treaties include State duties to give certain obligations direct horizontal effect in the national legal orders (see for example art. 5(f) of the International Convention on the Elimination of All Forms of Racial Discrimination (ICERD)).

139 See Jordan J. Paust, 'Human Rights Responsibilities of Private Corporations' (2002) 35 VJTL 801, 810ff.

140 Paust is of the opinion that private actors, in particular corporations, are directly responsible already according to current international human rights law (ibid., 802ff). He argues on the one hand with individual obligations and the clauses prohibiting abuse of rights in international human rights law, and on the other hand with the existing national legislations that impose such obligations upon private actors (see ibid., 809).

141 Bourquain (n. 117) 110.

commentators argue that transnational corporations are—or at least should be—subject to human rights obligations.[142] However, on the level of positive law, little if anything has materialized.[143] The Organization for Economic Co-Operation and Development (OECD), which has issued the Guidelines for Multinational Enterprises,[144] has consistently emphasized that compliance with these Guidelines, which constitute no more than recommendations, is voluntary. The same applies to the Global Compact which was launched as an initiative of then-UN Secretary-General Kofi Annan, who, in an address to the World Economic Forum in January 1999, had invited business leaders to promote and respect a number of key principles relevant to economic activities, including human rights.[145]

To sum up, the existing international instruments that aim at corporate human rights responsibility are not binding, but form voluntary commitments. In addition, they are solely addressed to internationally operating corporations, thereby ignoring the fact that locally operating small and medium enterprises can threaten human rights to a considerable extent too.[146] Therefore, no legal action can be initiated based on the ground of corporate social

---

142 See Menno T. Kamminga and Saman Zia-Zarifi, *Liability of Multinational Corporations under International Law* (Kluwer 2000); Ralph G. Steinhardt, 'Corporate Responsibility and the International Law of Human Rights: The New Lex Mercatoria' in P. Alston (ed.), *Non-State Actors and Human Rights* (OUP 2005); Paust (n. 139) 801ff; Steven R. Ratner, 'Corporations and Human Rights: A Theory of Legal Responsibility' (2001) 111 YLJ 443; Beth Stephens, 'Expanding Remedies for Human Rights Abuses: Civil Litigation in Domestic Courts' (1997) 40 German Yearbook of International Law; Beth Stephens, 'Translating Filártiga: A Comparative and International Law Analysis of Domestic Remedies for International Human Rights Violations' (2002) 27 YJIL 1; Christian Tomuschat, 'Grundpflichten des Individuums nach Völkerrecht' (1983) 21 AVR 289; Marion Weschka, 'Human Rights and Multinational Enterprises: How Can Multinational Enterprises Be Held Responsible for Human Rights Violations Committed Abroad?' (2006) 66 HILL 625.

143 Tomuschat (n. 2) 107.

144 The 2011 update of the Guidelines for Multinational Enterprises can be found online at <http://www.oecd.org/daf/internationalinvestment/guidelinesformultinationalenterprises/48004323.pdf> accessed 27 August 2013.

145 Thousands of enterprises worldwide responded to the call. However, the initiative has remained entirely voluntary and does not purport to establish a binding legal regime. More information about this initiative is available online at <http://www.unglobalcompact.org/AboutTheGC/index.html> accessed 27 August 2013. See also Oliver F. Williams, 'The UN Global Compact: The Challenge and the Promise' (2008) 25 Issues in Business Ethics 229.

146 Bourquain (n. 117) 110 with further references.

responsibility against a foreign investor who is discriminating against particular societal groups.

Legal Actions Against the Host State in the Event of a Discrimination by the Foreign Investor

As has been shown, the citizen who is deprived of his right to housing in a discriminatory way by the foreign investor cannot initiate any legal action against the foreign investor if the host State has not recognized the right to housing at the national level. Thus, the citizen is *de facto* deprived of its right to housing. As the host State is however obliged to enforce respect for the right to housing pursuant to the ICESCR, it could be argued that the citizen can undertake legal actions against the host State.

The discrimination was undertaken by the foreign investor, a private entity. In order to apply the law on State responsibility, it is necessary to attribute an international wrongful act to the State. Attribution of acts committed by individuals to a State is governed by customary international law, as codified in the non-binding ILC Articles.[147] Whereas any organ of the State may engage the responsibility of the State,[148] the act of a person who is not an organ of the State will be attributed to the State only if (a) that person is empowered by the law of that State to exercise elements of the governmental authority and has acted in that capacity in the particular instance.;[149] or (b) that person has in fact acted on the instructions of, or under the direction or control of, the State in carrying out the conduct;[150] or (c) the State has acknowledged and adopted the conduct in question as its own.[151]

None of these possibilities is applicable to the situation in which foreign investors discriminate against certain societal groups with regard to the right to housing. Although the State primarily bears the duty to provide its citizens with the right to housing pursuant to the ICESCR and the ACHPR, the foreign

147 The Articles on Responsibility of States for Internationally Wrongful Acts, adopted by the International Law Commission (ILC) on 9 August 2001 (see UN Doc A/56/10 (2001)). GA Res. 56/83 of 12 December 2001 annexed the text of the Articles on State Responsibility and commended them to governments (see also GA Res. 59/35, and James Crawford and Simon Olleson, 'The Continuing Debate on a UN Convention on State Responsibility' in 54 ICLQ 959 (2005)). For more information about the Articles on State Responsibility just see James Crawford, *The International Law Commission's Articles on State Responsibility* (CUP 2002).

148 Art 4 of the Articles on State Responsibility (n. 147).

149 Ibid., 5.

150 Ibid., 8.

151 Ibid., 11.

investor, who is engaging in a PPP aiming at guaranteeing the right to housing, does not automatically exercise elements of governmental authority. The investor will still act as a private entity carrying out its own business. It is rather unlikely that a host State will instruct the foreign investor to discriminate against certain societal groups with regard to the right to housing. As the investor is not a State organ, the rules on *ultra vires* acts are inapplicable. Similarly, it is rather unlikely that a host State acknowledges and adopts the discrimination against certain societal groups as its own conduct. Consequently, the discrimination against certain societal groups by a foreign investor with regard to the right to housing and other socio-economic rights will in most cases not be attributable to the State.

However, States do not bear only the obligation to respect socio-economic rights, but also the duty to enforce respect of these rights.[152] As has been shown above, enforcing respect of socio-economic rights might be problematic if the right in question has not been recognized at the national level and is for example not incorporated in the concession or PPP agreement.[153] If an enforcement of socio-economic rights is not possible in a State, the State is in breach of its obligations arising out of the ICESCR and the ACHPR.

3.1.3 Conclusion on the Compliance with the General Provisions of the ICESCR

Guaranteeing socio-economic rights through PPPs generally complies with the more general provisions of the ICESCR. None of the obligations in Articles 2(1), 2(2) and 3 of the ICESCR exclude this possibility, on the contrary, some obligations even promote the use of PPPs to guarantee socio-economic rights. However, it is up to the particular State to fulfill these obligations.

With regard to the Ghanaian Public Housing Project, it can be doubted whether this project complies with the general provisions of the ICESCR. The lack of recognition of the right to housing at the national level is for example problematic, as an enforcement of the right to housing against a discriminating foreign investor is rather difficult. Therefore, the Ghanaian Public Housing Project did not comply with the general provisions of the ICESCR.

3.2 *Compliance with the General Provisions of the ACHPR*

As Ghana has not only ratified the ICESCR but also the ACHPR, it has to be determined whether the Ghanaian Public Housing Project in particular, and the possibility to guarantee socio-economic rights through PPPs in general, is

152 Ibid., pp. 14–5.

153 Ibid., p. 14.

in accordance with the general provisions of the ACHPR. These provisions are contained in Articles 1 and 2 of the ACHPR.

Article 1 of the ACHPR contains the obligation of Member States to adopt legislative or other measures to give effect to the various rights contained in the ACHPR. It could be assumed that Article 1 of the ACHPR corresponds with Article 2(1) of the ICESCR. However, whereas Article 2(1) of the ICESCR urges Member States to 'particularly' adopt legislative measures, thus subordinating 'other measures', both are not in any way ranked by Article 1 of the ACHPR. In practice though, whereas administrative and judicial measures will protect the granted rights,[154] legislative measures will be generally the most efficient measure to give effect to the rights contained in the ACHPR,[155] especially in dualist States such as Ghana, where international law has to be transformed into domestic law. As Ghana has not recognized the right to housing at the national level,[156] the right to housing contained in the ACHPR is not given effect in Ghana in the meaning of Article 1 of the ACHPR.

In addition, Article 2 of the ACHPR contains a prohibition on discrimination similar to the prohibition incorporated in Articles 2(2) and 3 of the ICESCR. Comparable to the provisions of the ICESCR, discrimination based on race, ethnic group, color, sex, language, religion, political or any other opinion, national and social origin, fortune, birth or other status is prohibited. However, the procedure for complaints about discriminations or other violations of rights contained in the ACHPR by States is quite different to the procedure with regard to the ICESCR. Communications can be sent to the African Commission on Human and Peoples' Rights pursuant to Article 56 of the ACHPR bearing in mind that local remedies have to be exhausted prior to sending the communication to the Commission 'unless it is obvious that this procedure is unduly prolonged'.[157] Local remedies with regard to the enforcement of the right to

154 See African Commission on Human and Peoples' Rights (n. 52) para. 4.

155 See ibid., 36. In 1989 the African Commission on Human and Peoples' Rights adopted at its Fifth Ordinary Session in Benghazi (Libya) the Resolution on the Integration of the Provisions oft he African Charter on Human and Peoples' Rights into National Laws of States, which stressed the importance oft he integration oft he provisions oft he ACHPR into the national laws of States, and recommended Member States to introduce arts 1 to 29 'in their constitutions, laws and regulations and other acts relating to human rights'. The resolution is available at <http://www.achpr.org/sessions/5th/resolutions/3/> accessed 27 August 2013.

156 Ibid., 14–15.

157 This point was addressed by the Inter-American Court of Human Rights, Advisory Opinion on Exception to Domestic Remedies in Cases of Indigency (CHECK) or Inability to Obtain

housing and other socio-economic rights face are however hardly available in Ghana.[158] Consequently, with regard to legal actions against the State by an individual, who is discriminated against by a foreign investor with regard to her or his right to housing, there is no difference between the right to housing contained in the ACHPR and the right to housing contained in the ICESCR. If the respective State has not recognized the right to housing at the national level or has not ensured in the concession or PPP agreement that the right to housing is provided in a non-discriminatory way by the foreign investor, legal remedies are hardly available. Similar to the ICESCR, legal actions against the State are possible at the international level, if the State itself discriminates against certain societal groups.

4 Outlook

It is general possible to guarantee socio-economic rights such as the right to housing through PPPs. However, States aiming at guaranteeing socio-economic rights through PPPs should be aware of the various obligations arising out of international human rights law. States have to observe these obligations when negotiating new BITs and PPP agreements. Articles 12 and 13 of the 2012 United States Model Bilateral Investment Treaty,[159] which already incorporate certain environment and labor related human rights into a BIT, illustrate that States are observing these obligations when drafting new BITs. Even more rights are included in the 2005 IISD Model International Agreement on Investment for Sustainable Development.[160]

In addition, the number of multinational enterprises voluntarily complying with instruments such as the UN Global Compact, the OECD Guidelines for Multinational Enterprises or the UN Guiding Principles on Business and

Legal Representation Because of a Generalized Fear Within the Legal Community, Advisory Opinion OC-11/90 of 10 August 1990, Ser A No 11.

158 Ibid., 14–21.

159 2012 United States Model Bilateral Investment Treaty <http://www.ustr.gov/sites/default/files/BIT%20text%20for%20ACIEP%20Meeting.pdf> accessed 27 August 2013.

160 International Institute for Sustainable Development (IISD), 'IISD Model International Agreement on Investment for Sustainable Development' (International Institute for Sustainable Development 2005) <http://www.italaw.com/sites/default/files/archive/ita1027.pdf> accessed 27 August 2013.

Human Rights,[161] is constantly increasing. Although all these instruments are 'soft law' and thus not enforceable, multinational enterprises are recognizing human rights as applicable law regardless of the fact whether the particular human right has been recognized at the national level. Voluntarily complying with international human rights standards is even considered to be a competitive advantage,[162] as customers are becoming more aware of corporate social responsibility and might take the compliance with human rights into consideration when deciding which product they want to buy.[163]

5 Conclusion

It is possible to guarantee socio-economic rights such as the right to housing through PPPs. Neither do the specific provisions on the right to housing in the ICESCR and the ACHPR, nor do the more general provisions in both international human rights treaties prohibit a State from concluding a PPP aiming at guaranteeing the right to housing. The State's obligation of international cooperation and assistance even encourages States to undertake a PPP. However, the particular State has to fulfill the other obligations arising out of international human rights treaties, such as the ICESCR and the ACHPR. None of these obligations exclude the possibility to guarantee socio-economic rights through PPPs but they impose certain limitations States have to observe which were elaborated above.

Although the Ghanaian Public Housing Project was not carried out, it still is an illustrative example for other States aiming at guaranteeing socio-economic rights through PPPs. Despite the failed project, also Ghana is aiming to pursuit its national housing policy by agreeing on PPPs with foreign investors. This gives Ghana the chance to avoid previous mistakes and to observe the various obligations arising out of international human rights law.

---

161 Just see UN Human Rights Council, 'Report of the Special Representative of the Secretary-General on the Issues of Human Rights and Transnational Corporations and other Business Enterprises, John Ruggie—Guiding Principles on Business and Human Rights: Implementing the United Nations 'Protect, Respect and Remedy' Framework' UN Doc A/HRC/17/31 (21 March 2011) available at <http://www.business-humanrights.org/media/documents/ruggie/ruggie-guiding-principles-21-mar-2011.pdf> accessed 27 August 2013.

162 See Williams (n. 145).

163 Ibid.

CHAPTER 7

Determination of Compensation in Investor–State Arbitrations: Is There a Place for Human Rights Arguments?

Filip Balcerzak[1]

1 Introduction

For many years international investment law and international human rights law developed along separate paths, each system having created specific dispute settlement mechanisms.[2] The present chapter falls within a broad subject of possible interrelations between the two fields. Although currently 'connecting human rights considerations to investment arbitration is still in its infancy',[3] the intersections between both fields of law have started to raise interest in the literature.[4]

The ongoing expansion of international investment law and the existence a global web of investment treaties is a fact.[5] Typically, international investment

1 The author can be contacted via e-mail: balcerzak@icam.es.

2 Valentina Vadi, 'Reconciling Public Health and Investor Rights: The Case of Tobacco' in P.-M. Dupuy, E.-U. Petersmann, F. Francioni (Eds)s *Human Rights in International Investment Law and Arbitration* (OUP 2009) 481. Although it may be observed that human rights and international investment law have the joint roots in the protection of aliens.

3 Jasper Krommendijk and John Morijn, '"Proportional" by What Measure(s)? Balancing Investor Interests and Human Rights by Way of Applying the Proportionality Principle in Investor–State Arbitration' in P.-M. Dupuy, E.-U. Petersmann, F. Francioni (Eds)s *Human Rights in International Investment Law and Arbitration* (OUP 2009) 446.

4 In 2009 a first collective work focusing exclusively on the interrelations between human rights and investment law was published—P.-M. Dupuy, E.-U. Petersmann and F. Francioni (Eds) *Human Rights in International Investment Law and Arbitration* (OUP 2009). Before that, the issue was discussed only in separate articles published in various places.

5 Freya Baetens, 'The Kyoto Protocol in Investor–State Arbitration: Reconciling Climate Change and Investment Protection Objectives' in M.-C. Segger, M. Gehring and A. Newcombe (Eds), *Sustainable Development in World Investment Law* (Kluwer 2011) 683. According to UNCTAD, as for the end of 2011 the exact number of international investment agreements, including free trade agreements with investment chapters, but excluding double taxation treaties was 3164. See UNCTAD, *World Investment Report 2012* (United Nations Publication 2012) <http://www.unctad-docs.org/files/UNCTAD-WIR2012-Full-en.pdf> accessed 27 August 2013.

 | DOI 10.1163/9789004270190_008

agreements (IIAs)[6] contain no provisions that specifically allow an arbitrator to counterbalance the behavior of an investor which violates international human rights standards.[7]

At the same time, the possibility for a host state to raise human rights arguments in arbitral proceedings as a defence to an alleged breach of an international investment treaty can become important in some proceedings. The UN Special Representative of the Secretary General on the issues of Human Rights and Transnational Corporations and other Business Enterprises (SRSG) has noted that business activities 'can affect virtually all internationally recognized rights'.[8]

There are strong policy reasons for why human rights actions, undertaken in the course of performing states' obligation to respect, protect and fulfil human rights, should not be totally ignored by arbitrators in investment disputes.[9] The complete disregard by arbitral tribunals of the human rights of the individuals within the host states' territories would undermine the legitimacy of the whole

---

6 The term 'International Investment Agreements' encompass Bilateral investment Treaties (BITS) as well as Free Trade Agreements with an Investment Chapter. See Anne van Aaken, 'Primary and Secondary Remedies in International Investment Law and National State Liability: A Functional and Comparative View' in S. Schill (Ed.), *International Investment Law and Comparative Public Law* (OUP 2010) 721.

7 In an arbitration based on an investment treaty a counter-claim of a host state typically will not fall within jurisdiction of an arbitral tribunal. A specific consent of an investor would be necessary.

8 John Ruggie, 'Protect, Respect and Remedy: a Framework for Business and Human Rights: Report of the Special Representative of the Secretary-General on the issue of human rights and transnational corporations and other business enterprises', (2008) UN Doc A/HRC/8/5, para. 34. In his subsequent Report it is added for example that 'companies can affect the entire spectrum of rights, as documented in the Special Representative's mapping of nearly 400 public allegations against companies.' See John Ruggie, 'Business and human rights: Towards operationalizing the 'protect, respect and remedy' framework: Report of the Special Representative of the Secretary-General on the issue of human rights and transnational corporations and other business enterprises, John Ruggie' (2009) UN Doc A/HRC/11/13, para. 52.

9 'While it is debatable whether investment tribunals should systematically address a State's human rights obligations each time an investment contract derives into a dispute, such tribunals should at the very least be aware of the negative implications that upholding investment treaties may have on the realization of human rights or on the likelihood of human rights violations that may occur should a State insist on upholding investment contracts in the midst of social and generalized economic strife'. See Jorge Daniel Taillant, Jonathan Bonnitcha, 'International Investment Law and Human Rights' in M.-C. Segger, M. Gehring and A. Newcombe (Eds), *Sustainable Development in World Investment Law* (Kluwer Law International 2011) 80.

investor–state arbitration system in the eye of public opinion, leading to a general perception of the system as being biased towards interests of investors, at the expense of the public interest. The future development of the investment arbitration should provide an answer to these concerns, rather than be silent on them.

Possible interrelations between international investment arbitration and international human rights may be analyzed from various perspectives, such as for example: (i) a conflict of norms in international law and a related question of whether human rights can overcome provisions of investment treaties, (ii) possible influence of international human rights law on the interpretation of standards of investors' protection included in IIAs, and (iii) possible influence of human rights on the determination of compensation for a breach of an IIA which has already been established by the arbitral tribunal at the merits phase of the proceedings. The present chapter focuses on the third of these perspectives.

The compensation stage is 'a strategic stage of the arbitral award'.[10] It should be neither underestimated nor considered as less important than merits phase. The moment of determining compensation can be the appropriate stage when states' international human rights obligations may exert influence on the awards rendered in investor—state arbitration, at least on the determination of compensation for a violation of the fair and equitable treatment (FET) standard.[11]

Within such defined scope, the present chapter seeks to answer the specific question of whether states' obligation to respect, protect and fulfil human rights may reduce the compensation due for a breach of a standard of protection guaranteed in an IIA. It differentiates between two situations, in which: (i) investors are involved in human rights violations in the territories of the host states, and when (ii) no human rights violations have been committed by investors, but nevertheless host states invoke their human rights obligations in an attempt to justify measures breaching investment treaties.

---

10 Ioana Knoll-Tudor, 'The Fair and Equitable Treatment Standard and Human Rights Norms' in P.-M. Dupuy, E.-U. Petersmann and F. Francioni (Eds), *Human Rights in International Investment Law and Arbitration* (OUP 2009) 340. This can be illustrated by the number of cases where the compensation stage was split into a separate procedural phase.

11 'In the specific case of the FET, the last scenario, where the non-investment obligations are taken into account at the stage of compensation, appears to be promising.' See ibid. 340. Similarly Lahra Liberti 'Investissements et droits de l'homme' in P. Kahn and T. Wälde (Eds), *New Aspects of International Investment Law* (Martinus Nijhoff 2007) 833; Krommendijk and Morijn (n. 3) 423.

For the purposes of this analysis, it is assumed that a claim arises under an IIA (allegation of a breach of the treaty) and that the applicable law is international law.

2 Compensation in Investor–State Arbitrations

Awards rendered in investor–state arbitral proceedings almost always comprise of monetary compensation.[12] It is the situation even though under international law adjudicating bodies can award non-pecuniary remedies, such as specific performance.[13]

There are various reasons for that. Whilst the arbitral tribunals' authority to order remedies other than monetary compensation is at the first place determined by the substantive law applicable to the dispute, some investment treaties preclude any kind of relief other than monetary compensation.[14] Additionally, disregarding other relief which may be available on the ground of a particular IIA, investors almost exclusively ask for monetary compensation,[15] which is within their rights as claimants. Arbitrators cannot go beyond what they are asked for, which is expressed by the maxim *non ultra petita.*[16] As long

12 Carole Malinvaud, 'Non-pecuniary Remedies in Investment Treaty and Commercial Arbitration' in A.J. van den Berg (Ed), *50 Years* of the New York Convention: ICCA International Arbitration Conference (Kluwer Law International 2009) 210, see also Articles on Responsibility of States for Internationally Wrongful Acts, adopted by the International Law Commission (ILC) on 9 August 2001 (see UN Doc A/56/10 (2001), 99 (ILC Arts).

13 Christoph Schreuer, 'Non-Pecuniary Remedies in ICSID Arbitration' (2004) 20:4 Arbitration International 332; see also *Enron Corporation and Ponderosa Assets LP v Argentina*, Decision on Jurisdiction, ICSID Case No ARB/01/3, IIC 92 (2004), 11 ICSID Rep. 273, 14 January 2004, paras 79, 81; *Texaco Overseas Petroleum Company and California Asiatic Oil Company v Government of the Libyan Arab Republic*, Award on the Merits, 53 ILR 389, 19 January 1977, paras 509 and 511. The ILC Arts recognize a broad concept of 'reparation', divided into the subcategories of restitution, satisfaction and compensation. See ILC Arts ibid. 86.

14 For example art. 1135 of the North American Free Trade Agreement Between the Government of Canada, the Government of Mexico and the Government of the United States, 17 December 1992 (NAFTA), art. 10.26 of the Dominican Republic—Central America—United States Free Trade Agreement, 5 August 2004 (CAFTA).

15 Malinvaud (n. 12) 221; Schreuer (n. 13) 329.

16 Thomas Wälde and Borzu Sabahi, 'Compensation, Damages and Valuation' in P. Muchlinski, F. Ortino, and Christoph Schreuer (Eds), *The Oxford Handbook of International Investment Law* (OUP 2008) 1059.

as the investors do not seek any remedy other than monetary compensation, the arbitral tribunals are bound by their choice. In addition, if the controversial measures are undertaken by states in pursuit of their international human rights obligations, it is probable that the states will not be willing to change these measures instead of paying compensation.[17]

Although the issue of compensation in investor–state arbitrations is still relatively unexamined when compared to issues of jurisdiction and merits, some general observations can be made.[18]

The starting point for any discussion on compensation is the decision of the Permanent Court of International Justice from 1928 in the *Chorzów Factory* case, according to which reparation for an internationally illegal act:

> must, as far as possible, wipe out all the consequences of the illegal act and reestablish the situation which would, in all probability, have existed if that act had not been committed.[19]

In other words, the general principle is that the award should put an investor back in a position in which it would have been 'but for' the breach of the investment treaty.[20] In consequence, compensation for the internationally wrongful act must reflect the damage (loss, harm) actually suffered by the claimant.[21]

---

17 More appropriate in this context is to pay the compensation and not to change the state's policies. However, this observation is true only to some extent. Firstly, there may be at least two different ways of achieving the human rights goals. Secondly, if the state faces excessive compensation, it could value the outcome of the undertaken human rights activities and that of the compensation and as a result decide to withdraw from its activities.

18 Todd Weiler and Luis Miguel Diaz, 'Causation and Damages in NAFTA Investor–State Arbitration', in T. Weiler (Ed), *NAFTA Investment Law and Arbitration: Past Issues, Current Practice, Future Prospects* (Transnational Publishers 2004) 179.

19 *Factory at Chorzów*, Merits, 1928 P.C.I.J. (Set. A) No 17, 47.

20 Weiler and Miguel Diaz (n. 18) 188.

21 Rudolf Dolzer and Christopher Schreuer, *Principles of International Investment Law* (OUP 2008) 272. According to the classification present in many domestic legal systems, the term 'actual damage' in this context would mean both, *damnum emergens* and *lucrum cessans*. See Dolzer and Schreuer, 272–273. However, this differentiation is not necessarily applicable in investment law. It is argued that it was the traditional remedy for breach of contract, and that the *lucrum cessans* was meant to compensate for the shortcomings of a purely historic and cost-based focus on individual items, considered separately rather than as a 'package'. However, some modern valuation methods already incorporate lost profits in the value. If such valuation method is used, 'a separate payment in recognition of lost profit would amount to double recovery'. See Wälde and Sabahi (n. 16) 1066–1067.

Undoubtedly, there must be a causal relationship between the damage suffered by the investor and the state measures which are in the breach of the investment treaty.[22]

The relevance of the principle established in the *Chorzów Factory* has been confirmed in investor–state arbitrations.[23] Additionally, the principle of 'full reparation' is expressed in Article 31 of the International Law Commission Draft articles on Responsibility of States for Internationally Wrongful Acts (ILC Articles).

3 Compensation for Expropriation and Non-Expropriatory Standards

Rules applicable to the compensation for expropriation are well developed if compared with the rules for non-expropriatory standards of protection of investments, such as the fair and equitable treatment. It is a result of a debate over the standard of compensation for expropriation which took place during the last 80 years.[24] Nowadays, it is agreed that under modern customary international law the compensation for expropriation should be full compensation, expressed by terms such as 'prompt, adequate, and effective'.[25] In addition, many investment treaties expressly include this standard in their wording regarding compensation for legal expropriation.[26]

The amount of compensation for expropriation may differ, depending on whether it was lawful, in which case the due compensation is typically the fair market value of the investment, or unlawful, then the compensation is for the damage occurred. Although it may be that the only damage sustained

---

It may be concluded that the term 'actual damage' includes lost profits, but does not have to be based on the *damnum emergens/lucrum cessans* concept.

22 Wälde and Sabahi (n. 16) 1093. Causation is also included in the ILC Arts (n. 12) 91.

23 For example in *SD Myers Inc v Canada*, First Partial Award and Separate Opinion, Ad hoc—UNCITRAL Arbitration Rules, IIC 249 (2000), 13 November 2000, para. 311.

24 Visible at the example of the discussion concerning the Hull formula and the Calvo doctrine. See Wälde and Sabahi (n. 16) 1068.

25 Also known as the Hull formula. It can be also called as 'market value' or 'genuine value'. ibid. 1069—1070. See also Abby Cohen Smutny, 'Principles relating to compensation in the investment treaty context' (IBA Annual Conference, Investment Treaty Arbitration Workshop, Chicago, 19 September 2006) <http://www.josemigueljudice-arbitration.com/xms/files/02_TEXTOS_ARBITRAGEM/01_Doutrina_ScolarsTexts/investment_arbitration/compensation_in_inv_treaties-_abbey_cohen_smutny.pdf> accessed 27 August 2013, 8.

26 Dolzer and Schreuer (n. 21) 274; Irmgard Marboe, *Calculation of Compensation and Damages in International Investment Law* (OUP 2009) 47–48.

due to the unlawful expropriation was the loss of the value of the taken property, when there is no difference in the amount of compensation between lawful and unlawful expropriation because the compensation would in that case amount to the fair market value of the property anyways, it is not always the situation.[27]

The notion of 'full compensation' must be assessed in an objective way. Arbitral tribunals determine the amount by applying one of the methods of investment valuation, such as market-based valuation, discounted cash flow or book value and related methods focusing on historic cost and income information.[28] Although the methods themselves are based on objective criteria and do not represent different standards of compensation, the choice between application of one and not another method may result in different outcomes.[29] This grants arbitral tribunals a certain margin of discretion.

Despite the significance of the compensation stage of the arbitral proceedings, there is 'little precedent and even less theoretical analysis' of the rules applicable to compensation for breaches of the non-expropriatiory standards.[30] Among this type of standards, the fair and equitable treatment is the most relevant when considering possible impact of human rights on investor–state arbitration.[31]

IIAs are typically silent on the standard of compensation for breaches of the FET standard.[32] This grants the arbitral tribunals discretion when deciding the issue,[33] strengthened by the fact that when assessing the FET standard,

27 Cohen Smutny (n. 25) 17–18.

28 Wälde and Sabahi (n. 16) 1070—1079.

29 It is even suggested that 'the choice of valuation methodology favouring a lower-end outcome or of compensation-reducing concepts (eg mitigation, contributory negligence) can be used to achieve consensus' between the arbitrators in order to render a unanimous decision. See ibid. 1064.

30 Ibid., 1082.

31 Basically, human rights obligations may be relevant to the issues of expropriation and of the fair and equitable treatment. Other typical standards of protection included in IIAs offer much less space for such considerations. Because of space limits, they cannot be analysed in the present chapter.

32 See for example *CMS Gas Transmission Company v Argentina*, Award, ICSID Case No ARB/01/8, IIC 65 (2005), 12 May 2005, para. 409 (*CMS v Argentina*), *MTD Equity Sdn. Bhd. and MTD Chile S.A. v Chile*, Award, ICSID Case No ARB/01/7, IIC 174 (2004), 25 May 2004, para. 238 (*MTD v Chile*).

33 'It is obvious that in both of these earlier cases (Pope & Talbot and S.D. Myers—FB), which as here involved non-expropriation violations of Chapter 11, the tribunals exercised considerable discretion in fashioning what they believed to be reasonable approaches to damages consistent with the requirements of NAFTA.' *Feldman Karpa v Mexico*, Award and separate opinion, ICSID Case No ARB(AF)/99/1, IIC 157 (2002), 16 December 2002,

tribunals take into consideration a broad number of elements.[34] The discretion of the arbitrators at the moment of determining the compensation can also be seen at the moment of choosing a proper method of valuation of the damage suffered by the investor. Although the methods are based on objective criteria, the choice between them can result in different outcomes.[35] Even if we assume that the pure valuation of damages can be achieved in a perfectly objective way, the assessment of an investor's situation before and after the breach, necessary for the purposes of such valuation, is at least to a certain extent subjective.[36]

In practice, tribunals tend to determine the quantity of compensation for breaches of the FET standard in an analogous way as in cases of expropriation[37] or breaches of contractual obligations.[38] In many situations, a breach of the FET standard takes place together with an indirect expropriation, which allows calculation of the compensation in accordance with the rules established in the context of the latter.[39] Such situation makes it possible to avoid the problematic issue of calculating compensation for the breach of the FET standard separately. Not entering here into the analysis whether it is correct, the typical

para. 197. In *AMT v Zaire* the tribunal first appointed an expert to determine the loss suffered by the investor. Then it treated it as one of 'circumstances' before it: 'The tribunal proceeds to exercise its discretionary and sovereign power to determinate the quantum of compensation that the republic of Zaïre shall pay to AMT, taking into account all the circumstances of the case before it'. *American Manufacturing & Trading, Inc v Zaire*, Award and separate opinion, ICSID Case No ARB/93/1, IIC 14 (1997), 11 February 1997, para. 7.21. Similarly: 'What is required to effect full reparation in any particular case will be solely within the discretion of the tribunal'. See Meg Kinnear, 'Damages in Investment Treaty Arbitration' in K. Yannaca-Small (Ed.), *Arbitration under international investment agreements: a guide to the key issues* (OUP 2010) 560.

34 Knoll-Tudor (n. 10) 340.

35 See (n. 29).

36 Wälde and Sabahi (n. 16) 1115.

37 *CMS v Argentina*, *supra* note 30, para. 410; *Azurix v Argentina*, Award, ICSID Case No ARB/01/12, IIC 24 (2006), 23 June 2006, para. 423 (*Azurix v Argentina*).

38 *Nykomb Synergetics Technology Holding AB v Latvia*, Award, SCC Case No 118/2001, IIC 182 (2003), 16 December 2003, section. 5.1.

39 Ioana Tudor, 'Balancing the Breach of the FET standard' (2007) 4:6 Transnational Dispute Management 1. This observation is especially important when one takes into consideration that legitimate expectations can play role in determining whether there has been a breach of both standards of protection: the FET and prohibition of (indirect) expropriation. In addition, Mayeda suggests even that 'the fair and equitable treatment should not provide protection against financial losses that do not amount to expropriation'. See Graham Mayeda, 'Playing Fair: the Meaning of Fair and Equitable Treatment in Bilateral Investment Treaties' (2007) 41:2 Journal of World Trade 275.

approach is that when the same measures of the state give rise for allegations of breaches of the FET and expropriation at the same time, the compensation is due for all the breaches of an IIA taken, and calculated, together.

4 Possible Impact of Human Rights on Determination of Compensation

4.1 *Reduction of Compensation and the Obligation of States to Protect Human Rights*

The moment of determination of compensation is often argued to be the one which creates the possibility of introducing human rights considerations into investor—state arbitrations.[40]

Possible relevance of human rights for the compensation stage of the arbitral proceedings cannot be properly analyzed without a distinction between two scenarios. The first of them concerns situations in which investors are involved in human rights violations in the territories of the host states. The second scenario concerns situations in which no human rights violations have been committed by investors, but nevertheless host states invoke their human rights obligations in an attempt to justify measures breaching investment treaties.

4.1.1 The Meaning of the Obligation to Protect Human Rights

The first scenario may be seen from the perspective of the host states' obligation to protect human rights. It requires states to exercise due diligence to prevent violations of human rights by private persons.[41] States are thus required to 'take measures—such as by legislation and administrative practices—to control, regulate, investigate and prosecute actions by non-state actors that violate the human rights of those within their territory [and those subject to the state's jurisdiction].'[42] States are in a breach of the obligation to protect human rights when their acts or omissions enable private persons, including foreign investors, to act within their territories in violation of human rights.[43]

40 See (n. 11).

41 Manfred Nowak, *Introduction to the International Human Rights Regime* (Martinus Nijhoff 2003) 50, Janusz Symonides, 'Cultural rights' in J. Symonides (Ed.), *Human Rights: concept and standards* (Ashgate 2000) 201.

42 Robert McCorquodale and Penelope Simons, 'Responsibility Beyond Borders: State Responsibility for Extraterritorial Violations by Corporations of International Human Rights Law', (2007) 70:4 Modern Law Review 618.

43 Ibid.

In the light of states' obligation to protect human rights the question arises whether the compensation for a breach of an investment treaty may be reduced because of violations of human rights committed by the investors.

4.1.2 Relevance of the Behavior of Investors When Determing the Compensation

In general terms, the practice of arbitral tribunals in investor—state arbitrations shows that arbitrators have the power to take investors' behaviour into consideration when calculating the compensation.[44] Thus, for example, in *MTD v. Chile* the arbitral tribunal decided that the investor behaved in a negligent way, by paying up-front the full price for land without appropriate legal protection. For that reason the tribunal reduced the compensation due.[45] Similarly, in *Bogdanov v. Moldova* the tribunal deducted part of the compensation for breach of the FET standard due to the investor's behavior. It was decided that the investor was partially responsible for its loss by not ensuring that the privatization contract at hand contained 'appropriately precise regulation of the compensation' due in case of a breach of the contract.[46] Another example can be seen in *Azurix v. Argentina.* In principle, the tribunal decided to calculate the fair market value of the investment by applying the actual investment method. However, it took into account the unreasonable behavior of the investor, who paid for the concession a price which 'no well-informed investor' would have paid. For that reason, the tribunal determined the fair market value of the investment only after reducing the outcome of the applied valuation method, by 'adjusting' it to the 'real value' of the investment.[47]

These arbitral awards illustrate that tribunals can use their discretion to reduce the compensation, based on behavior of investors. At the same time, they provide no explanation as to the legal basis of this authority.

4.1.3 The Concept of the Contribution to the Injury

Although the above examples relate to the negligent behavior of the investors from an economic perspective, there appears to be no reason preventing arbitral tribunals from applying the same discretionary powers where investors have engaged in behavior that violates international human rights standards.

---

44 Dolzer and Schreuer (n. 21) 273.

45 *MTD v Chile* (n. 31) paras 242–243. The tribunal decided to reduce the compensation by 50%.

46 *Iurii Bogdanov v Republic of Moldova*, Award, Ad hoc—SCC Arbitration Rules; IIC 33 (2005), 22 September 2005, point 5.2.

47 *Azurix v Argentina* (n. 36) paras 425–426.

The legal basis for such discretionary power, for both economic negligence and violations of human rights by investors, seems to be expressed in the wording of Article 39 of the ILC Articles:

> In the determination of reparation, account shall be taken of the contribution to the injury by wilful or negligent action or omission of the injured State or any person or entity in relation to whom reparation is sought.[48]

However, two potential problems may arise with a direct application of this rule.[49] The first one relates to the nature of investment obligations, as Article 39 applies only to obligations owed to states.[50] The question therefore arises as to the nature of the obligations emerging from investment treaties. The debate is illustrated by the *Sweeteners* cases, which were arbitral proceedings based on NAFTA Chapter 11, in which Mexico defended its measures, among others, on the ground of countermeasures undertaken against the US.[51] The arbitral tribunals analyzed the issue of whether investors' rights under IIAs are the investors' own substantive and procedural rights (being therefore states' obligations towards investors), or only procedural rights, applied to trigger proceedings for breach of substantive obligations towards the state of the investor's nationality (being therefore substantive obligations towards the other contracting states). In *Corn Products v. Mexico* the tribunal decided that 'NAFTA confers upon investors substantive rights separate and distinct from those of the State of which they are nationals'.[52] The tribunal in *Cargill v. Mexico* did not consider it 'fruitful' to characterize the investors' rights as substantive or merely

48 ILC Arts (n. 12) 109.

49 Another potential problem is related to the fact that the ILC Arts do not have a binding legal character. Despite this, they are commonly referred to as a 'codification' of customary international law and as authoritative statements as to the content of the international legal principles. In consequence, although they cannot be considered as a 'legal ground' in a strict sense, they provide significant authority for legal reasoning present in investor—state arbitrations.

50 ILC Arts (n. 12) 87–88. See also art. 33.

51 *Cargill, Inc v Mexico*, Award, ICSID Case No ARB(AF)/05/2, IIC 479 (2009), 13 August 2009 (*Cargill v Mexico*); *Corn Products International Inc v Mexico*, Decision on Responsibility, ICSID Case No ARB(AF)/04/1, IIC 373 (2008), 15 January 2008 (*Corn Products v Mexico*); *Archer Daniels Midland Company and Tate & Lyle Ingredients Americas, Inc v Mexico*, Award and Separate Opinion, ICSID Case No ARB(AF)/04/05, IIC 329 (2007), 26 September 2007 (*Archer Daniels v Mexico*).

52 *Corn Products v Mexico* para. 167.

procedural, but observed that 'it is the investor that institutes the claim, that calls a tribunal into existence, and that is the named party in all respects to the resulting proceedings and award'.[53] In consequence, both tribunals concluded that countermeasures cannot preclude wrongfulness of actions undertaken in breach of NAFTA Chapter 11 obligations.[54] Different approach was adopted in *Archer Daniels v. Mexico*, where the tribunal supported the second approach, that NAFTA Chapter 11 'sets forth substantive obligations which remain inter-State, without accruing individual rights for the Claimants', agreeing on general applicability of countermeasures in investor—state arbitration, although it did not find its prerequisites fulfilled in the case.[55]

Not entering here into the analysis which approach is correct, if the approach of the tribunal in *Archer Daniels v. Mexico* is followed, *ie* obligations emerging from IIAs remain owed by states towards other states, the rule illustrated in Article 39 of the ILC Articles can be invoked as the express basis for the reduction of the compensation for the investors' behavior.[56] In consequence, violations of international human rights committed by investors could be considered as 'contribution to the injury' within the meaning of Article 39 of the ILC Articles.

The conclusion must be different if the other approach prevails, i.e., that under investment treaties investors have their own substantive and procedural rights. Then, Article 39 of the ILC Articles cannot be invoked as the express basis for the reduction of the compensation due to the investors' behavior because it applies only to inter—state obligations.

However, even in such situation the relevance of the legal norm reflected in the wording of the referred provision of the ILC Articles is not necessarily unimportant for the present analysis. Keeping in mind that a typical investment treaty does not contain any provision regulating standard of compensation for breaches of non-expropriatory standards, the solution is to be found in customary international law and principles of law. For such purposes the ILC Articles, considered as 'codification' of customary international law,[57] are often

53 *Cargill v Mexico* (n. 51) paras 385, 429.

54 Ibid., para. 424; *Corn Products v Mexico* (n. 51) para. 161.

55 *Archer Daniels v Mexico* (n. 51) paras 168, 171–173, with strong concurring opinion by Arthur W. Rovine on this issue.

56 Although phrasing it as 'express basis' may be misleading, as the whole document is not legally binding, as it was observed in the footnote 49.

57 ILC Arts (n. 12) 31. It must be noted that the ILC Arts are an attempt of 'codification and progressive development', which may cause doubts whether particular provision is a 'codification', or rather a proposal for 'progressive development' of international law.

relied on in the course of investor—state arbitrations. In this sense, the principle expressed in Article 39 can be found useful and may be applied *per analogiam*, or may have at least an indirect influence on the tribunal's analysis.

The second of the problems with the norm expressed in Article 39 of the ILC Articles is related to the issue of whether human rights violations committed by investors can be considered as 'contributing to the injury' emerging from a breach of an investment treaty committed by host states. As illustrated in the examples above, a typical situation is that 'contribution to the injury' refers to a business activity, such as a payment of an elevated price or a lack of mitigation of the loss on the investors' side.

The answer to this question depends on facts of a particular case. If a state undertakes measures which are in a breach of an IIA, but at the same time they are undertaken in a genuine pursuit of the state's obligation to protect human rights, then the measures are a direct response to human rights violations committed by the investor. During the proceedings the investor may claim that its damage has emerged from the measures which violate the IIA in question, even though these measures were provoked by the behavior of the investor itself. Because of this relation, there seems to be no obstacle to consider violations of human rights committed by the investor as a 'contribution to the injury', leading to the conclusion that the tribunal has the power to reduce the compensation.

4.1.4 The 'Caveat Investor' Principle and the 'Clean Hands' Doctrine

This reasoning is in accordance with the 'caveat investor' principle proposed by Muchlinski, according to which the behavior of the investor bears relevance for its claims concerning breaches of the FET standard.[58] Muchlinski argues that investors have three major duties regarding the FET standard: (i) a duty to refrain from unconscionable conduct, (ii) a duty to engage in the investment in the light of an adequate knowledge of its risks, and (iii) a duty to conduct business in a reasonable manner.[59] He differentiates the consequences of breaches of these duties. Whilst the breach of the first duty could lead to exemption of the state's liability, the breach of the latter two duties would be relevant for the compensation stage only.[60] The duty to conduct business in a reasonable manner is understood to be related not only to the duty to manage the investment in the best interests of the investor's shareholders, but also to

---

58 Peter Muchlinski, ' "Caveat Investor"? The Relevance of the Conduct of the Investor under the Fair and Equitable Treatment Standard' (2006) 55:3 ICLQ 527.

59 Ibid., 530.

60 Ibid.

'a corporate responsibility to act in the best interests of the host country and its economic development'.[61] Thus, the 'caveat investor' principle supports the idea that the violations of human rights by the investors may lead to a reduction of the compensation.[62]

Also Knoll-Tudor argues that in the context of the FET standard, the behavior of the investors is relevant for the compensation stage of arbitral proceedings.[63] Although she underlines that the FET is not a reciprocal obligation between the state and the investor, she justifies her position by the concepts of fairness and equity.[64] According to the 'clean hands' doctrine, the investor should not receive full compensation for damage emerging from a situation to which it had contributed.[65] She agrees on the possible relevance of human rights for the determination of compensation, concluding that the amount of compensation may be reduced 'proportionally' to the investors' violations of human rights.[66]

Although the 'clean hands' doctrine is not generally considered as part of international law,[67] the arguments of Muchlinski and Knoll-Tudor strengthen the idea that the human rights violations committed by investors can be

---

61 Ibid., 548.

62 At least the violations which take place once the investment is established. Separate issue relates to human rights violations committed before or at the moment of making investments. In such situation, if treated as the investments contrary to law, a claim may be inadmissible. See *Phoenix Action Ltd v Czech Republic*, Award, ICSID Case No ARB/06/5, IIC 367 (2009), 9 April 2009, paras 101–105.

63 Tudor (n. 39) 20.

64 'Since fairness and equity imply that each one of the Parties receives what it deserves, only an investor who respects human rights deserves full compensation.' See ibid. 21.

65 Knoll-Tudor (n. 10) 341.

66 Ibid., 342.

67 The 'clean hands' doctrine is not considered as 'an institution of general international law'. Additionally, it 'appears to operate as a ground of inadmissibility rather than as a circumstance precluding wrongfulness or responsibility.' See James Crawford, 'Second report on State responsibility', (1999) II:2 Yearbook of the International Law Commission, A/CN.4/SER.A/1999/Add.1 (Part 1) 83, paras 333, 336. ILC Arts acknowledge that the doctrine of 'clean hands' has been applied 'rarely'. See ILC Arts (n. 12), p. 72. The tribunal in *Guyana v Suriname* case stated that 'the ICJ has on numerous occasions declined to consider the application of the doctrine, and has never relied on it to bar admissibility of a claim or recovery. However, some support for the doctrine can be found in dissenting opinions in certain ICJ cases, as well as in opinions in cases of the Permanent Court of International Justice(…)'. At the same time it acknowledged that 'no generally accepted definition of the clean hands doctrine has been elaborated in international law.' See *Guyana and Suriname*, award of the arbitral tribunal, 17 September 2007, para. 418.

regarded as a 'contribution to injury' emerging from a breach of the FET. If the investor violates human rights and the state undertakes measures to stop these violations, or to prevent future ones, it acts in conformity with its obligation to protect human rights. Theoretically, therefore, a state could successfully invoke its obligation to protect human rights at the moment of determining the compensation for the breach of the FET standard guaranteed in the IIA, which could result in reduction of the amount of compensation due.[68]

This conclusion does not apply to the lawful expropriation, which demands the compensation to be based on the totality of the determined value of the investment. Following this 'all or nothing approach', if the tribunal determines that there has been a lawful expropriation, full compensation is to be paid. Here, the compensation is due not for a breach of an IIA, but rather as one of the elements of the lawful expropriation. This conclusion changes in case of an unlawful expropriation. Then, the reduction of compensation seems to be possible, however only regarding compensation due for a breach of an IIA. In other words, the reduction could be possible only to the extent of the amount of compensation which exceeds the value of the taken property, i.e., the potential difference of compensation between lawful and unlawful expropriation.

4.2 *Valuation Methods and the Obligation of States to Fulfil Human Rights*

The second scenario in the analysis of possible influence of human rights on the compensation stage in the investor—state arbitrations relates to situations when investors have not violated human rights. It concerns invocations of human rights by host states to justify measures breaching IIAs, independently of the investors' behavior.

Such situation can be considered from the perspective of the states' obligation to fulfil human rights, understood as the obligation to take measures to ensure that human rights are implemented to the greatest extent possible. These measures may be of a constitutional, legislative, executive

68 Another possible explanation of the availability of the deduction of the compensation lies in the theory that an injury can exist without monetary damages. See Kinnear (n. 33) 555. According to this opinion, the fact that the injury can exist without compensation and does not entail monetary damages does not imply that there is no injury. If one applies the argumentations *a maiore ad minus*, if the injury can exist without the compensation, it can exist also with reduced ('balanced') compensation.

(administrative), judicial or practical nature,[69] and 'special emphasis in this context is placed on the concept of prevention'.[70]

Within that context, Article 39 of the ILC Articles cannot provide any basis for a reduction of compensation, as there is no 'contribution to the injury' on the part of the investor. Thus, in the context of the second scenario there seems to be no legal basis for arbitral tribunals to formally deduct anything from the compensation due, even in the context of the FET standard.[71]

Keeping in mind that the compensation must be based on the objectively proven loss of the investor, the only possible discretion of the arbitrators may lie in the choice of the valuation method of the loss. It is observed that the choice of the valuation methodology which favors a lower-end outcome of the proceedings can be used to achieve a consensus amongst arbitrators and to render a unanimous award.[72] The same discretion can be used to lower the quantum of compensation and achieve the objective of 'balancing' the breach of an IIA on one side, and the obligation to fulfil human rights on the other side. Such situation can be also considered as 'equitable considerations'.[73]

However, it must be remembered that the arbitrators have this discretion only within the scope of the principle of full compensation. Additionally, it cannot be forgotten that the choice between various methods of valuation must be reasonable, and not depending solely on the will of the arbitrators. However, within such defined borders, human rights may be considered as

---

69 Jean-Bernard Marie, 'National Systems for the Protection of Human Rights' in J. Symonides (Ed), *Human Rights: International Protection, Monitoring, Enforcement* (Ashgate 2003) 258–262.

70 Nowak (n. 41) 49; Henry J. Steiner, Philip Alston, Ryan Goodman, *International Human Rights in Context. Law, Politics, Morals* (OUP 2008) 1089–1092. The third element of the tripartite obligation to respect, protect and fulfil human rights, the obligation to respect, imposes a duty on states to refrain from acting in contravention of human rights, as long as it is not permissible under relevant legal limitation or reservation clause. It is therefore not relevant for the purposes of the present analysis.

71 There are opinions that the arbitral tribunals can detach from the standard of full compensation if the measure undertaken by the state is adopted in pursuit of the state's positive obligations in the field of human rights. This would allow the tribunal to 'balance' the interests of the investor and the state. See Liberti (n. 11) 845. Although it can be considered 'just' and based on equity, this theory is not based on a legal justification.

72 Wälde and Sabahi (n. 16) 1064.

73 Ibid., 1105. 'Equitable considerations' can moreover correct the excessive results of an already applied method and 'serve as emergency brake'. However, application of 'equitable considerations' not when choosing the method, but once the method is already applied, is more controversial.

circumstances influencing the choice of a particular method. Thus, in that context their relevance for the valuation of compensation would emerge more from 'facts' of the case, than from legal grounds.

5 Conclusions

International human rights can influence the compensation stage of the investor–state arbitrations.

Violations of human rights by investors can be considered from the perspective of states' obligation to protect human rights. Then, such behaviour of the investors could be considered as 'contribution to the injury'. Depending on how one defines the nature of obligations arising from the investment treaties, Article 39 of the ILC Articles provides a direct or indirect basis for claiming that compensation may be reduced. This observation is valid regarding compensation for breaches of the FET standard. With reference to the expropriation, as long as an expropriation is lawful, there is no possibility of reducing the due compensation based on human rights considerations. However, with regard to an unlawful expropriation compensation may be reduced, as long as such reduction would not affect the full market value of the expropriated investment, but rather the damages exceeding this amount.

If there is no violation of human rights by the investor, the principle of full compensation applies and there is no formal basis for any reduction of compensation based on human rights considerations. In consequence, the only way arbitral tribunals may use their discretionary power to consider the states' international obligation to fulfil human rights is at the moment of choosing one of various available valuation methods. These informal considerations would introduce an element of 'balancing' the states' and the investors' interests at the compensation stage. However, the final outcome of determining the amount of compensation must remain based on objective criteria, which are to be chosen in an unbiased and reasonable way. This is why such discretion may be applied only when choosing valuation methods which are objectively available for a particular case.

The purpose of the investor—state arbitration is to solve an investment dispute. This mechanism grants arbitrators a very specific mandate. If its scope is ignored, the awards can be subject to annulment, setting aside or denial of enforcement, depending on the circumstances. However, even within these limits, human rights considerations can influence the compensation stage of the arbitral proceedings.

CHAPTER 8

Are Feed-in Tariff Schemes with Local Content Requirements Consistent with WTO Law?

Jan-Christoph Kuntze and Tom Moerenhout

1 Introduction

Various support mechanisms for the diffusion and development of renewable energy have been implemented all over the world, in particular during the past decade. Today, at least 127 countries have some sort of renewable energy support in place.[1] The support mechanism that has triggered particularly strong growth of the national renewable energy sectors is the feed-in tariff (FIT).[2] It is often favored by investors as it guarantees generators the purchase of their renewable electricity and grants them bonus payments for renewable electricity for a long period of time.[3]

With the increasing competition on the global renewable energy market in recent years and with renewable energy firms from certain countries dominating the market, more and more countries with yet uncompetitive renewable energy industries opted for national support instruments to develop their national renewable energy sectors. They have in particular resorted to FIT schemes with attached local content requirements (LCR).[4] These schemes guarantee renewable electricity producers a determined price per KWh over a certain period of time, usually between 15 and 20 years. They often include degression rates, which stipulate that the level of FIT rates decreases in subsequent years. At the same time, as a condition for financial support, they require renewable electricity generators to source a previously defined share of components for their final products from local manufacturing or assembly.

---

1 REN21, 'Global Status Report 2013' (2013) 14 <http://www.ren21.net/> accessed 16 June 2013.

2 Ibid., 72.

3 Miguel Mendonca, David Jacobs and Benjamin Sovacool, *Powering the Green Economy: The Feed-in Tariff Handbook* (Routledge, 2009) 15–39.

4 Jan-Christoph Kuntze and Tom Moerenhout, 'Local Content Requirements and the Renewable Energy Industry: A Good Match?' (2013) ICTSD Working Paper 21–34 <http://ictsd.org/downloads/2013/06/local-content-requirements-and-the-renewable-energy-industry-a-good-match.pdf> accessed 04 June 2013.

 | DOI 10.1163/9789004270190_009

From a political point of view, a state's decision for a FIT with LCR might be perfectly rational. FITs without LCR could mainly sponsor foreign manufacturers of renewable energy components while adding little value for domestic businesses. Labor unions and local industry representatives would likely object to such ways of using public money and could question the value of renewable energy development for the local population. The integration of LCR might therefore be a compromise solution for the national governments of 'late-comer countries' to put FIT schemes for renewable energy development in place, particularly in times of budgetary constraints. In many cases, if governments were to not implement any FIT schemes, renewable electricity generators would potentially be unable to compete in national electricity markets that are dominated by conventional energy producers towards whom they have initial competitive disadvantages.

For WTO Members, the use of LCR in FITs will, however, be difficult to align with their WTO commitments. While FITs with LCR may help the development of renewable energy and potentially the mitigation of climate change the WTO's free trade rationale seems to be incompatible with support policies aimed at creating local industries. A precise analysis of the treatment of FIT schemes with LCR under WTO law will be beneficial to highlight potential flexibilities for the use of such schemes by WTO Members, or to point to those WTO provisions that are irreconcilable with FITs that contain LCR.

This chapter will assess whether FIT schemes with LCR are consistent with certain WTO provisions, and will look for provisions inside and outside the WTO realm that could potentially exempt these schemes from violating WTO law.

2 Design of Feed-in Tariffs with Local Content Requirements

WTO Members have implemented FITs with LCR in mainly two different ways. On the one hand, the Canadian province of Ontario and the Indian government, among others, have defined the use of local content as a general precondition for the receipt of a FIT. The Ontarian Green Energy Act requires wind and solar photovoltaic (PV) projects to source respectively 50 and 60 per cent of their project components locally in order to be eligible for FIT payments.[5] Renewable electricity producers must regularly prove their

5 Ontario Power Authority, 'Feed-in tariff Program, FIT Rules Version 2.1' (14 December 2012) para. 8.4(a) <http://fit.powerauthority.on.ca/sites/default/files/page/FIT_Rules_Version_2.1.pdf> accessed 01 June 2013.

compliance with the local content requirements to the administering body, the Ontario Power Authority.[6] The Ontarian scheme has been subject to two WTO disputes brought by Japan and the European Union against Canada.[7] India has put in place a similar financing scheme with LCR for solar PV and solar thermal production. Since 2011, the Indian Jawaharlal Nehru National Solar Mission (JNNSM) requires the manufacturing of PV cells and their assembly to PV modules to happen locally in order to be eligible for FIT payments. It further requires that 30 per cent of solar thermal projects be sourced locally. The US has challenged the JNNSM before the WTO and has requested consultations with India.[8]

On the other hand, the WTO Members Turkey and Malaysia have incentivized the use of local content with a progressive increase in support according to the percentage of local content used in renewable energy projects. The FIT scheme with LCR in Turkey consists of two different components, a fixed and a variable one. Depending on the renewable energy technology used, the Turkish Renewable Energy Law grants certain fixed amounts of FIT payments to all renewable energy producers. Those producers that use a high share of local components in their projects can receive additional FIT payments on top.[9] For PV solar projects, for instance, bonus payments are granted for the use of local modules, cells, invertors and tracking systems.[10] The Malaysian Renewable Energy Bill 2010 foresees a FIT with LCR on similar conditions. The scheme grants the payment of a basic feed-in tariff rate to all renewable energy producers. A bonus feed-in tariff share is available for solar PV producers that use locally manufactured or assembled modules or inverters.[11]

6 Green Energy and Green Economy Act Bill 150 (2009) Legislative Assembly of Ontario (Canada) Chapter S.O. 2009 C. 12.

7 *Canada-Certain Measures Affecting the Renewable Energy Generation Sector* WT/DS412/R WT/DS426/R (24 May 2013).

8 India—Certain Measures Relating to Solar Cells and Solar Modules' wt/DS456/1 (6 February 2013).

9 Law No 5346 'On utilization of renewable energy sources for the purpose of generating electrical energy' (2010) Parliament of Turkey, art. 6/B.

10 Ibid., Schedule II.

11 DR 47/2010 Renewable Energy Bill 2010 'Renewable resources, feed-in tariff rates, effective period and annual degression rates' (2010) Parliament of Malaysia, Schedule (Section 2).

3 Feed-in Tariffs with LCR under WTO law

This section shall assess whether FITs with LCR are consistent with specific WTO rules. Among others, WTO law disciplines the use of subsidies and of internal taxes, internal charges, laws, regulations and requirements. FITs with LCR shall be analyzed under three specific WTO provisions, namely Article III:4 and III:5 of the GATT, Article 2.1 of the TRIMs Agreement, and Article 3.1(b) of the SCM Agreement. As FITs with LCR will be found to be inconsistent with two, and potentially all, of these provisions, it will be necessary to expand the analysis to the exceptions contained in GATT Article XX and the 'infant industries' exception in GATT Article XVIII.

3.1 *Inconsistencies of FITs Containing LCR with WTO Law*

3.1.1 Violation of National Treatment under the GATT?

One of the cornerstone provisions of the GATT is the non-discrimination clause contained in GATT Article III.[12] GATT Article III:4 determines that 'foreign products shall be accorded treatment no less favourable than that accorded to like products of national origin'. No less favorable treatment must be provided 'in respect of all laws, regulations and requirements affecting the (…) internal sale, offering for sale, purchase, transportation, distribution or use [of imported products]'. The Appellate Body held that three elements needed to be given in order to find a violation of GATT Article III:4: (i) the imported and domestic product must be 'like products', (ii) the measure must be a 'law, regulation, or requirement affecting their internal sale, offering for sale, purchase, transportation, distribution, or use', and (iii) the imported product must be accorded 'less favourable' treatment than the like domestic product.[13] The domestic and imported products would in this case be renewable energy components, for instance solar PV modules, cells or inverters or raw materials, such as steel or silicon.

In order to determine whether FIT schemes with LCR may violate GATT article III:4, a WTO panel would likely first affirm that imported and domestic

12 GATT art. III:4 demands that imported products 'shall be accorded treatment no less favorable than that accorded to like products of national origin in respect of all laws, regulations and requirements affecting their internal sale, purchase, transportation, distribution or use.' General Agreement on Tariffs and Trade 1994 (GATT) Marrakesh Agreement Establishing the World Trade Organization, Annex 1A (15 April 1994) art. III:4.

13 Appellate Body Report *Korea—Measures Affecting Imports of Fresh Chilled and Frozen Beef* WT/DS169/AB/R (11 December 2000) para. 133.

renewable energy components constitute 'like products'. The following criteria would be used for the assessment of 'likeness':

> (i) the physical properties of the products; (ii) the extent to which the products are capable of serving the same or similar end-uses; (iii) the extent to which consumers perceive and treat the products as alternative means of performing particular functions in order to satisfy a particular want or demand; and (iv) the international classification of the products for tariff purposes.[14]

A panel would further look at 'the competitive relationship' of the products.[15] None of these criteria supplies a good argument to distinguish between imported and domestic renewable energy components. Each of them would support the 'likeness' of these products.

In a second step, a panel would determine whether a FIT with LCR constitutes a 'law, regulation or a requirement' affecting the internal sale, offering for sale, purchase, transportation, distribution or use of imported renewable energy components. As FITs with LCR are usually implemented in a law, and spelled out in more specific degrees, they will be found to be 'laws' or 'regulations'.[16] They clearly 'affect' the 'internal sale' of imported components, as they contain incentives for developers to use domestic instead of imported renewable energy components.[17]

In a third step, a panel would assess whether FITs with LCR accord imported components 'less favorable treatment' than components of national origin. It would specifically determine 'whether a measure modifies the conditions of

---

14 Appellate Body Report, *European Communities—Measures Affecting Asbestos and Asbestos-Containing Products* WT/DS135/AB/R (12 March 2001) para. 101.

15 Ibid., 103.

16 The Panel in Canada—FIRA finds that the term 'regulations' encompassed 'mandatory rules applying across-the-board', but that a measure did not need to be 'mandatory' and 'apply across-the-board' in order to be subject to art. III:4. Panel Report, *Canada-Administration of the Foreign Investment Review Act*, BISD 30S/140 (7 February 1984) para. 5.5.

17 The Panel in EC—Bananas III clarifies that 'The word 'affecting' covers not only measures which directly regulate or govern the sale of domestic and imported like products, but also measures which create incentives or disincentives with respect to the sale, offering for sale, purchase, and use of an imported product 'affect' those activities'. Panel Report *European Communities—Regime for the Importation, Sale and Distribution of Bananas* WT/DS27/R (19 May 2008) para. 7.175.

competition in the relevant market to the detriment of imported products'.[18] When comparing the competitive position of imported and domestic components, a panel would likely find that imported renewable energy components are 'less favorably treated' as they do not receive the same benefits as domestic components. In fact, FITs with LCR usually determine that renewable energy producers only receive FIT payments in case they source a sufficient share of components from national production. Domestic components are therefore clearly given favorable treatment that is meant to strengthen their competitive position to the disadvantage of imported components.[19]

As all three assessed elements seem to be fulfilled, it may be concluded that FITs with LCR would likely be found inconsistent with GATT Article III:4. In support of this, the Panel in the *Canada-Administration of the Foreign Investment Review Act* explicitly stated that 'the purpose of GATT Article III:4 [was (...)] to ensure that goods originating in any other contracting party benefit from treatment no less favourable than domestic goods, in respect of the requirements that affect their purchase.'[20] The same Panel considered a 'requirement to purchase goods of Canadian origin [...] contrary to GATT Article III:4'.[21] Precisely such a requirement is contained in FITs with LCR.

In addition to GATT Article III:4, FIT schemes with LCR could further be inconsistent with GATT Article III:5. This provision might be violated if a FIT with LCR is found to constitute, as stated in GATT Article III:5,

> [an] internal quantitative regulation relating to the mixture, processing or use of products in specified amounts or proportions which requires, directly or indirectly, that any specified amount or proportion of any product which is the subject of the regulation must be supplied from domestic sources.[22]

---

18 Appellate Body Report, *Korea Beef* (n. 13) para. 137.

19 The Panel in *China-Audiovisuals* clarifies that 'Less favourable treatment of imported like products may arise from laws, regulations, or requirements which provide domestic products more favourable treatment than imported products or from laws, regulations, or requirements which place additional burdens on imported products that are not placed on domestic products'. Panel Report *China-Measures Affecting Trading Rights and Distribution Services for Certain Publications and Audiovisual Entertainment Products* WT/DS363/AB/R (21 December 2009) para. 7.1472.

20 Panel Report *Canada-Administration* (n. 16) paras 2.2, 2.3.

21 Ibid.

22 GATT art. III:5.

First, it is likely that a panel would find a FIT with LCR to constitute an 'internal quantitative regulation', as it determines a certain amount of local content to be fulfilled. The Panel in *US-Tobacco*, for instance, argued in this context that the measure in question set a minimum specified proportion of 75 per cent for the use of US tobacco in manufacturing cigarettes.[23] Second, it would need to be proven that a FIT with LCR 'requires' the sourcing of local content. In the US-Tobacco case, such a 'requirement' was found as the US government made any producer that failed to source the required amount of local content subject pay penalties.[24] On FITs with LCR a Panel could argue along similar lines that these schemes may involve an 'indirect' penalty, as renewable energy producers not fulfilling the demanded local content quota would not receive equal support and would thereby have a competitive disadvantage towards other producers that fulfill the quota. FITs with LCR could then be found inconsistent with GATT Article III:5. It should be noted, however, that in past cases panels have often refrained from assessing a violation of Article III:5 due to reasons of judicial economy when they had found a violation of GATT Article III:4 already.[25]

Both Article III:4 and III:5 GATT can only apply to FITs with LCR if they are not precluded by Article III:8(a) GATT.[26] This provision has, for instance, been invoked by Canada in defense of the FIT scheme with LCR in Ontario.[27] GATT Article III:8(a) determines that GATT Article III:4 shall not apply to 'laws, regulations or requirements governing the procurement by governmental agencies of products purchased for governmental purposes and not with a view to commercial resale (…)'.

In order to assess whether GATT Article III:8(a) can be invoked, a panel will in a first step determine whether FITs with LCR can be characterized as 'laws, regulations or requirements *governing* procurement'. In a second step, it will define the meaning of the term '*procurement* by governmental agencies'. The Appellate Body stated that 'procurement' referred 'to the process pursuant to which a government acquires products'.[28] It further stated that the term

23 Panel Report *United States—Measures Affecting the Importation, Internal Sale and Use of Tobacco* WT/DS44/R (4 October 1994) para. 67.

24 Ibid., 68.

25 Panel Report *China—Measures Affecting Imports of Automobile Parts* WT/DS342/R (18 July 2008) para. 7.275.

26 Appellate Body Report *Canada-Certain Measures Affecting the Renewable Energy Generation Sector* WT/DS412/R wt/DS426/R (24 May 2013) para. 5.56.

27 First Written Submission Canada in *Canada—Certain Measures Affecting the Renewable Energy Generation Sector* WT/DS412 (22 December 2011) paras 62, 67, 101.

28 Appellate Body Report *Canada—Renewable Energy* (n. 26) para. 5.59.

'governmental agency' had to be 'determined by the competences conferred on the entity concerned and by whether that entity acts for or on behalf of government'.[29] In a third step, a panel would analyze whether a governmental agency 'purchases' electricity through the FIT scheme with LCR 'for governmental purposes and not with a view to commercial resale'. The Appellate Body determined that 'products purchased for governmental purposes' in Article III:8(a) GATT referred to goods consumed by government or acquired by government in order to hand them to recipients to discharge public functions. It held that Article III:8(a) GATT required there to be a 'rational relationship between the product and the governmental function being discharged'.[30] It further required an assessment of 'commercial resale' to consider whether it was 'oriented at generating a profit for the seller' in the short or long term.[31]

With regard to the first step, the Appellate Body interpreted the term 'governing' as 'constitut[ing] a law or rule for', based on its dictionary meaning.[32] It inferred that 'the act of procurement [needs to be] undertaken within a binding structure of laws, regulations, or requirements'.[33] The Appellate Body considered that 'the product being procured is electricity, whereas the product discriminated against for reason of its origin is generation equipment'. These two products were not in a competitive relationship. Although FIT schemes with LCR spelled out conditions for energy generation equipment, they did not contain conditions for electricity as the procured end-product. Therefore, the Appellate Body concluded that a 'binding structure' did not exist between the procured product (electricity) and the FIT schemes with LCR.[34] In the *Canada—Renewable Energy* case, the Appellate Body therefore stopped its analysis at this point and concluded that the FIT scheme with LCR at issue did not fall within the ambit of GATT Article III:8(a).[35]

Based on this reasoning, a panel will reject the application of GATT Article III:8(a) to potential violations of GATT Article III:4 and III:5. A FIT with LCR will therefore most likely be found inconsistent with these two provisions.

29 Ibid., 5.60.

30 Ibid., 5.68.

31 Ibid., 5.71.

32 Oxford English Dictionary online, 'governing' <*http://www.oedcom/view/Entry/80304*> accessed 01 June 2013.

33 Appellate Body Report, *Canada Renewable Energy* (n. 26) para. 5.58.

34 Ibid., 5.79.

35 Ibid., 5.79, 5.85.

3.1.2 Violation of TRIMs Agreement?

Second, FITs with LCR might also be inconsistent with provisions of the WTO's TRIMs Agreement. This agreement contains an Illustrative List that specifies which measures constitute violations of GATT Article III:4.[36] Based on Article 2.1 and 2.2 TRIMs Agreement, the Illustrative List qualifies those trade-related investment measures as inconsistent with GATT Article III:4

> which are mandatory or *enforceable under domestic law* or under administrative rulings, or *compliance with which is necessary to obtain an advantage*, and which require: (a) the *purchase or use by an enterprise of products of domestic origin* or from *any domestic source*, whether specified in terms of particular products, in terms of volume or value of products, or in terms of a proportion of volume or value of its local production (...).[37]

In an assessment of Article 2.1 and 2.2 TRIMs Agreement a panel will determine (i) whether FITs with LCR constitute 'trade-related investment measures', and (ii) whether they fall under the provision above in the Illustrative List.[38]

First, a FIT with LCR will likely be considered an 'investment measure' as it has 'a significant impact on investment' in the renewable energy sector. FIT schemes with LCR can have a large positive effect on investment into domestic manufacturing facilities of renewable energy components, while they potentially have a negative impact on investments into manufacturing facilities in other countries from which components would otherwise be imported.[39] The FIT with LCR in Ontario, for instance, explicitly aims to '[e]nable new green industries through new investment and job creation' and to '[p]rovide

36 The Panel Report *Canada—Certain Measures Affecting the Renewable Energy Generation Sector* WT/DS412/R (19 December 2012) para. 7.118 finds that art. III:8(a) GATT will need to be analyzed first, as it could preclude the application of art. III:3 GATT and art. 2.1 TRIMS.

37 Emphasis added Agreement on Trade-Related Investment Measures (TRIMs Agreement) Marrakesh Agreement Establishing the World Trade Organization, Annex 1A (15 April 1994) para. 1 Annex: Ill.

38 Before these two steps, the Panel in Canada Renewable Energy requires the assessment of art. III:8(a) GATT conducted above, as that provision could preclude the application of both art. III:4 GATT and art. 2.1 TRIMS. See Panel Report, *Canada Renewable Energy* (n. 36) paras 7.118, 7.119.

39 Panel Report *Indonesia—Certain Measures Affecting the Automotive Industry* WT/DS64/R (2 July 1998) paras 14.73–14.81.

incentives for investment in renewable energy technologies'.[40] The Panel in *Canada—Renewable Energy* found evidence of specific cases in which the scheme had 'motivated' several manufacturers to move their production of renewable energy equipment from overseas to Ontario.[41]

FIT schemes with LCR will further be considered 'related to trade'. The Panel in *Indonesia—Autos* clarified that measures with LCR necessarily constituted trade-related investment measures, because such requirements 'by definition, always favour the use of domestic products over imported products, and therefore affect trade'.[42] FIT schemes with LCR will therefore fall under the scope of the TRIMS Agreement.

Second, a Panel will find FIT schemes with LCR to fall under the above-mentioned provision in the Illustrative List of the TRIMS Agreement. The schemes are usually 'mandatory under domestic law' as they are spelled out in binding legal documents and they demand compliance with their provisions to 'obtain an advantage', namely the receipt of FIT payments. They also explicitly demand the 'purchase or use' of products of domestic origin from renewable electricity generators as they require a minimum share of local content in their projects.[43] FIT schemes with LCR will therefore likely be inconsistent with Article 2.1 and 2.2 of the TRIMS Agreement.

The GATT requires that a FIT scheme with LCR that is found to be inconsistent with GATT Article III:4, GATT Article III:5, and/or Article 2.1 TRIMS Agreement must be brought into conformity with these provisions, provided that their inconsistency is not justified by another GATT provision, such as Article XX GATT or Article XVIII:C and D (assessed in section 3.2.). The Appellate Body stated that be above-mentioned Article III:8(a) GATT could also be applicable to Article 2.1 and 2.2 TRIMS Agreement. It reasoned that the 'TRIMS Agreement as a whole' mainly clarified the application of GATT Articles III and XI to a specific set of measures and would 'safeguard rights recognized in the GATT'.[44]

40 Minister of Energy and Infrastructure of Ontario, Letter to Ontario Power Authority Regarding FIT Program (24 September 2009) 1 <http://www.powerauthority.on.ca/ sites/default/files/page/15420_FIT_Directive_Sept_24_09.pdf> accessed 04 June 2013.

41 Panel Report, *Canada Renewable Energy* (n. 36) para. 7.110.

42 Panel Report, *Indonesia Automotive* (n. 39) paras 14.82, 14.83. This view was affirmed by the Panel in Canada Renewable Energy. See Panel Report, *Canada Renewable Energy* (n. 36) para. 7.111.

43 Panel Report, *Canada Renewable Energy* (n. 36) paras 7.163, 7.166.

44 Appellate Body Report, *Canada Renewable Energy* (n. 26) para. 5.32.

An issue that has been controversial is in which sequence a Panel should assess the consistency of FIT schemes with LCR with Article III:4 GATT and Article 2.1 and 2.2 TRIMS.[45] While the Panel in *Indonesia—Autos* claimed that the TRIMS provisions had to be assessed first, as the TRIMS Agreement was 'more specific' than Article III:4,[46] the Panel in *EC-Bananas* insisted on a prior assessment of Article III:4 GATT.[47] In several cases, panels dealt with inconsistencies with Article III:4 GATT first and, due to 'judicial economy' reasoning, refrained from assessing violations of the TRIMS Agreement afterwards.[48] The Panel in *Canada—Renewable Energy* assessed whether GATT Article III:8(a) may exclude an application of GATT Article III:4 and subsequently inferred from an analysis of Article 2.1 and 2.2 TRIMS that FITS with LCR were inconsistent with GATT Article III:4.[49]

3.1.3 Violation of the Agreement on Subsidies and Countervailing Measures?

Apart from their inconsistency with the GATT and the TRIMS Agreement, FITS with LCR could further constitute 'prohibited subsidies' under the WTO's SCM Agreement. The first question to be asked is whether a FIT with LCR constitutes a 'subsidy' in the definition of the SCM Agreement. Only if that is the case, the scheme might constitute a 'prohibited subsidy'.

Article 1.1 SCM Agreement lists two requirements for the qualification of a measure as a 'subsidy', namely the existence of a 'financial contribution by a government or any public body within the territory of a Member', or an 'income or price support in the sense of Article XVI of GATT 1994', and the conferment of a 'benefit'.

A FIT scheme with LCR would be found a 'financial contribution' where:

(i) a government practice involves a direct transfer of funds (e.g. grants, loans, and equity infusion), potential direct transfers of funds or liabilities (e.g. loan guarantees);

---

45 First Written Submission by the European Union *Canada—Measures Relating to the Feed-in Tariff Program* (2012) WT/DS426 (14 February 2012) paras 142–47.

46 Panel Report, *Indonesia Automotive* (n. 39) para. 14.93.

47 Panel Report, *EU Bananas* (n. 17) para. 7.185–7.186.

48 Panel Report *Canada—Certain Measures Affecting the Automotive Industry* (2000) WT/DS142/R (11 February 2000) para. 10.91; Panel Report *India—Measures Affecting the Automotive Sector* (2001) WT/DS175/R (21 December 2001) para. 7.324; Panel Report, *China Automobile Parts* (n. 25) para. 7.368.

49 Panel Report, *Canada Renewable Energy* (n. 36) paras 7.152–7.167.

(ii) government revenue that is otherwise due is foregone or not collected (e.g. fiscal incentives such as tax credits);
(iii) a government provides goods or services other than general infrastructure, or purchases goods;
(iv) a government makes payments to a funding mechanism, or entrusts or directs a private body to carry out one or more of the type of functions illustrated in (i) to (iii) above which would normally be vested in the government and the practice, in no real sense, differs from practices normally followed by governments.[50]

One approach to assess FIT schemes with LCR as 'financial contributions' is to consider them as involving 'purchases' of electricity under Article 1.1(a)(1)(iii) SCM Agreement. One could argue that the government pays for the amount of electricity delivered to the grid, receives control of the electricity in the grid in return, and can sell it to any customer. Once the producer has delivered electricity to the grid, it loses control over its use and sale and is reimbursed for each kWh injected into the grid. As noted above, the Panel in *Canada-Renewable Energy* argued that the term 'to purchase' could encompass the gain of 'possession of' a product. As a government agency would pay a FIT and receive 'possession' of electricity in return, the agency could be argued to 'purchase goods'.[51] The Appellate Body considered it irrelevant whether the tasks to pay for electricity and to receive and transmit it lay with different government institutions or not, as long as all of them could be defined as 'public bod[ies]' in the meaning of Article 1.1(a)(1) SCM Agreement.[52] The Panel concluded from its analysis of Article 1.1(a)(1)(iii) SCM Agreement that the Ontario FIT therefore involves a 'financial contribution'.[53]

The Appellate Body in *Canada—Renewable Energy* emphasized that 'a transaction may fall under more than one type of financial contribution' and that the different types listed in Article 1.1(a)(1) SCM Agreement are not mutually exclusive.[54] Therefore, a FIT scheme could also, and at the same time, constitute a 'direct transfer of funds' under Article 1.1(a)(1)(i) SCM Agreement. The Appellate Body defined that a 'direct transfer of funds' may exist in the form

50 Agreement on Subsidies and Countervailing Measures Marrakesh Agreement Establishing the World Trade Organization, Annex 1A (15 April 1994) art. 1.1(a).

51 Panel Report, *Canada Renewable Energy* (n. 36) paras 7.231–7.239.

52 Appellate Body Report, *Canada Renewable Energy* (n. 26) para. 5.124. Also Panel Report, *Canada Renewable Energy* (n. 36) paras 7.234, 7.235, 7.239,

53 Panel Report, *Canada Renewable Energy* (n. 36) paras 7.225–7.230.

54 Appellate Body Report, *Canada Renewable Energy* (n. 26) paras 5.120, 5.131, 5.132.

of a 'conditional grant' and that 'what is captured is a government's provision [...] of funds, irrespective of whether this is done gratuitously or in exchange for consideration'.[55] Based on this definition, Japan and the EU argued that the FIT scheme with LCR in Ontario could fall under Article 1.1(a)(1)(i) SCM Agreement as it involved the payment of a price to electricity generators, which is alleged to be above the market price, in return for the production of electricity with sufficient local content.[56] The Appellate Body in *Canada—Renewable Energy* dismissed this argument—it reasoned that Ontario's FIT scheme issued payments for the quantity of electricity that is actually delivered into the electricity grid, it did not grant lump-sum payments.[57]

Most FIT schemes with LCR are different with regard to the extent that the government is involved in the payment of the FIT premium. In relatively liberalized and privatized electricity markets, a FITs with LCR could equally be found to involve a 'financial contribution' under Article 1.1(a)(1)(iv) SCM Agreement even if the responsible institutions were not 'public bod[ies]'. This could be the case, provided that the government 'entrusts or directs' a private utility to grant FIT payments to renewable electricity generators, and provided that this task 'would normally be vested in the government and the practice, in no real sense, differs from practices normally followed by governments'. The conditions of FIT schemes with LCR are generally implemented and supervised by governmental entities—individual electricity consumers and utilities would not offer such conditions to renewable electricity generators on their own.[58] This argument suggests that the government may 'entrust or direct' a private body through its FIT with LCR.

With regard to the question of whether the distribution of FIT payments is a function that 'would normally be vested in the government and in no real sense, differs from practices normally followed by governments', a panel will conduct a case-by-case analysis 'of the core features of the [private] entity concerned, and its relationship with the government in the narrow sense'.[59] On the one hand, the Appellate Body clarified that '[i]f a public body did not

55 Appellate Body Report, *US—Large Civil Aircraft (Second Complaint)* WT/DS353/AB/R (23 March 2012) paras 617–618.

56 Second Written Submission Japan in *Canada—Certain Measures Affecting the Renewable Energy Generation Sector* WT/DS412 (15 May 2012) para 45; EU First Submission, *Canada Feed-in Tariff Program* (n. 45) paras 49–50.

57 Appellate Body Report, *Canada Renewable Energy* (n. 26) para. 5.131, 5.132.

58 See Case C-379/98 *Preussen Elektra AG v Schleswag AG* (2001) ECR I-2099, para. 20–21.

59 Appellate Body Report *United States-Definitive Anti-Dumping and Countervailing Duties on Certain Products from China* WT/DS379/AB/R (11 March 2011) paras 297, 318.

itself dispose of the relevant authority or responsibility, it could not effectively control or govern the actions of a private body or delegate such responsibility to a private body'.[60] On the other hand, there is an argument that most FIT schemes with LCR that are administered by private utilities should be considered a financial contribution, as a government could otherwise circumvent the disciplines of the SCM Agreement by setting up a private intermediary, which would then be obliged to carry out the support scheme.[61]

Alternatively to the analysis of a 'financial contribution', a panel could also assess whether FIT schemes with LCR may amount to 'income or price support in the sense of Article XVI of GATT 1994' and under Article 1.1(a)(2) SCM Agreement. Japan and the EU both argued that the Ontario FIT scheme functions as a 'price support system' as the government contractually agreed on a price above market level with eligible electricity generators. They reasoned further that, due to its local content quota, the scheme reduced imports of renewable energy components into Ontario and thereby potentially supported the income of Ontario businesses.[62] The Appellate Body in *Canada—Renewable Energy* did not analyze this argument due to judicial economy considerations; therefore the interpretation of Article 1.1(a)(2) SCM Agreement with regard to FITs with LCR remains unclear.[63]

Following the analysis of Article 1.1(a)(1)(iii) SCM Agreement, many FIT schemes would be considered to involve a 'financial contribution'. In order to constitute a subsidy under the SCM Agreement, a FIT with LCR would further need to 'confer a benefit' under Article 1.1(b) SCM Agreement. The essential question here is whether electricity producers from certain renewable energy technologies receive FIT rates on 'more favorable terms' than the 'prevailing market conditions for the good or service in question in the country of provision or purchase'.[64] Interpreted in the context of Article 14(d) SCM Agreement, a 'benefit analysis' requires a comparison between actual remuneration and a market-based benchmark or proxy, and thus between amounts.[65] First, a

---

60 Ibid., 294.

61 Panel Report, *United States-Definitive Anti-Dumping and Countervailing Duties on Certain Products from China* WT/DS379/R (22 October 2010) para. 8.79.

62 EU First Submission, *Canada Feed-in Tariff Program* (n. 45) paras 32–42; First Written Submission Canada in *Canada—Certain Measures Affecting the Renewable Energy Generation Sector* WT/DS412 (22 December 2011) paras 205–214.

63 Appellate Body Report, *Canada Renewable Energy* (n. 26) para. 5.139.

64 SCM Agreement art. 14(d). see Appellate Body Report *US-Final Countervailing Duty Determination with Respect to Certain Softwood Lumber from Canada* WT/DS257/AB/R (17 February 2004) para. 86.

65 Appellate Body Report, *Canada Renewable Energy* (n. 26) para. 5.165.

'benefit' analysis will need to identify appropriate 'market conditions' as basis for comparison.[66] Second, it will need to define determinants for whether the conditions of a FIT scheme are 'more favorable' than these market conditions.

Firstly, identifying an appropriate benchmark for the 'benefit' analysis, the Panel in *Canada—Renewable Energy* reviewed several wholesale electricity markets in Ontario. It also resorted to in-province and out-of province 'market' benchmarks in order to replicate competitive market conditions, adjusting the underlying conditions to the market of purchase.[67] However, as the Panel found distortions in all these markets, it considered them inappropriate for a 'benefit' analysis of FIT schemes for renewable energy technologies.[68] Instead, the Appellate Body suggested taking a 'separate wholesale market for electricity generated from solar PV and windpower technologies' as benchmark.[69] In the concrete analysis of the FIT scheme with LCR in Ontario, neither the Panel, nor the Appellate Body in *Canada—Renewable Energy* were able to complete the 'benefit' analysis on the basis of that benchmark due to insufficient factual evidence.[70]

Secondly, a panel will assess whether the conditions of a FIT scheme are 'more favorable' than the 'prevailing market conditions'. The outcome may be different depending on the level at which the benefit analysis is conducted (wholesale level or retail level). The Appellate Body in *Canada—Renewable Energy* reasoned that while final consumers mostly did not distinguish between energy technologies (as price and shape of electricity were the same to them) the government's purchase patterns of electricity (at the wholesale level) were often shaped by the objective to achieve a certain energy supply-mix. According to the Appellate Body, the cost structures of different energy technologies could justify their differentiated treatment in terms of remuneration of generated electricity. Wind and solar PV technologies, for instance, had much higher capital costs than other technologies and fewer economies of scale.[71] Therefore, electricity from different energy sources was not to be seen as substitutable at the wholesale level.[72] Rather, the Appellate Body reasoned that a government could legitimately choose a certain supply-mix of electricity generation technologies and grant each technology an adequate remunera-

66 Ibid., 5.169.

67 Appellate Body Report, *US Softwood* (n. 64) paras 87, 103.

68 Panel Report, *Canada Renewable Energy* (n. 26) para. 7.320.

69 Appellate Body Report, *Canada Renewable Energy* (n. 26) para. 5.190

70 Ibid., 5.244.

71 Ibid., 5.178.

72 Ibid., 5.219.

tion to 'recover their costs' and achieve a 'reasonable margin'. The definition of a certain supply-mix by the government was not to be considered '*in and of itself* as conferring a benefit within the meaning of Article 1.1(b) of the SCM Agreement'.[73]

The Appellate Body further considered government objectives such as 'reducing reliance on fossil fuels to secure the sustainability of electricity markets' (*inter alia* because of their exhaustibility) and 'addressing the negative and positive externalities that are associated with conventional and renewable electricity production' as distinguishing factors for the 'benefit' analysis.[74] Further, it viewed as legitimate such government interventions that aim to secure long-term access to electricity through renewable energy.[75]

As the Panel and the Appellate Body in *Canada—Renewable Energy* were unable to complete the 'benefit' analysis, it remains open whether FIT schemes with LCR may constitute a 'subsidy' in terms of Article 1.1. SCM Agreement. Energy economists and trade lawyers have criticized the reasoning of both instances, particularly with regard to their choice of a market benchmark. It will be interesting to see whether future panels will successfully conclude the 'benefit' analysis on the basis of a different benchmark, for instance, based on the national market for solar and wind energy (as suggested both by the Panel and the Appellate Body).

Generally, the subsidy definition is decisive for whether FITs with LCR might be inconsistent with the SCM Agreement. In case they would amount to a financial contribution and confer a benefit, they will likely constitute a 'prohibited subsidy'. Article 3.1(b) SCM Agreement defines subsidies as prohibited if they are 'contingent (…) upon the use of domestic over imported goods'. As FITs with LCR condition their premium payments upon the use of a certain percentage of local content they would violate this provision. 'Prohibited subsidies' would need to be withdrawn by the host Member 'without delay'.[76]

3.2 *Potential Justifications for Inconsistencies with WTO Law*

From the analysis above one can derive that FITs with LCR would likely be inconsistent with different WTO provisions, namely with Article III:4 GATT and Article 2.1 and 2.2 TRIMs Agreement. The following section shall assess whether the use of FITs with LCR could be justified under certain provisions in

73 Ibid., 5.175.
74 Ibid., 5.176.
75 Ibid., 5.187.
76 SCM Agreement art. 3.2 and 4.7.

WTO law, i.e., with GATT Article XX or with GATT Article XVIII:C and D, and be legally used by WTO Members.

3.2.1 Justification through GATT Article XX?

First, GATT Article XX may be invoked to justify the use of FITs with LCR. This provision is meant to exempt certain measures, otherwise inconsistent with WTO law, in case they are 'necessary for' or 'related to' the achievement of certain legitimate policy aims by a WTO Member and in case they are applied in a non-discriminatory manner.

The application of GATT Article XX to justify violations of Article III:4 and III:5 GATT is non-controversial. Its applicability to the TRIMS Agreement has been affirmed by the Appellate Body in *China—Various Raw Materials*.[77] However, there is much debate on whether Article XX GATT could potentially be applied to the SCM Agreement. On the one hand, the finding of the Appellate Body in *China—Various Raw Materials* suggests that it may not be applicable to the agreement. The Appellate Body found that Paragraph 11.3 of China's Accession Protocol, at issue in this case, did 'not contain any reference to other provisions of the GATT 1994, including Article XX'.[78] The Panel specified that 'it is reasonable under these circumstances to assume that, were GATT Article XX intended to apply to Paragraph 11.3 of China's Accession Protocol, language would have been inserted to suggest this relationship'.[79] The SCM Agreement does not contain such 'language to suggest [a] relationship' to Article XX GATT. It can be assumed that Article XX GATT would therefore currently not be applicable to its violations. On the other hand, several relevant arguments have been made that suggest that the applicability of Article XX GATT to the SCM Agreement might be confirmed in a future decision.[80]

---

77 The Appellate Body found a cross-reference in the TRIMS Agreement that it regarded sufficient to allow for justifications of TRIMS violations through art. XX GATT. art. 3 of the TRIMS states that '(a)ll exceptions under GATT 1994 shall apply, as appropriate, to the provisions of this Agreement'. Appellate Body Report *China—Measures Related to the Exportation of Various Raw Materials* WT/DS398/AB/R (30 January 2012) para. 303.

78 Appellate Body Report, *China Raw Materials* (n. 77) para. 303, 304.

79 Panel Report *China—Measures Related to the Exportation of Various Raw Materials* WT/DS398/R (5 July 2011) para. 7.154.

80 See Christopher Tran, 'Using GATT, art. XX to Justify Climate Change Measures in Claims Under the WTO Agreements' (2010) 27 EPLJ 355–358; Amicus Curae Submission by IISD, CELA Ecojustice *Canada—Certain Measures Affecting the Renewable Energy Generation Sector* (10 May 2012) 6–19 <www.iisd.org/pdf/2012/ecojustice_amicus_curiae_brief.pdf> accessed 27 August 2013.

Two specific exception provisions of Article XX GATT might exempt FIT schemes containing LCR from the disciplines of Article III:4 and 5 GATT and Article 2.1 and 2.2 TRIMS Agreement. On the one hand, Article XX GATT paragraph (b) could potentially justify FITS with LCR as 'necessary to protect human, animal or plant life or health'. On the other hand, paragraph (g) could do so as 'relating to the conservation of exhaustible natural resources, if [they] are made effective in conjunction with restrictions on domestic production or consumption'. Following a two-step analysis, a Panel would first examine the specific exceptions in both paragraphs and would then assess compliance of FITS with LCR with Article XX's introductory clause, the *chapeau*.[81]

(a) *Applicability of Article XX(b)* GATT

The application of subparagraph (b) depends on whether the defendant WTO Member can demonstrate that the measure protects (or aims to protect) 'human, animal or plant life or health' and, if so, that the measure is 'necessary' to achieve that objective.

With regard to the objective of FITS with LCR, the Member could potentially argue that they help to offset negative effects on 'human, animal or plant life or health' from fossil fuel production by incentivizing clean renewable energy production. The link between fossil fuel production and climate change, as well as the negative effects of climate change on human health have been widely recognized.[82] A FIT with LCR that serves to promote renewable energy production could be justified on a similar base as the Appellate Body's argument in *Brazil—Tyres* that the waste of tyres 'carries risks for public health [...]' and that 'governments, legitimately, take actions [including preventive measures] to minimize the adverse effects of waste tyres'.[83] In the same lines, a WTO Member could potentially argue that its FIT with LCR is a preventive measure to minimize negative health effects from climate change and that the measure therefore contributes to the protection of public health.

81 This two-step analysis was set out by the Appellate Body in US-Gasoline. Appellate Body Report *United States—Standards for Reformulated and Conventional Gasoline* WT/DS2/R (29 January 1996) 22. See Appellate Body Report *United States—Import Prohibition of Certain Shrimp and Shrimp Products* WT/DS58/AB/R (6 November 1998) para. 157.

82 See WHO 'Climate change and human health—risks and responses' (2010) Chapter 7 <www.who.int/entity/globalchange/environment/en/chapter7.pdf> accessed 27 August 2013.

83 Appellate Body Report *Brazil—Measures Affecting Imports of Retreaded Tyres* WT/DS332/AB/R (17 December 2007) para. 171.

In a second step, a panel will undertake a balancing test between the contribution of a FIT with LCR to human, animal or plant life or health and its potential negative trade impact. This is made in order to assess whether the measure is 'necessary to protect human, animal or plant life or health'.[84] According to the Appellate Body, a 'contribution to the achievement of the objective must be material, not merely marginal or insignificant (...)'. With regard to the trade impact of the measure the Appellate Body takes into consideration whether [less trade restrictive] measures are 'reasonably available' to achieve the same objective, in case such measures are alleged by the complainant.[85] Without further consideration of the contribution of FITs with LCR to avoid negative health effects, the availability of 'less trade restrictive measures' than FITs with LCR shall directly be looked at.

Several economic models show the potential trade distorting effect of local content requirements.[86] Although there might be contrary arguments, a panel could argue that LCR in a FIT scheme contribute little to the protection of 'human, animal or plant life or health', and may even constitute a barrier for renewable energy projects instead. It could therefore suggest that FITs without LCR would be a less trade restrictive alternative to FITs with LCR, which could achieve the same objective. Based on such an assumption, FITs with LCR would not pass the balancing test on necessity.[87] GATT Article XX(b) would therefore likely not be available to justify the use of FITs with LCR.

(b) *Applicability of Article XX(g) GATT*

For the application of subparagraph (g), the measure must be found to 'relate to the conservation of exhaustible natural resources'. Further, the measure must be 'made effective in conjunction with restrictions on domestic production or consumption'.

An argument for the existence of a link between a FIT with LCR for the promotion of renewable energy and the 'conservation of exhaustible natural resources' could read as follows. Fossil fuel power plants emit large amounts of greenhouse gases into the 'clean air'. 'Clean air' has been recognized as an

84 Ibid., 210.

85 Ibid.; Appellate Body Report *European Communities and Certain Member states—Measures Affecting Trade in Large Civil Aircraft* (2011) WT/DS316/AB/R (18 May 2011) para. 172.

86 See Vladimir Tomsik and Jan Kubicek, 'Can local content requirements in international investment agreements be justified?' (2006) NCCR Trade Working Paper 2006/2 <http://papers.ssrn.com/sol3/papers.cfm?abstract_id=1092840> accessed 27 August 2013.

87 See J-C Kuntze and T Moerenhout, Local Content Requirements (n. 4).

'exhaustible natural resource'.[88] It could be 'conserved' if fossil fuel plants were replaced by renewable energy plants. The promotion of renewable energy plants is precisely the objective of FITs with LCR, see for instance the FIT scheme in Ontario.[89]

In a second step, a panel would assess whether 'the means [of a measure] are, in principle, reasonably related to the ends'.[90] A 'reasonable' relation between a FIT with LCR and the conservation of 'clean air' could likely be established, although the attached LCR would potentially be found as hindering rather than promoting the 'conservation of exhaustible natural resources'.[91] As an overall scheme, however, a FIT with LCR might pass the 'reasonably related' test.

In a third step, a panel requires the even-handedness of the FIT scheme with LCR in question between foreign and domestic production, meaning that its restrictions must be placed both upon domestic and imported products.[92] The Panel in *China—Raw Materials* held that 'Article XX(g) cannot be invoked for GATT-inconsistent measures whose goal or effects is to insulate domestic producers from foreign competition in the name of conservation'.[93] As FITs with LCR usually have the explicit objective to increase domestic share in the production of renewable energy components in the market vis-à-vis imported components, they will not pass the even-handedness test. GATT Article XX(g) would therefore likely not be available to justify the use of FITs with LCR.

(c) *Application of the 'chapeau'*

In the unlikely case that FITs with LCR would be found to fall under GATT Article XX(b) or (g), their compliance with GATT Article XX's *chapeau* would need to be assessed. The *chapeau* requires state measures to not be 'applied in a manner which would constitute a means of arbitrary or unjustifiable discrimination between countries where the same conditions prevail, or a disguised restriction on international trade (...).' [94] An 'arbitrary or unjustifiable discrimination' is deemed to exist

88 'Clean air' was recognized to be an 'exhaustible resource' in the US-Gasoline case. Appellate Body Report, US Gasoline (n. 81) III.C.

89 Appellate Body Report, *Canada Renewable Energy* (n. 26) para. 4.9.

90 Appellate Body Report, *US Shrimp* (n. 81) 135, 141.

91 J.-C. Kuntze and T Moerenhout, Local Content Requirements (n. 4).

92 Appellate Body Report, *US Gasoline* (n. 81) 19.

93 Panel Report, *China Raw Materials* (n. 79) para. 7.408.

94 GATT, art. XX.

> when a Member seeks to justify the discrimination resulting from the application of its measure by a rationale that bears no relationship to the accomplishment of the objective that falls within the purview of one of the paragraphs of GATT Article XX, or goes against this objective.[95]

The two objectives that a WTO Member could use in order to justify its support scheme with LCR are either the 'prevention of health effects' (under Article XX(b)) or 'the conservation of clean air' (under Article XX(g)). However, a panel would likely argue that the discrimination against imported renewable energy components through FITs with LCR, found under Article III:4 GATT, does not benefit the achievement of either of the two objectives. Instead it could even find that LCR impede the achievement of these two objectives as they worsen investment conditions for foreign manufacturing firms (due to a restricted availability and choice of inputs for renewable energy generation plants) and therefore potentially reduce their engagement in renewable energy projects.[96]

Even if FITs with LCR would pass the previous criteria of GATT Article XX, they could therefore be found to constitute an 'arbitrary or unjustifiable discrimination' and would then still not be justifiable under GATT Article XX.

3.2.2 Justification through Infant Industries Exception?

A second provision that might justify inconsistencies of FITs containing LCR with WTO law is the so-called 'infant industries' exception in GATT Article XVIII:C and XVIII:D. The availability of GATT Article XVIII:C is limited to those WTO Members 'the economy of which can only support low standards of living and is in the early stages of development'.[97] Article XVIII:D is only available to WTO Members 'the economy of which is in the process of development'.[98] In case a WTO Member fulfills the criteria of one of the two provisions, it may use certain 'governmental assistance' measures that are inconsistent with the GATT, in order to 'promote the establishment of a particular industry'.[99] As

---

95 In US-Shrimp the Appellate Body found that the requirement to use exactly the same methods as employed in the USA is insufficiently connected to the 'declared objective of protecting and conserving sea turtles'. Appellate Body Report, *US Shrimp* (n. 81) 165. In Brazil—Tyres the Appellate Body reached the result that the import ban of retreaded and used tyres was not sufficiently related to the objective of reducing the exposure to risk from waste accumulation. Appellate Body Report, *Brazil Tyres* (n. 83) para. 246.

96 See EU First Submission, *Canada Feed-in Tariff* (n. 45) para. 5.

97 GATT art. XVIII.4. See also Henning Jessen *WTO-Recht und 'Entwicklungsländer'* (Berliner Wissenschaftsverlag, 2006) 237.

98 GATT art. XVIII.4(b); GATT art. XVIII.22.

99 Ibid., art. XVIII.13.

in the case of GATT Article XX the provisions will apply to Article III:4 and 5 GATT, and likely to Article 2.1 and 2.2 TRIMs Agreement. Their applicability to the SCM Agreement would, however, need to be clarified. As yet, no precedent exists on the interpretation of GATT Articles XVIII:C and D.

Certain WTO Members whose economies are in the 'process of development' could potentially justify the implementation of their FITs with LCR under Article XVIII:C or Article XVIII:D. When notifying the implementation of the measure to other WTO Members, they must prove that their FITs with LCR serve to 'rais(e) the general standard of living of (their) people' and that no other measure that is consistent with the GATT provisions would be 'practicable to achieve that objective'.[100] They could argue that their people benefit from the implementation of a FIT with LCR with regard to their 'general standard of living', as there can be more jobs in domestic firms that produce renewable energy components than without such a scheme and as there might be spill-over effects from the development caused by the success of such firms to other sectors of the domestic economy. As mentioned above, FITs with LCR will nevertheless not always have such positive effects. In certain cases they might even hinder the development of the domestic renewable energy sector, if the required shares of local content are set too high and if the local renewable energy components are too expensive compared to imported ones.[101]

A developing country with a poorly developed renewable energy industry could further argue that LCR are necessary to shield its renewable energy firms from direct competition with large and far-advanced producers of renewable energy components, for instance from Europe or China. If an LCR clause was not attached to a national FIT scheme, the renewable energy industry of that developing country could lose the competitive race for not having received the time to develop. Obviously, this is rather the case for larger developing countries and economies in transition, as poor countries will likely not have the capacity to implement expensive FIT schemes with LCR.

Before resorting to GATT Article XVIII:C and GATT Article XVIII:D, a WTO Member must notify all WTO Members of its FIT scheme and must enter into consultations with other Members if requested.[102] The other Members can request consultations on the measure and can, under certain conditions,

100 The country will have to prove here that neither section A nor section B of art. XVIII GATT are 'practicable' to achieve the objective of their measure. GATT art. XVIII:3.

101 See J-C Kuntze and T Moerenhout, Local Content Requirements (n. 4).

102 A WTO Member must inform other Members of those special difficulties that it aims to meet with its measure and must supply the Member States with details on the measure. See GATT art. XVIII:14. See See also Jessen (n. 97) 237.

suspend concessions on their side as means of compensation if the measure is implemented. Only if all WTO Members agree that 'there is no measure consistent with the [GATT] which is practicable in order to achieve the objective' and give their consent to the proposed FIT with LCR, a Member could justify its scheme under GATT Articles XVIII:C and D.[103] The other WTO Members still reserve the right to equally suspend concessions against the implementing country if they are affected by the schemes.[104] FITs with LCR that are justified under Article XVIII:C and Article XVIII:D may only be used 'to deviate temporarily from the provisions [of the GATT]'[105] and will be reassessed annually by the WTO Member States.[106] These notification requirements significantly limit the practical availability of GATT Articles XVIII:C and D to justify FITs with LCR. It is unlikely that WTO Members would consent to a FIT with LCR that potentially disadvantages their local component manufacturers. Further, the fact that other WTO Members can suspend concessions in response to the scheme may prevent a developing country from implementing a FIT with LCR in the first place.

It follows that the infant industries exception as it exists in Article XVIII:C and D GATT could potentially justify the use of FITs with LCR, however, it is highly unlikely to do so.

3.3 *Preliminary Conclusion*

Overall, the analysis shows that FIT schemes with LCR will violate GATT Article III:4 and 5 and Article 2.1 and 2.2 TRIMs Agreement. None of the potential justifications that were assessed would be available to those wishing to argue in favour of FIT schemes with LCR. GATT Articles XVIII:C and D might apply but have very limited practical significance. It remains uncertain whether Article 3.1(b) SCM Agreement may also be breached by certain FIT schemes with LCR.

103 GATT art. XVIII:15, 17. After notification, Member states have a period of 30 days to request consultation with the state on its measure with regard to potential alternatives and the measure's potential effect on the other state's 'commercial and economic interests'.

104 Ibid., art. XVIII:21, 22.

105 Ibid., art. XVIII:4(a).

106 Ibid., art. XVIII:6.

4 Status of International Agreements Including FIT with LCR in WTO Law

The previous section concluded that FITs with LCR are inconsistent with WTO law. This begs the question of how WTO law interacts with other international law regimes that potentially permit the use of FIT with LCR. In what follows, we will give a brief and general introduction to the topic and its main issues, to be further developed in future scholarly work.

4.1 *Regional Trade Agreements Permitting the use of FIT with LCR*

4.1.1 A Constitutionalist or Contractualist Approach?

In general, there are two theoretical and opposing understandings of the nature of WTO law. From one side, 'constitutionalists' argue that obligations under WTO law are integral and multilateral. In effect, breaking such obligations is a violation of a constituting document and derogating from such a document is only possible when all contracting parties agree to an amendment.[107] From another side, 'contractualists' think of WTO obligations as a collection of reciprocal agreements between the WTO Members. Even though concessions are made to the entire WTO community via the MFN principle, the collective of obligations following from such concessions are bilateral in nature.[108] For them, it is theoretically easier to breach the contractual terms. They hold that since most non-constitutional trade obligations in general, and those in GATT specifically, are bilateral in nature, it is also permitted and possible for two WTO Members to derogate from WTO law by stipulating different obligations in other international treaties, which can then serve as *lex posterior* and *lex specialis* to the bilateral WTO rights and obligations of the FTA members.[109]

Then again, Langille argues convincingly that WTO rules and obligations are of such a complex nature that it is not opportune to position them in either a constitutionalist or contractual understanding. Rather, she gives priority to investigate the specific relationship between FTAs and WTO law on a case-by-case basis. In general, she finds that contracting out from WTO

107 In particular Ernst-Ulrich Petersmann has developed this approach. See, among others: Ernst-Ulrich Petersmann, 'Ten years of the WTO Dispute Settlements System: Past, present, and future' (2006) 3 J INT'LL & POL'Y 1:1.

108 Joost Pauwelyn, 'The Nature of WTO Obligations' (2002) Jean Monnet working paper <http://centers.law.nyu.edu/jeanmonnet/papers/> accessed 10 August 2013.

109 Joost Pauwelyn, *Conflict of Norms in Public International Law: How WTO Law Relates to Other Rules of International Law* (CUP 2006).

obligations could be possible, but not without respecting judicial review and non-discrimination.[110] It is in the latter—in particular under National Treatment—that FTAS permitting FITS with LCR might violate WTO law.

4.1.2 LCR in FTAS and Their Effects on Bounded and Third Parties

The legal relationship between FTAS permitting FITS with LCR and WTO law is mainly guided by general international law and the WTO itself. Regarding general international law, the VCLT contains a set of customary rules that guide the interaction of treaties. In US-Gasoline, the Appellate Body confirmed that such rules can be applicable to interpret the WTO covered agreements.[111] The VCLT is important in confirming that treaties must be followed (*pacta sunt servanda*) and that no rights or obligations are created for third states that did not consent to the treaty.[112] More important to the LCR question, however, is Article 30(4) VCLT. This article stipulates that certain parties to an earlier treaty can modify their rights and obligations in a later treaty, which then prevails between them, while the earlier treaty remains applicable between members and non-members of the later treaty. This article could suggest that derogating from WTO law on the basis of a later treaty outside the WTO realm is possible.[113]

However, VCLT Article 41 puts constraints on the possibility of derogating from multilateral treaties with a few member parties only. Two requirements need to be met. First, the possibility of modification needs to be foreseen by the multilateral treaty. This is the case for the WTO. GATT Article XXIV permits the derogation from WTO rules in regional trade agreements. Second, inter-party amendments to a multilateral treaty in a later agreement must not 'relate to a provision, derogation from which is incompatible with the effective execution of the object and purpose of the treaty as a whole'.[114] This is where regional FTAS between a few WTO Members that permit FITS with LCR may very well become illegal. In this case, it would not be a violation of the Most-Favoured-Nation (MFN) clause[115] that is found (as Article XXIV allows for exemptions), but rather a prohibition above the flexibilities of Article XXIV.

110 Joana Langille, 'Neither constitution nor contract: Understanding the WTO by examining the legal limits on contracting out through regional trade agreements' (2011) 86 NYU Review 1482.

111 Appellate Body Report, *US Gasoline* (n. 81) 23.

112 Art 26, 34 Vienna Convention Law of Treaties (adopted 23 May 1969, entered into force 27 January 1980) 1155 UNTS 331 (VCLT).

113 Ibid., art. 30 (4).

114 Ibid., art. 41.

115 MFN is a principle that stipulates that WTO Members cannot discriminate between their trading partners, which is relevant in regional trade agreements. National treatment

As non-discrimination through national treatment is a constituting object and purpose of the WTO, permitting LCR that discriminate against foreign component producers in inter-party modifications is not permitted. A permission of such schemes would be incompatible with the object and purpose of the WTO agreements of prohibiting protectionism, as shown in the analysis of GATT Art. III:4 and III:5, as well as TRIMS Art 2.1 and Art 2.2 described above.

This conclusion is reached not only by assessing the Vienna Convention on the Law of Treaties, but also by scrutinizing GATT Article XXIV. In Turkey-Textiles, the Appellate Body indeed found that under certain conditions Article XXIV may 'justify the adoption of a measure which is inconsistent with certain other GATT provisions, and may be invoked as a possible defence to a finding of inconsistency'.[116] GATT Article XXIV:5(b) allows for FTAs derogating from the WTO treaty if their 'duties and other regulations of commerce' on third countries are not 'higher or more restrictive than the corresponding duties and other regulations of commerce existing in the same constituent territories prior to the formation of the free-trade area'. As a condition, Marceau and Wyatt rightly point to the definitional requirements of RTAs, one of which is that RTAs should 'not raise trade barriers vis-à-vis WTO Members not party to the RTA'.[117] It can well be argued that LCR do not comply with this first condition.

A second condition can be found in the definition of FTAs in GATT Article XXIV. This definition states that FTAs are intended to eliminate 'duties and other restrictive regulations (…) on substantially all the trade between the constituent territories in products originating in such territories'.[118] FTAs permitting LCR would be inconsistent with this requirement, as they explicitly create restrictions on imported products (in this case renewable energy components). For example, the Appellate Body has made clear that non-discrimination is an important element when assessing a defense under GATT Article XXIV. In Turkey-Textiles and other cases, it established a necessity requirement (FTA measures need to be necessary for the conclusion of an FTA), that FTA membership does not justify discrimination in tariff treatment, and that safeguard measures and import restrictions have to be applied uniformly to FTA

(GATT art. III as described above) is about discriminating between imported and locally-produced goods.

116 Appellate Body Report, *Turkey—Restrictions on Imports of Textile and Clothing Products* WT/DS34/AB/R (19 November 1999) para. 45.

117 Gabrielle Marceau and Julian Wyatt, 'Dispute Settlement Regimes Intermingled: Regional Trade Agreements and the WTO' (2010) 1 JIDS 67.

118 GATT art. XXIV.

members and FTA non-members.[119] In sum, in a potential dispute settlement, WTO Panels and the Appellate Body would not go lightly over FTAs permitting some form of FITs with LCR.

4.2 *International Agreements Covering WTO Membership Allowing FIT with LCR*

4.2.1 Applicability of International Agreements in the WTO

As Doha has proven, WTO legal reform can be a long and uncertain process. In addition, the trade negotiation culture has, to date, relatively little experience with including environmental considerations to the paradigms the WTO has been built on.[120] Therefore, some have suggested the use LCR in climate change agreements outside of the WTO, either as a political tool to reach such an agreement or because they believe this may lead to more renewable energy deployment in the medium-term. Despite the fact that amending WTO rules outside of the WTO is a controversial topic, it is legally possible for international agreements outside the WTO to have legal effect within WTO adjudication. Dealing with FITs with LCR outside of the WTO does require in the first place that WTO Members are parties to the concerned agreement or protocol. In general there are two visions on the topic.

From one side, an outside-the-WTO approach to justifying inconsistencies of FITs with LCR with WTO rules would be based on the position that WTO law is one subsection of public international law instead of a self-contained regime. Pauwelyn points out that, despite what is often (implicitly) claimed, there is no hierarchy between different sources of international law with the WTO on top.[121] This means that WTO law is only one part of a wider unified yet decentralized system that follows general rules of international law such as *pacta sunt servanda*, *lex posterior* and *lex specialis*. Under these general principles, it is able to interact with other 'sub-systems' of international law, including legally permitted local content agreements in other international agreements.[122] Within this understanding, a multilateral agreement on

---

119 Langille (n. 110).

120 Luzius Wasescha, 'A Word of Introduction from the Trade Negotiator Perspective' in J. Pauwelyn (ed.), *Global Challenges at the Intersection of Trade, Energy and the Environment* (CEPR 2010) 11–12.

121 In US-Reformulated Gasoline, the Appellate Body solidly confirmed: 'the General Agreement is not to be read in clinical isolation from public international law'. Appellate Body Report, *US Gasoline* (n. 81) 17.

122 See Pauwelyn, 'Conflict of Norms' (n. 105) 25–88; see also Carlos Justino Lopez Hurtado, 'The WTO Legal System and International Human Rights' (2006) 140–188.

climate change action could theoretically include a legally binding section that requires its members to derogate from certain WTO obligations. FITs with LCR could be justified in such a way. As all WTO members would, however, need to be part to the multilateral agreement before such provisions on LCR could serve as *lex specialis* within WTO dispute settlement, these legal trade-related renewable energy provisions would technically look like an amendment to the WTO Agreements. In a dispute settlement, the defendant using FITs with LCR could then use this agreement as applicable law to justify the otherwise violation of the WTO agreements. Considering the complexity and multitude of WTO provisions that would likely be violated by FITs with attached LCR, it is clear that the hypothetical provisions allowing such measures with the multilateral climate agreement would have to be highly detailed so that conflict with WTO law could be resolved by using *lex posterior* and *les specialis.*

From another perspective, opponents of this applicable law doctrine hold that such trade related issues primarily fall under a WTO mandate and that WTO Courts cannot just simply apply other international law as *lex specialis* within WTO dispute settlement. For them, WTO law is already a set of *lex specialis.*[123] Under this understanding, an international agreement admitting LCR for renewable energy could be used in the interpretation of Article XX. In this case, a Panel would find a violation of GATT and then use the international climate agreement for interpretation, instead of using it as *lex specialis* that is applicable in WTO dispute settlement and potentially prevails over GATT. However, in light of the analysis above, it is questionable whether an LCR could ever pass the *chapeau* of Article XX. It must be noted that until today, there has been no clear case in WTO Dispute Settlement that has explicitly dealt with the question of applicable law that would prevail over GATT. In general, the Appellate Body has followed the road of using other international law for the interpretation of WTO Articles.

4.2.2 Political Questions in Dealing with LCR Outside the WTO

Clearly, few legal scholars would consider an attempt to justify FITs with LCR outside of the WTO more appropriate than taking action within the WTO. However, because of the pressing need to take action on climate and energy issues, as well as the long process that lead to the conclusion of the Doha negotiations, LCR proponents do occasionally suggest such an approach. They realize it could be unwise to open the Pandora's box of WTO legal reform to renegotiate LCR. Instead, some would propose the option of writing LCR as a

123 Gabrielle Marceau, 'WTO Dispute Settlement and Human Rights' (2002) 13 EJIL 753.

(small) part of a political package deal in a comprehensive protocol of a climate change agreement that is subsequently ratified by all WTO member states.

The authors do not argue for such an approach, but merely point to the theoretical possibility of dealing with the issue outside of the WTO while assuring its applicability within WTO dispute resolution. However, if there needs to be action taken on renewable energy-related trade issues, it is preferable to deal with such problems within the WTO. Cottier, for example, argues that instead of sectoral negotiations on different WTO provisions, an integrated approach is needed in the shape of a Framework Agreement on Energy. Like the Agreement on Agriculture, an Agreement on Energy would be *lex specialis* to other provisions and would clarify the application of current existing provisions to energy-related goods and services. Like the TRIPS agreement refers to the Berne and Paris Conventions, the energy agreement would also be able to refer to outside WTO law such as the UNFCCC and its protocols.[124] In theory, it would be possible to set up a detailed, technical standard for FITS with LCR that are permitted under strict conditions and override traditional WTO provisions on national treatment, subsidies or exceptions.

Whether or not FITS with LCR are treated outside of or within the WTO, the discussion ultimately comes down to their political importance. As noted, in the current legal framework, FITS with LCR are not consistent with WTO rules. However, in case these schemes serve as politically necessary tools in countries with budgetary constraints, a non-legal argument needs to be included in the debate: The sustainability of free trade and the WTO regime depends on delivering the promise of economic growth and greater prosperity. FITS with LCR for renewable energy generation, if useful and politically important, may serve as one way of keeping up political support, especially from developing and emerging economies, for free trade. Looking at trade liberalization as a goal in itself, instead of a means to employment and economic goals, may end up carving out the free trade regime even more. That said, however, one should nuance and consider the many elements related to LCR that warrant caution in their use and potential usefulness in actually attaining objectives such as employment and industrial growth.[125]

124 Thomas Cottier, Garba Malumfashi, Sofya Matteotti-Berkutova, Olga Nartova, Joëlle De Sépibus and Sadeq Z. Bigdeli, 'Energy in WTO Law and Policy' in Thomas Cottier (ed.) *The prospects of international trade regulation* (2009) 211–244.

125 A complete analysis can be found in: J.-C. Kuntze and T Moerenhout, Local Content Requirements (n. 4).

5 Conclusion

This chapter has assessed whether FITs with LCR are consistent with WTO law. The analysis suggests that FITs with LCR violate provisions from two WTO agreements. First, they go against the national treatment principle in GATT Article III:4 and 5, as they promise to grant renewable electricity producers premium payments if they source locally manufactured or assembled components. Second, FITs with LCR may violate Article 2.1 and 2.2 of the TRIMs Agreement as they will constitute trade-related investment measures that require 'the purchase or use of products of domestic origin or from any domestic source' as a condition to obtain an advantage. In addition, FITs with LCR may also constitute 'prohibited subsidies' under Article 3.1(b) SCM Agreement, as 'contingent (…) upon the use of domestic over imported goods'. It has been found that the violations of these WTO provisions may not be justified with other WTO provisions, neither with GATT Article XX nor with GATT Article XVIII:C and D.

Because FITs with LCR violate the constituting principle of non-discrimination through national treatment, it is unlikely that regional free trade agreements have the legal capacity to exempt them from WTO prohibition. While infringing upon the MFN principle is accepted in GATT Article XXIV, a lack of practical implementation of WTO oversight over the content and scope of free-trade agreements has led to many FTAs also infringing upon non-discrimination within the national treatment principle. However, legally, FTAs permitting LCR would be in contradiction to both WTO law and public international law. In case all WTO Members agreed on rules to legally use FITs with LCR for renewable energy projects, modifications inside or outside the WTO could, of course, be possible.

Whether or not the strict WTO discipline on FITs with LCR should be reconsidered depends on their potential benefits to achieve global public goods. It is important to note that this analysis falls outside the scope of this chapter. However, it must be concluded that the WTO leaves ample space for any potential action in this regard. Not only in the debate on FITs with LCR, but also in general, the linkages between trade, energy and sustainable development are becoming increasingly prevalent and important. Treating them in the current framework could turn out troublesome to maintain the support for free trade considerations, in particular for developing economies that want to invest in renewables. Therefore it is valuable to debate the usefulness of LCR and options such as, for instance, redesigning the 'infant industries' exception. Furthermore, a new energy agreement in the WTO *à la* the Agreement on Agriculture could provide a mechanism to accommodate FITs with LCR in the WTO, were it deemed necessary by its Members.

PART FOUR

Regulating Energy Transit and New Technologies

CHAPTER 9

Energy Transit in International Law—Concept and Challenges

Beatriz Huarte Melgar

1 Introduction

The controversial question of transit in international law, whose *raison d'être* and regulation are still being discussed by the doctrine, gains even more relevance concerning the issue of energy transit. Thus, this survey examines the notion of energy transit in international law to understand its implications in the current international scenario. After the rescission of the provisional application of the Energy Charter Treaty (ECT) pursuant to Article 45 by Russia on 18 October 2010,[1] and the intention of the EU to reset the negotiations on the Energy Charter Treaty Protocol on Transit (ECTP), it is crucial to find a legal alternative to achieve energy security and energy independence.[2]

The author divides the chapter into seven sections. After this brief introduction, Section Two explores the notion of transit in international law to conclude with energy transit. Section Three describes freedom of transit under the WTO/GATT, as well as under the ECT, to understand its implications. Next, Section Four introduces the current Doha Round negotiations on trade facilitation and its relationship with energy transit to finish, before the conclusions, with Section Five analyzing the ECTP. The survey concludes with Section Six exploring the challenges of energy transit, based on the current situation of energy transit *vis-à-vis* the ECTP's negotiations.

1 Concerning the gas crisis of 2009, the Russian President, Dmitry Medvedev, condemned the ECT stating that it was inefficient in order to prevent and resolve the crisis.

2 Anna Aseeva, 'EU-Russia Energy Relations: the Role of International Law from Energy Investment and Transit Perspective' (Institut Europeen de l'Université de Genève, Collection Euryopa, vol 65–2011, 7) <http://www.unige.ch/gsi/Bienvenue/publications/euryopa/aseeva.pdf> accessed 10 August 2013.

 | DOI 10.1163/9789004270190_010

2 Concept of (Energy) Transit in International Law

There are several theories about transit in international law. Based on the principle of sovereignty, it is assumed that States may prevent the construction or use of objects designated to the transit of goods.[3] However, because of the necessity of trade and communication, which creates interdependence among States, there have been numerous attempts to qualify the notion of transit as a right or freedom. The challenge is finding the balance between the convenience of transit and the legitimate right of States to protect their national interests by avoiding any kind of transit that can be prejudicial for the transit State.

Independently of the discussion about the existence of a right of transit in customary international law, interpretations of multilateral conventions in different realms of law defend the idea about the necessity of transit regulation. Thus, the first important multilateral agreement in this regard was the 1921 Barcelona Convention and Statute on Freedom of Transit (Barcelona Statute), which describes transit in Article 3 as follows '[t]raffic in transit shall not be subject to any special dues in respect of transit (including entry and exit). Nevertheless, on such traffic in transit there may be levied dues intended solely to defray expenses of supervision and administration entailed by such transit.'[4] This provision exempts transit from custom duties as well as from import and export duties. Furthermore, Article 2 of the Barcelona Statute establishes the freedom of transit: 'the measures taken by Contracting States [...] shall facilitate free transit by rail or waterway on routes in use convenient for international transit.' As observed, Article 2 sets up the duty to facilitate transit only 'by rail or waterway on routes in use convenient for international transit', which excludes transit by roads or pipelines and the creation of new routes that can be convenient for international transit.[5]

There are other multilateral conventions concerning transit. With regard to air law, there is the 1944 Chicago Convention, which establishes the right of transit for non-scheduled flights (Article 5) under certain conditions. The right of transit for non-scheduled flights is 'subject to the right of the State flown

3 See E. Lauterpacht, 'Freedom of Transit in International Law', in The Grotius Society Transactions for the years 1958 & 1959, Problems of Public and Private International Law (London: Longmans, Green, 1945–1959), vol 44, 313–356.

4 Convention and Statute on Freedom ofTransit (Barcelona, 20 April 1921) Un Doc I-16908, art. 3.

5 John Merryman and Edgar Ackerman, *Transit Trade of Landlocked States* (Alfred Metzner Verlag 1969).

over to require landing'[6] The GATT 1947[7] established in Article V the freedom of transit of goods, vessels and other means of transportation, which, due to its relevance in energy transit, will be examined in the next section.

In relation to transit trade of landlocked States, the 1965 New York Convention establishes the freedom of transit in Article 2 based on the principle of non-discrimination and 'on routes in use mutually acceptable for transit to the Contracting States concerned.' Following the same line than the other multilateral conventions, there is no obligation under this convention to create new routes for transit. This lack of obligation is a crucial element that characterizes the current controversial regulation of transit in international law.

Concerning the Law of the Sea, the 1982 United Nations Convention on the Law of the Sea (UNCLOS)[8] codifies the right of transit passage in straits used for international navigation (Article 38). Pursuant to the Convention, the right of transit passage implies the freedom of navigation and over flight for the purpose of continuous and expeditious transit of the strait. The right of innocent passage (Arts. 8, 17, 52), as the 'right of the ships of all States to pass—in the various forms and manners indicated—innocently through the territorial sea',[9] and the right of freedom of transit for landlocked States (Article 125) are also significant parts of the notion of transit in international law. It is also important to emphasize, concerning energy transit, that this Convention regulates only the construction and management of cross-border pipelines regarding submarine pipelines.[10]

Taking into consideration the evolution of the concept of transit in international law, for the purpose of this chapter, the following sections will analyze the particular subject of energy transit in detail.

6 Moreover the International Air Services Transit Agreement and the International Air Transport Agreement in art. I, Section 1 denominate the freedoms of the air as 'privileges' in relation to scheduled international air services. Art 15 of the Convention on International Civil Aviation (Chicago 7 December 1944) ICAO Doc 7300 states that 'no fees, dues or other charges shall be imposed' for the purpose of transit.

7 With the advent of the WTO at the end of the Uruguay Round the GATT 1947 became, *mutatis mutandis*, the GATT 1994. In this case it is important to note that the GATT 1994 keeps the same text of Art. V GATT 1947.

8 The 1982 United Nations Convention on the Law of the Sea (Montego Bay, 10 December 1982) UN Doc I-31363 is based on the Convention on the High Seas (Geneva, 29 April 1958) UN Doc I-6465, which established free transit on a basis of reciprocity (Art. 3).

9 Francis Ngantcha, *The Right of Innocent Passage and the Evolution of the International Law of the Sea* (Printer Publishers, 1990) 56.

10 See Arts 58(1), 79 and 112 of the UN Convention on the Law of the Sea (n. 7).

3 The Freedom of (Energy) Transit Provisions and Their Inter-relationship

3.1 *The Article V of GATT 1994*

The freedom of transit on a non-discriminatory basis is enshrined in Article V of the GATT 1994, based on the 1921 Barcelona Transit Convention. GATT Article V:2 states: 'There *shall* be freedom of transit through the territory of each contracting party, via the routes most convenient for international transit'.

Under WTO/GATT, Contracting Parties may only apply either transportation charges or charges for administrative expenses and services (Article V:3), which have to be reasonable (Article V:4) and non-discriminatory (Article V:5).[11] Due to the fact that the *Colombia—Ports of Entry case* is the only WTO case related to the freedom of transit till now which has been solved by a Panel and owing to the lack of definition of 'freedom of transit' in the WTO/GATT, it is interesting to note that this Panel accepted the definition of freedom of transit proposed by Colombia, namely, the 'unrestricted access via the most convenient routes for the passage of goods in international transit'.[12]

The scope of application of the freedom of transit in WTO/GATT applies in Article V:1 to the transit of goods. However, can one consider energy a good?[13] Some authors argue that energy is not a good because drafters did not intend to include energy within the purpose of the WTO/GATT referencing the strategic importance of energy in the economic world[14]—regarding security and economic growth—, which makes it necessary to regulate energy separately. The significance of energy transit can be observed in the period after the oil crisis of 1973, when energy was *de facto* treated as an issue outside of the WTO/GATT rules.[15] In spite of this kind of treatment for energy, there is another view, which defends the consideration of energy as a good pursuant to the GATT 1994. It is based on the fact that there is WTO jurisprudence relating

11 GATT ArtV(5): '... treatment no less favorable than the treatment accorded to traffic in transit to or from any third country.'

12 WTO Panel Report, *Colombia—Indicative Prices and Restrictions on Ports of Entry* (*Colombia—Panamá*) WT/DS366/R (27 April 2009) para. 7.401, 176.

13 Martha M. Roggenkamp, 'Transit of Network-bound Energy: The European Experience' in T. Wälde (Ed), *The Energy Charter Treaty: An East-West Gateway for Investment and Trade* (Kluwer, London 1996) 507.

14 Danae Azaria: 'Energy Transit under the Energy Charter Treaty and the General Agreement on Tariffs and Trade' (2009) 27(4) J Energy & Nat Resources L 559, 565.

15 Roggenkamp (n. 13) 507.

to petroleum,[16] and that energy goods are not specifically excluded from the scope of application of either the GATT 1947 or the GATT 1994.[17]

In addition, the *Services Sectorial Classification List*[18] includes petroleum, solid fuels, natural liquefied gas and the primary as well as secondary production of electricity (as raw material) within the scope of application of the GATT 1994.[19] This results in the question whether energy can be considered a service. Since the GATS[20] does not define the concept of *service* it is interesting to mention the Hill's definition of 'service':

'A change in the condition of a person, or of a good belonging to some economic unit, which is brought about as the result of the activity of some other economic unit, with the prior agreement of the former person or economic unit. This definition [...] is consistent with the underlying idea which is inherent in the concept of a service, namely that one economic unit performs some activity for the benefit of another.'[21]

This definition is based on the notion of 'ownership', which is a crucial condition to differentiate 'production of a good' and 'production of a service'; thereby, the production of goods by an entity which is the owner of the raw material is not considered a service and therefore it does not fall within the scope of application of the GATS.[22] Nevertheless, the GATS covers a variety

16 See for example Appellate Body Report *United States—Standards for Reformulated and Conventional Gasoline* WT/DS2/AB/R, adopted on 20 May 1996.

17 Azaria (n. 14) 565.

18 The Sectorial Classification List (1991) W/120 is a point of reference of WTO Members for the classification of energy services.

19 WTO, *Energy Services* (Background Note by the Secretariat, S/C/W/311, 12 January 2010) 3.

20 The General Agreement on Trade in Services (GATS) applies to 'trade in services', which is defined by GATS ArtI as 'the supply of a service' through four modes of supply: '(a) from the territory of one Member into the territory of any other Member; (b) in the territory of one Member to the service consumer of any other Member; (c) by a service supplier of one Member, through commercial presence in the territory of any other Member; (d) by a service supplier of one Member, through presence of natural persons of a Member in the territory of any other Member.' (GATS ArtI:2). The notion of 'supply of a service' is defined by GATS Art. XXVIII(b) as 'the production, distribution, marketing, sale and delivery of a service'.

21 T.P. HIll, 'On Goods and Services', Review of Income and Wealth 23, 315–338, December 1977, in Mireille Cossy, 'Energy Services under the General Agreement on Trade in Services', *Regulation of Energy in International Trade Law—WTO, NAFTA and Energy Charter*, ed. Yulia Selivanova, Wolters Kluwer Law & Business, vol. 34 (The Netherlands, 2011) 150.

22 Mireille Cossy, 'Energy Services under the General Agreement on Trade in Services', in Y. Selivanova (Ed.) *Regulation of Energy in International Trade Law—WTO, NAFTA and Energy Charter* (Kluwer 2011) 151.

of services related to production. According to the *United Nations Central Product Classification* (CPC) the production on a fee or contract basis is a service.[23] Moreover, the WTO Members are guided by the abovementioned *Service Sectorial Classification List* (W/120), which includes three sectors directly related to the energy sector, namely, services related to the mining industry (CPC 883 and CPC 5115); services related to the energy distribution (CPC 887); and transportation of fuels (CPC 7131). In addition to that, it is remarkable that the ECT created a Draft, which has been not adopted by any ECT Contracting Party yet, focused on energy services and based on the classification of the CPC and the W/120. The relevance of this Draft is the impetus of the ECT to classify the energy services on the grounds of the WTO rules.[24] Concerning that, it is interesting to note that the GATS is opened to the inclusion of new services, because it applies to all services, with the exception of those provided 'in the exercise of governmental authority',[25] as well as WTO Members have a certain degree of flexibility to schedule GATS commitments on energy services.[26] This supports the idea that energy can also be considered a service.

Coming back to the consideration of energy materials and products as goods, the Doha Round negotiations on trade facilitation make reference to goods transported via pipelines and grids, which means that proposals cover oil, gas and electricity. In fact, in 2006 a group of countries together with the European Communities—Armenia, Canada, Kyrgyzstan, Mongolia, New Zealand, Paraguay and Moldova—launched a proposal to clarify 'traffic in transit' in order to explicitly include the definition of goods moved via fixed infrastructure.[27] Moreover, in 2009 another group of countries—Switzerland, Macedonia, Mongolia and Swaziland—launched another proposal in order to include goods moved via fixed infrastructure within the definition of 'traffic in transit'.[28] The requirement of including 'goods moved via fixed infrastructure' of both proposals has been accepted so far and consequently it is included in the Draft of Trade Facilitation Agreement (TFA) Article 11, which supports the

---

23 See the United Nations Statistics Division <http://unstats.un.org/unsd/cr/registry/regcst.asp?Cl=3> accessed 27 August 2013.

24 Beatriz Huarte Melgar, 'Influencia del Caso 'Colombia—Puertos de Entrada' en la Liberalización del Tránsito Energético' (2012) 2(2) Revista de Derecho Económico Internacional 63, 75.

25 Cossy (n. 22) 155.

26 Ibid., 176.

27 Negotiating Group of the WTO in Trade Facilitation, TN/TF/W/79 (15 February 2006).

28 Negotiating Group of the WTO in Trade Facilitation, TN/TF/W/133/Rev3 (26 June 2009).

idea that energy is a good covered by GATT Article V.[29] The exception for the consideration of energy as a good is hydroelectric power, which is considered a service.[30] In this way, the last version of the Draft of the TFA in Article 11 (freedom of transit) covers the transit of oil and gas via fixed infrastructure,[31] which means that gas and oil are part of the definition of 'traffic in transit' established by GATT Article V:1.

Furthermore, in the SIOT case[32] the ECJ ruled that although GATT Article V does not have direct effect in relation to third countries nor applies to transit within the European Union, the importance of Article V with regard to transport of network bound energy, *i.e.*, oil, natural gas and electricity, was not further put in question.[33]

Accordingly, on the basis of previously mentioned arguments and taking into account the evolution of the negotiations on trade facilitation within the WTO, it can be interpreted that energy falls within the scope of application of WTO/GATT being considered a good: consequently, it is covered by the freedom of transit provision of GATT Article V.[34]

3.2 *Relationship between Both Legal Provisions*

The scope of application of ECT Article 7 and GATT Article V is the same, that is, both legal provisions regulate transit of goods. However, whereas the GATT Article V refers to goods in general, the ECT regulates 'transit of goods' in relation to the issue of energy, which is considered a good.[35] The relationship

---

29 Art. 11 of the Draft of the TFA: '*Article 11: Freedom of Transit. 1. Goods subject to the provisions on Freedom of Transit of GATT 1994 and of this Agreement include those moved (via fixed infrastructure) (inter alia pipelines and electricity grids).*', TN/TF/W/165/Rev11 (7 October 2011).

30 Owen Saunders, 'Energy, Natural Resources and the Canada. United States Free Trade Agreement' (1990) 8(1)J Energy & Nat Resources L, 7.

31 Ar. 11(1) of the Draft of the TFA (n. 29): '*Freedom of Transit. 1. Goods subject to the provisions on Freedom of Transit of GATT 1994 and of this Agreement include those moved (via fixed infrastructure) (inter alia pipelines and electricity grids)*'.

32 Case 266/81 SIOT v Ministero delle Finanze (1983) ECR 731.

33 Roggenkamp (n. 13) 507.

34 Assuming that energy materials and products are considered 'goods' within the scope of application of the WTO/GATT, it is fundamental that Russia—as one of the most important energy exporters of the world—joins the WTO for a trade liberalization of energy. See Anders Åslund, 'Why Doesn't Russia Join the WTO?' (2010) 33(2) The Washington Quarterly 49.

35 See the last section and the explanation about energy as a good and energy as a service in Melgar (n. 24) 76.

between the ECT and the GATT is governed by ECT Article 4, which provides that '[n]othing in this Treaty shall derogate, as between particular Contracting Parties which are parties to the GATT, from the provisions of the GATT and Related Instruments as they are applied between those Contracting Parties.' At the same time, ECT Article 7(1) links energy transit to the principle of freedom of transit.

Furthermore, since not all Parties to the ECT have ratified the GATT 1994, ECT Article 29 establishes interim measures for those States that are not Members of the WTO/GATT. Thus, they are treated, concerning energy material and products, as if they would be Parties thereof. It is clear that WTO/GATT rules apply to international trade in general and that ECT rules refer to international trade in energy.[36] This would mean that ECT is a *lex specialis* to GATT 1994. According to this argument, it is likely that a WTO Panel or Appellate Body will take the ECT into consideration in cases dealing with energy transit under the GATT Article V.[37] However this interpretation does not appear to be appropriate because not all ECT Contracting Parties are WTO Members and *vice versa*, which means that the ECT Article 7 could only be applied as *lex specialis* to the GATT 1994 in cases that solely involved States that are Contracting Parties to both international conventions.[38]

Another question about the relationship between both legal provisions concerns ECT Article 7 and its commonly referred name 'GATT-Plus' provision.[39] Thus, ECT Article 7 provides new features on the freedom of transit of GATT Article V. In this sense, ECT Article 7(2) and ECTP Article 9 grant the possibility of building new transit facilities. Thereby, whereas on the one hand the freedom of transit established by GATT Article V focuses on the concept of 'capacity' concerning the capacity of the transit facilities, on the other hand the freedom of transit of ECT Article 7 focuses on the notion of 'building' new transit facilities.[40] Likewise, ECT Article 7(5) grants the flows of energy materi-

---

36 Roggenkamp (n. 13) 507.

37 Azaria (n. 14) 594.

38 See Art. 31(3)(c) of the Vienna Convention on the Law of Treaties (adopted 23 May 1969, entered into force 27 January 1980) 1155 UNTS 331: (3) There shall be taken into account, together with the context: (c) any relevant rules of international law applicable in the relations between the parties. This legal provision indicates that in case of a dispute about energy transit where all involved States are Contracting Parties of the ECT as well as of the GATT 1994, the ECT Art. 7 will apply in the first place.

39 Craig S. Bamberger, 'An overview of the Energy Transit Treaty' in T. Wälde (Ed), *The Energy Charter Treaty: An East-West Gateway for Investment and Trade* (Kluwer, 1996) 6.

40 Melgar (n. 24) fn 13.

als and products. ECT Article 7(7) provides a conciliation procedure in case of dispute. Also, ECT Article 7(3) states: 'shall treat Energy Materials and Products in Transit in no less favourable a manner than its provisions treat such materials and products originating in or destined for its own Area', which grants a particular level concerning the principle of non-discrimination.

In spite of this, Danae Azaria thinks that the consideration of ECT Article 7 as a GATT-Plus provision has some limits because, firstly, ECT Article 7 does not make explicit reference to GATT Article V and, secondly, both legal provisions have different objects, purposes and scopes of application.[41] However, pursuant to ECT Article 4, GATT 1994 regulates trade between Contracting Parties of the ECT, as well as of the GATT 1994, because the ECT does not derogate from the WTO/GATT rules. Likewise, among ECT Parties that are not WTO Members their relations will be influenced by the WTO/GATT by virtue of ECT Article 29(2)(a). Even the Amendment to the Trade-Related Provisions of the Energy Charter Treaty, which is not in force yet, requires that Panels interpret the ECT based on the WTO/GATT rules.[42]

Consequently, even though the ECT Article 7 does not refer explicitly to the GATT Article V and the ECT as well as the GATT 1994 are different international conventions with different purposes, the ECT binds itself explicitly with the WTO rules. Owing to the fact that the object of both legal provisions is the same, namely the transit of goods—in case of ECT Article 7 only energy-related-goods—, one could conclude that ECT Article 7 is a GATT-Plus provision.[43]

3.3 *The Article 7 of ECT*

Like GATT Article V, ECT Article 7 defines energy transit as through-transit based on the principle of non-discrimination.[44] ECT Article 7(6) states that in case of a dispute a transit State shall not interrupt or reduce the existing flow of energy, which indicates the importance of protecting energy transit.[45]

41 Azaria (n. 14) 560.

42 See Art. 3(3)(a) of the Amendment to the Trade-Related Provisions of the Energy Charter Treaty, in Energy Charter Secretariat (Ed.), *The Energy Charter Treaty and Related Documents, A Legal Framework for International Energy Cooperation* (Brussels 2004) 177.

43 Melgar (n. 24) 67–68.

44 See Art. 7(1) ECT and Art. 7(3) ECT.

45 With regard to that, it is interesting to note that in the crisis of gas in 2009 between Russia and the Ukraine, Russia suspended the gas flow, which resulted in a lack of gas supply to Europe.

From the definition of ECT Article 7(10)(a)[46] it can be observed that it is not necessary that all States involved in the energy supply are ECT Contracting Parties. Thus, it is enough that either the transit State, the State of origin or the State of destination are ECT Contracting Parties. Likewise, the scope of application of the legal provision cover transit where the State of origin is the same as the State of destination, but transit takes place throughout a second territory.

According to some authors, unlike GATT Article V, ECT Article 7 emphasizes the principle of sovereignty.[47] It states that 'Contracting Parties shall take the necessary measures to facilitate transit [...] consistent with the principle of freedom of transit.' This expression is weaker than the WTO/GATT freedom of transit description.[48] Also, the right to construct transit facilities is limited by the national legislation of the transit State and such constructions may be suspended for reasons of security.[49] Therefore, although apparently it can be understood that the ECT includes a new characteristic of transit in comparison with GATT Article V, namely, the right to construct transit facilities,[50] this improvement is limited due to a nationalistic approach. However, the legal provision that actually establishes the principle of sovereignty within the ECT is Article 18, of which energy resources are the exclusive focus. The implications of this Article are that ECT Contracting Parties are free to develop energy resources implementing the objectives of their own national policies. At the same time, Contracting Parties are free to decide to what extent they want to open the energy sector to international investors, which facilitates access

46 ECT Art. 10(a): (i) the carriage through the Area of a Contracting Party, or to or from port facilities in its Area for loading or unloading, of Energy Materials and Products originating in the Area of another state and destined for the Area of a third state, so long as either the other state or the third state is a Contracting Party; or (ii) the carriage through the Area of a Contracting Party of Energy Materials and Products originating in the Area of another Contracting Party and destined for the Area of that other Contracting Party, unless the two Contracting Parties concerned decide otherwise and record their decision by a joint entry in Annex N. The two Contracting Parties may delete their listing in Annex N by delivering a joint written notification of their intentions to the Secretariat, which shall transmit that notification to all other Contracting Parties. The deletion shall take effect four weeks after such former notification.

47 See art. 18 ECT about sovereignty over energy resources.

48 Art V:2 GATT 1994 states that 'there shall be freedom of transit'.

49 See art. 7(5) ECT.

50 Roggenkamp (n. 13) 511.

to energy resources in a non-discriminatory manner.[51] Moreover, taking into consideration that in the relationship of transit the weakest party is the State over whose territory the transit takes place, but which is not the owner of the energy resources, the sovereignty argument should not be applied to the interpretation of ECT Article 7(1) as a limitation to the freedom of transit.[52] This is because, pursuant to ECT Article 18(4), the sovereignty principle does not pretend to difficult the access to energy resources; on the contrary, it assumes 'to facilitate access to energy resources' in a non-discriminatory manner by stating in paragraph 3 that:

> Each state continues to hold in particular the rights to decide the geographical areas within its Area to be made available for exploration and development of its energy resources, the optimalization of their recovery and the rate at which they may be depleted or otherwise exploited, to specify and enjoy any taxes, royalties or other financial payments payable by virtue of such exploration and exploitation, and to regulate the environmental and safety aspects of such exploration, development and reclamation within its Area, and to participate in such exploration and exploitation, inter alia, through direct participation by the government or through state enterprises.

ECT Article 7 requires Parties to take 'necessary measures to facilitate transit', which implies a positive action when necessary.[53] The meaning of 'measures' was clarified by the International Court of Justice (ICJ) in the *Fisheries Jurisdiction* case, which stated that due to the wide meaning of the word, it covers 'any act, step or proceeding, and imposes no particular limit on their material content'.[54] Among these measures might, therefore, be included the construction of new routes for energy transit, which are allowed under certain conditions, established by ECT Article 7, paragraphs 4 and 5. In addition, since there is no provision in the treaty explicitly addressing access to

51 Yulia Selivanova, 'The Energy Charter and the International Energy Governance' in Y. Selivanova (Ed.) *Regulation of Energy in International Trade Law—WTO, NAFTA and Energy Charter* (Kluwer 2011) 375–376.

52 Melgar (n. 24) 69–70.

53 Azaria (n. 14) 580.

54 *Case concerning Fisheries Jurisdiction* (Spain v Canada) (1998) ICJ Rep 714, para. 66. See also Danae Azaria, 'Energy Transit under the Energy Charter Treaty and the General Agreement on Tariffs and Trade', 27(4) J Energy & Nat Resources L 2009, 559–596, 2009, footnote 69.

energy transport facilities, ECT Article 7(1) could be interpreted as providing access to energy transport facilities as a component of the trade facilitation.[55] Nevertheless the principle of 'freedom of transit' in ECT Article 7(1) mirrors the connection between the WTO/GATT and the ECT. Thus, according to the rules of interpretation of the VCLT, especially Article 31(3)(c),[56] the interpretation of the ECT Article 7 includes GATT Article V, as well as other international standards.[57]

The WTO/GATT legal provision on transit is analogous to the fundamental principles of the ECT, and the transit provision in the ECT better specifies the transit obligations than the WTO/GATT. Thus, this more specific description as well as the conciliation procedure established by ECT Article 7(7), can help to solve energy transit conflicts more efficiently. Hence, ECT Article 7 establishes a particular transit regime with the obligation to permit and facilitate transit,[58] unlike GATT Article V, which creates the freedom of transit 'via the routes most convenient for international transit.' Thereby and on the ground of the previous arguments, Article 7 ECT is indeed a 'GATT-Plus' provision.[59]

4 Doha Round Negotiations on Trade Facilitation in WTO—the Trade Facilitation Agreement (TFA)

The Doha Round negotiations on trade facilitation began in 2004 to improve GATT Articles V, VIII and X.[60] The freedom of transit provision of GATT Article V presents several difficulties, especially concerning energy transit because it does not explicitly refer to it. Thus, as it has been already shown, the draft of the WTO Trade Facilitation Agreement (TFA) has additional language

55 Karl Peter Waern, 'Transit Provisions of the Energy Charter Treaty and the Energy Charter Protocol on Transit' (2002) 20(2) J Energy & Nat Resources L 172, 180.

56 VCLT (n. 38) art. 31(3)(c): 'There shall be taken into account, together with the context: (c) any relevant rules of international law applicable in the relations between the parties.'

57 Azaria (n. 14) 591.

58 Ibid., 580.

59 See the explanation of this paper in Chapter III.b and Danae Azaria 'Energy Transit under the Energy Charter Treaty and the General Agreement and the General Agreement on Tariffs and Trade', WTO Research and Analysis <http://www.wto.org/english/res_e/publications_e/wtr10_8june10_e.htm> accessed 27 August 2013.

60 WTO Trade Facilitation: 'Members are directed to clarify and improve GATT art. V (Freedom of Transit), art. VIII (Fees and Formalities connected with Importation and Exportation), and art. X (Publication and Administration of Trade Regulations)' <http://www.wto.org/english/tratop_e/tradfa_e/tradfa_e.htm> accessed 27 August 2013.

including 'pipelines and grids' when defining traffic in transit.[61] The question involved the issue of fixed infrastructure, which is the route as such and therefore it cannot be itself in transit. The phrase 'other means of transport' in GATT Article V:2 opens the door for the interpretation to include pipelines and grids; nonetheless, certain Delegations affirm that 'means of transport' covers only mobile means of transport.[62]

Whatever the case may be and, taking into account the object of GATT Article V, goods that are in transit within the fixed infrastructure should fall within the scope of the article. Thereby, and as explained in the Chapter Three, Article 11 of the draft of the TFA—the freedom of transit—provides in para. 1: '[g]oods subject to the provisions on Freedom of Transit of GATT 1994 and of this Agreement include those via fixed infrastructure, inter alia pipelines and electricity grids.'[63] As observed, the trade facilitation negotiations include goods that are moved *via fixed infrastructure* and it provides for a non-exhaustive list by stating: *inter alia pipelines and electricity grids*, which introduces flexibility in the subject of energy transit under the WTO/GATT.

The TFA is not finalized yet; however, if it still contains the reference to 'fixed infrastructure' when it comes into force, it will improve the freedom on energy transit under the WTO/GATT and, consequently, under the ECT and the ECTP.

5 The Energy Charter Treaty Protocol on Transit (ECTP)

After the dissolution of the Soviet Union internal transport routes were transformed into international transit systems, which sometimes provoked interruptions of energy transit flows.[64] In these circumstances the Energy Charter Conference suggested entering into negotiations of an energy transit protocol in December 1999. These negotiations started at the beginning of 2000. The end of 2002 brought an agreement regarding the Protocol's text. However, due to the EU-Russian differences, it has been impossible to finish the Protocol.[65]

---

61 Azaria (n. 14) 562.

62 WTO Negotiating Group on Trade Facilitation, TN/TF/W/133/Rev2 (10 October 2008).

63 WTO, Negotiating Group on Trade Facilitation, TN/TF/W/165/Rev11 (7 October 2011).

64 Energy Charter Secretariat, 'The Energy Charter Treaty a Reader's Guide', 31 <http://www.encharter.org/fileadmin/user_upload/Publications/ECT_Guide_ENG.pdf> accessed 27 August 2013.

65 There is only a draft of the Energy Charter Protocol on Transit. For economy of language, this art will only refer to 'the Protocol' or to the 'ECTP', but it always means the draft of the Protocol.

Taking into account that the 40% of the Russian gas imports go to Europe[66] and that the Russian company *Gazprom* has a natural monopoly over energy in Russian territory,[67] the importance of reaching an agreement on the ECTP is clear.[68]

5.1 *Object, Scope of Application and Its Relationship with the* ECT

The idea behind the Transit Protocol's negotiations is the creation of a legally binding document for fostering the transit-related obligations established by the ECT.[69] The transit-related provisions of the ECT and the Protocol as a whole form the Energy Charter's transit regime.[70]

The Preamble emphasizes the principle of freedom of transit as established by ECT Article 7. Thus, it is reasonable to infer that ECT Article 7 does not only provide for the notion of energy transit, but for the notion of freedom of transit for energy.

The ECTP recognizes 'the basic principles in international law establishing the freedoms of the high seas including the freedom to lay submarine cables and pipelines.'[71] This emphasis on the idea of 'freedom' supports also the notion of the establishment of the freedom of energy transit under the ECT.

---

66 Data from EuroStat 2009 in Johannes Fuchs, 'Kooperative Erdgassicherhei-Energietransit im Völkerrecht unter besonderer Berücksichtigung des Nabucco-Abkommens' (2011) fn 17 <http://beck-online.beck.de/> accessed 10 August 2013.

67 Independently of the ECT there are some gas pipeline projects so that Europe can be more independent of Energy transit States, such as Belarus or the Ukraine concerning gas supply: the Nord Stream (from Russia to Germany), the South Stream (from Russia to Italy and Austria). Some experts argue that the problem is that Europe will become more dependent on Russia. And the Nabucco Pipeline (from Turkey to Austria), which is considered as a rival to the South Stream Pipeline and whose main suppliers are expected to be Azerbaijan and Iraq, instead of Russia.

68 'On 20 August 2009 the Russian Federation has officially informed the Depository that it did not intend to become a Contracting Party to the Energy Charter Treaty and the Protocol on Energy Efficiency and Related Environmental Aspects. In accordance with Article 45(3(a)) of the Energy Charter Treaty, such notification results in Russia's termination of its provisional application of the ECT and the PEEREA upon expiration of 60 calendar days from the date on which the notification is received by the Depository' (Energy Charter) <http://www.encharter.org/index.php?id=414#c1338> accessed 27 August 2013.

69 Energy Charter Secretariat (n. 64) 32.

70 Ibid., 33.

71 See the Preamble of the Draft Protocol.

The scope of application (Article 4) applies to energy materials and products in transit as well as to energy transport facilities, which is limited to crude oil, oil products and natural gas or electricity.[72]

In order to appreciate the relevance of the Protocol, it is important to clarify its relationship with the ECT. The relationship established in Article 3 of the Draft of the ECTP states:

1. Nothing in this Protocol shall derogate from the provisions of the Treaty.
2. The provisions of this Protocol shall complement, supplement, extend or amplify the provisions of the Treaty.
3. The provisions of the Treaty pertaining to its Article 7 shall apply in accordance with this Protocol.

Thus, some aspects that involve the relationship ECT/ECTP can be mentioned. The Understandings No.2 of the Draft of the Final Act of the Energy Charter Conference with respect to the Energy Charter Protocol on Transit of 2003 indicates that 'this Protocol shall be in accordance with Article 6 of the Treaty'.[73] Thus, States applying the ECTP must respect the rules of free competition established by the ECT. Likewise Article 1(1) of the Draft of the Protocol defines 'Contracting Party' as 'a state or Regional Economic Integration Organization which has consented to be bound by this Protocol and for which this Protocol is in force.' This legal provision indicates that not all ECT Contracting Parties are automatically ECTP Contracting Parties; on the contrary, in order to become an ECTP Contracting Party it is necessary to consent to be bound by the Protocol. Nevertheless, in order to become an ECTP Contracting Party it is necessary to become an ECT Contracting Party first.[74]

Accordingly, as the ECTP regulates energy transit in depth, the fact that there are ECT Contracting Parties that are ECTP Contracting Parties and ECT Contracting Parties that are not ECTP Contracting Parties creates energy transit regulation at 'two speeds'.[75] In other words, a situation of this type would exist where a group of countries—signatories of the ECT as well as of the ECTP—would have a stronger integration of the regulation on energy transit, whereas other group of States—only ECT signatories—would have a lack of

72 Waern (n. 55) 179.

73 ECT Art 6 regulates the competition rules.

74 Melgar (n. 24) 77. Also, art. 31(2) of the Draft of the ECTP states that 'any Contracting Party that withdraws from the Treaty shall be considered to have withdrawn from this Protocol.'

75 Expression taken of Romano Prodi 'Two-Speed Europe', see Melgar (n. 24) 77.

an adequate energy transit regulation and a slower development on energy transit regulation.[76] This is a fundamental issue due to the significant weight of energy transit in energy trade and consequently in international energy law.

Even though the ideal picture would be a regulation of energy transit of one speed, since the ECTP is still a draft and the negotiations are on standby, a situation of energy transit of two speeds could mean more choices in a complex scenario where States have different interests. This gives more flexibility in order to negotiate and to make possible that the Draft of the ECTP comes into force.

5.2 *The* Colombia—Ports of Entry *Case and Its Influence on the ECT as well as on the Energy Transit Protocol*[77]

The *Colombia—Ports of Entry* case[78] was the first and only, until now, case dealing with GATT Article V that a Panel resolved.

According to the Panel, it is clear that GATT Article V:1 defines *goods* as 'traffic in transit';[79] however this is not entirely correct because GATT Article V:1 includes in the definition of 'traffic in transit': '[g]oods [...] and also vessels and other means of transport'. Obviously, it does not differentiate what means of transport could be considered 'traffic in transit'.[80] Applying the Panel's opinion to the draft ECTP, GATT Article V covers only energy materials and products. Conversely, after a careful reading of the GATT provision as well as of Article 4(1) of the ECTP, it could be concluded that energy transport facilities are subject to the Protocol. Hence, WTO/GATT likely considers them 'other means of transport'.

However, some commentators state that a fixed infrastructure, such as pipelines or grids, is not traffic in transit under the WTO/GATT because it is not in movement.[81] The Understandings of the draft Protocol with respect to Article 4 states:

> *Energy transport facilities used for transit* excludes *other fixed facilities* to the extent that such facilities are not necessary to secure the flow

76 Melgar (n. 24) 77.

77 For a deeper analysis of the relationship between the case WT/DS366 and the ECT as well as the ECTP, see Melgar (n. 24).

78 For more information about the case see Panel Report, *Colombia—Ports of Entry* (n. 12) para. 7.402.

79 Ibid., 7.392, para. 7.396.

80 Azaria (n. 14) 569.

81 Ibid., 569.

> of Energy Materials and Products in Transit through high-pressure gas transmission pipelines, high-voltage electricity transmission grids and lines, crude oil transmission pipelines, coal slurry pipelines and oil product pipelines.

This indicates that pipelines and grids are considered 'energy transport facilities' in the draft Protocol, which could be interpreted as 'other means of transport' under the GATT Article V. The GATT provision does not specifically exclude fixed infrastructure; therefore, it is interesting to analyze the general definition of 'means of transport'. Thus, 'means' is 'an action or a system by which a result is achieved; a method'[82] and 'transport' is defined as 'system or means of conveying people or goods from place to place.'[83] Since the Panel did not refer to this question, there are apparently no objections to interpret pipelines and grids as 'other means of transport' for the purposes of the WTO/GATT.

Concerning the concept of 'freedom of transit', pursuant to the Panel, GATT Article V:2 limits such a freedom by stating 'via the routes most convenient for international transit'.[84] The notion of convenience, which depends upon 'the geographical position of the consumer and the producer',[85] is relative in the case of fixed infrastructure because it depends on the existence, location and capacity of the fixed infrastructure. Assuming that the WTO/GATT does only apply to existing means of transport, Contracting Parties cannot decide what routes are the most convenient, but they have to use those existing routes.

The issue of non-discrimination, or 'identical level of access', is also controversial. The Panel found that GATT Article V:2 provides for non-discrimination treatment, and the second sentence 'requires that goods from all Members must be ensured an identical level of access and equal conditions when proceeding in international transit.'[86] International transit may be read as 'traffic in transit';[87] thus, to apply 'identical level of access' to fixed infrastructure it is necessary, following the principle of transparency, that the transit State sets up a system that provides identical possibilities of access to infrastructure to the owners of goods.[88]

---

82 Oxford Dictionaries online, 'means', <http://oxforddictionaries.com/definition/means> accessed 27 August 2013.

83 Ibid., 'transport'.

84 Panel Report, *Colombia—Ports of Entry* (n. 12) para. 7.400.

85 Azaria (n. 14) 571.

86 Panel Report, *Colombia—Ports of Entry* (n. 12) para. 7.402.

87 Azaria (n. 14) 572.

88 Ibid., 572.

When interpreting 'conditions when proceeding in international transit' in the case of a fixed infrastructure, it can be read as transit transport tariffs, which are economically different due to the differences in the characteristics of the pipelines.[89] This is the result of the Note to GATT Article V:5, which states that transportation charges refer to 'like products' under 'like conditions'. In relation to that, the Panel found that the second sentence of GATT Article V:2 'requires that goods from all Members must be ensured an identical level of access and equal conditions when proceeding in international transit.'[90] The equal conditions standard is consistent with Article 10(1) of the Protocol as tariffs 'are objective, reasonable, transparent and non-discriminatory' instead of 'equal'. Therefore, the particular context is adapted to the route and to the infrastructure.[91]

Although the Panel in the *Colombia—Ports of Entry* case did not make its conclusions based on energy transit via fixed infrastructure, its findings about GATT Article V affect energy transit according to the ECT (and the Transit Protocol) because of its relationship with the WTO/GATT. Thus, taking into account that energy materials and products can be considered 'goods' in WTO law and that ECT Article 4 incorporates GATT obligations into the ECT field by reference, a clarification of the concept of 'freedom of transit' in WTO law results in a better understanding of the 'freedom of energy transit'.

6 Challenges of Energy Transit in International Law

The relevance of the ECT and the ECTP for energy transit is clear. However, after the rescission of the provisional application of the ECT pursuant to Article 45(3) by Russia on October 18, 2009,[92] and the European Union's stance to reset the negotiations, the ECTP is in a standby situation.[93] In spite of that, international regulation is crucial because energy supply on low prices

89 Ibid.

90 Panel Report, *Colombia—Ports of Entry* (n. 12) para. 7.402.

91 Azaria (n. 14) 573.

92 Johannes Fuchs, *Kooperative Erdgassicherheit—Energietransit im Völkerrecht unter besonderer Berücksichtigung des Nabucco-Abkommens vom 13.7.2009* (2011) ZaöRV, 103 <beck-online.de> accessed 27 August 2013: 'Russisches Erdgas macht über 40 % der Importe in die 27 Europäischen Union (EU)-Staaten aus, der Energieträger Erdgas deckt mehr als ein Fünftel des gesamteuropäischen Energieverbrauchs ab.'

93 Energy Charter Secretariat, Transit Protocol <http://www.encharter.org/index.php?id=37> accessed 27 August 2013.

represents the key for energy security. Furthermore, the gas crisis has highlighted the relevance of a general legal framework to control energy transit and investments.[94]

While several legal instruments, in the case of energy transit, regulate transit in international law,[95] the construction and management of cross-border pipelines is only regulated concerning submarine pipelines,[96] but not in relation to land pipeline-transport. Thus, regulation is more and more important for the stability of energy transit, especially after the negative reaction of Russia towards the ECT and ECTP and the EU's position concerning the ECTP's negotiations. Therefore, it is fundamental to take into consideration the specific and regional projects to grant energy security in international law.[97] Accordingly, the *Nabucco Agreement* of 2009[98] establishes a new scenario without the ratification by Russia of the ECT and ECTP.[99]

Regarding energy transit, the Agreement is compatible with the ECT[100] and its Preamble states the purpose of securing the 'uninterrupted transportation of Natural Gas in and across their respective Territories' and 'at competitive prices and conditions'. Article 7(1) establishes the prohibition of 'specific taxes, or discriminatory tax or legal requirements, or ostensibly general measures that are of equivalent effect.' In addition, the Agreement sets up the freedom of energy transit in Article 7(2): 'States Parties shall not permit nor require the Interruption of or restriction on the freedom of Transportation of Natural Gas.' with the exception of a hazard 'if it directly arises from Project Activities.'[101]

In case of interruption of transit, Article 7(6) establishes the right to 'use all lawful and reasonable endeavours' for the restoration of the Project Activities.

---

94 Fuchs (n. 66).

95 See chapter II above.

96 Arts 58(1), 79 and 112 of the UN Convention on the Law of the Sea (n. 7).

97 Fuchs (n. 66).

98 States Parties of the Nabucco Intergovernmental Agreement (Ankara, 13 July 2009): Austria, Bulgaria, Hungary, Romania and Turkey. The European Union signed the Agreement on 13 July 2009 to decrease its dependence on Russian gas.

99 Fuchs (n. 66).

100 Art 3(1) of the *Nabucco* Agreement (n. 99): 'The Agreement shall not affect any treaty rights and obligations of the States Parties, including those deriving from the Energy Charter Treaty to which the States Parties are all party, and from the Treaties establishing the European Union for the Republic of Austria, the Republic of Bulgaria, the Republic of Hungary, and Romania.'

101 See Art 7(4) ibid.

The *Nabucco Pipeline*[102] is regulated through an Agreement that establishes the freedom of energy transit and 'provides the necessary legal certainty to conclude supply contracts'.[103] Thereby, this pipeline competes with the Russian South Stream Pipeline. As Russia revoked the ECT and it is a WTO Member since 22 August 2012, this can be positive for the energy independence of Russia,[104] which can result in a possible opening-up of the energy markets.

Conversely, as a result of the political conflict with Iran, provoked by the issue of nuclear energy, and considering that Iran is a fundamental energy supplier of the *Nabucco Pipeline*, it is very important to find other regional alternatives. Thus, Germany is currently negotiating with the MENA Region[105] based on the ECT in order to support the project 'Creating a Reliable Legal and Political Framework for Energy Investments in the MENA Region on the Basis of the Energy Charter Treaty'.[106] The active involvement of MENA countries within the ECT negotiations, which helps their full involvement in the Energy Charter Process,[107] has a significant meaning for energy diversification, which results in energy independence, due to the importance of these countries concerning reserves of petroleum and natural gas.

The relevance of the previously mentioned projects should be compatible with and take place at the same time that the EU-Russia negotiations on energy transit. In this sense, after the qualification of the ECT as inefficient to resolve the gas crisis of 2009 by the Russian President, Dmitry Medvedev, he proposed in April 2009 the creation of a new legal framework of international

102 The main energy suppliers are expected to be Azerbaijan and Iraq due to the complicated relationships with Iran. However it is also expected the participation of other Middle Eastern countries. See *EU Countries sign geopolitical Nabucco Agreement* (EurActivcom, 14 July 2009) <http://www.euractivcom/energy/eu-countries-sign-geopolitical-nabucco-agreement/art-184062> accessed 27 August 2013.

103 See *EU Countries sign geopolitical Nabucco Agreement* (EurActivcom, 14 July 2009) <http://www.euractivcom/energy/eu-countries-sign-geopolitical-nabucco-agreement/art-184062> accessed 27 August 2013.

104 There is also the North stream pipeline (from Russia to Germany), which was promoted by the Russian government. The company owner of the pipeline is Nord Stream AG, whose main shareholders are Russians, with the 51% of shares.

105 MENA (Middle East & North Africa). The MENA Region is formed by the North of Africa and Middle East Countries that have vast reserves of petroleum and natural gas.

106 'The Energy Charter Welcomes Germany's Voluntary Contribution in Support of the Organisation's Closer Working Relations with the MENA Region' (Energy Charter News, 30 November 2011) <http://www.encharter.org/index.php?id=21&id_art=257&L=0> accessed 8 January 2012.

107 Ibid.

energy governance, the so-called 'Conceptual Approach to the New Legal Framework for Energy Cooperation' (the Concept or Conceptual Approach). *The Concept* would have an Annex that describes the elements of the transit agreement establishing obligations to ensure uninterrupted flow of energy resources. However, this Proposal is legally very similar to the ECT/ECTP system. Therefore, being the ECT the only legal binding multilateral agreement regarding energy materials and products, it seems unreasonable the creation of a new multilateral agreement that covers all the essential issues of the ECT. Consequently, it would be crucial to take into consideration the Russian Proposal so that it can be integrated into the Energy Charter Treaty forum, adapting the ECT to the new reality of the energy world.[108]

7 Conclusions

The consideration of energy materials and products as goods within WTO law is very important because it strengthens the relationship ECT/GATT. Thus, it makes possible the clear application of the freedom of transit to energy transit, giving certainty and legal security.

Furthermore, the adoption of the TFA would foster the notion of energy transit since, it will include in Article 11(1) of the draft TFA 'fixed infrastructure, inter alia pipelines and electricity grids'. As a result, due to the relationship between the WTO/GATT and the ECT as well as the ECTP, the TFA will clarify the issue of energy transit under the WTO/GATT, which, consequently, affects the ECT.

The insertion of this clarification into the TFA indicates that the interpretation of GATT Article V concerning energy transit is not clear; therefore, it is necessary to include it explicitly. Conversely, according to the interpretation of the SIOT case by the ECJ and WTO case law dealing with petroleum,[109] it could also be stated that energy materials and products could be covered by the WTO/GATT. Similarly the phrase of 'other means of transport' in GATT Article V should be understood as covering fixed infrastructure, as it has been explained above.

Although the matter of energy transit is still open to differing opinions, the conclusion of the TFA as well as of the ECTP will strengthen the relationship between the WTO/GATT and the ECT until the time that the freedom of transit provision in the WTO/GATT fully encompasses the transit provision

108 Selivanova (n. 51) 399.

109 See Appellate Body Report, *US Gasoline* (n. 16).

of the ECT, which would mean the liberalization of energy transit. Nevertheless, the Russian rescission of the ECT, and the EU's support of a reset of the ECTP negotiations, complicates the situation of the liberalization of energy transit; hence, a solution like the *Nabucco Agreement* can be effective for the short term and consequently an adaptation of the ECT/ECTP to the new Russian Proposal could facilitate the EU-Russia negotiations on energy transit. Thus, taking into account the Doha Round Negotiations[110] on Trade Facilitation and the TFA, as well as the ECT and ECTP, the issue of energy transit in international law can be regulated in a comprehensive manner, which will give legal clarification on the interpretation of this matter.

---

110 According to the current Doha Round Negotiations on Trade Facilitation, the issue of 'the routes most convenient for international transit' should be agreed on the basis of bilateral agreements. See WTO Negotiations on Trade Facilitation, Compilation of Members' Textual Proposals: 'Members shall promote bilateral and regional transit agreements or arrangements with a view to reducing trade barriers and enhance freedom of transit', TN/TF/W/43/Rev19 (30 June 2009) 30.

CHAPTER 10

Energy Transit in the Tangled Web of RTAs: The Relationship between GATT Articles V and XXIV in the Context of Energy Goods

Mikella Hurley[1]

1 Introduction

At the close of the Uruguay Round of negotiations in 1994, the World Trade Organization was comprised of 123 Members, with only a handful among them representing States vital to the global supply of energy resources. Uruguay-era negotiations pertaining to trade in goods focused primarily on the reduction of import tariffs, as well as regulatory restrictions that could hinder trade flows, particularly in key sectors such as agriculture and textiles. The negotiators accorded comparatively little focus to trade in natural and raw materials, including energy goods.[2] In contrast to agricultural and manufactured products, importing States rarely find it in their best interest to impede the flow of energy goods such as oil and natural gas. Indeed, such restrictions are uncommon in the energy sector; States typically seek to obtain energy goods at the lowest possible price, seldom imposing high tariffs or costly regulatory restrictions.[3]

---

1 The author wishes to thank Professor Gabrielle Marceau, Dr. Yulia Selivanova, Professor Joost Pauwelyn, and Marina Murina for their insightful comments on earlier versions.

2 It should be noted that negotiators from key developed country Members, like the United States, pushed to include specific disciplines within the final agreement on access to natural resources. These proposals were rebuffed by the developing country negotiating bloc. See Terence P. Stewart, *The GATT Uruguay Round: A Negotiating History, Volume I: Commentary* (Kluwer Law, 1993) 489–90. See also *Statement by the Informal Group of Developing Countries*, GATT Doc No MTN.TNC/W/19 (9 April 1990).

3 As Yanovich points out, while bound tariffs on fuel imports may be relatively high in some countries, on balance, actual applied tariffs are relatively low, with an average of 0.5% in developed countries and 6.7% in developing countries in 2007. See Alan Yanovich, 'WTO Rules and the Energy Sector' in Y. Selivanova (ed.) *Regulation of Energy in International Trade Law* (Kluwer 2011) 4.

 | DOI 10.1163/9789004270190_011

It is of little surprise that the existing WTO Agreement lacks provisions that specifically address the particular challenges of the energy sector.[4]

Since Uruguay, the times have changed, even if the rulebook has not. Within the WTO, energy is now a matter of highest priority. The mounting global dependence on oil and gas reserves found in remote and land-locked areas, paired with the fragmentation of transit routes between many different jurisdictions,[5] has 'increased the importance of transit pipeline issues in global oil and gas markets and politics.'[6] In parallel with this trend, several important producers of oil and natural gas have acceded to the WTO,[7] as have States that serve as critical conduits for the transit of these products.[8] While the WTO Agreement sets out general rules applicable to the transit of all goods in Article V of the GATT 1994, these provisions have only been subject to minimal interpretation by the WTO Dispute Settlement Body,[9] and they have never been applied in the context of energy transit. Over the past decade, the European region has experienced several high-profile disputes over the transit of hydrocarbons,[10]

---

4 World Trade Organization, *2010 World Trade Report* (2010) 194 <http://www.wto.org/english/res_e/booksp_e/anrep_e/anrep10_e.pdf> accessed 10 August 2013.

5 Most markedly demonstrated in the former Soviet Union (FSU) and former Yugoslavia.

6 Paul Stevens, 'Transit Troubles: Pipelines as a Source of Conflict' (A Chatham House Report, 2009) 4 <http://www.chathamhouse.org/publications/papers> accessed 10 August 2013.

7 Ecuador (acceded in 1996), Oman (2000) and Saudi Arabia (2005). The Russian Federation joined the WTO as its 156th Member, following formal approval of the Ministerial Conference on 16 December 2011 <http://www.wto.org/english/news_e/news11_e/acc_rus_16dec11_e.htm> accessed 27 August 2013. Russia is one of the World's most important producers of oil, topping out at an estimated 9.2 million barrels of crude per day in 2008 (a figure on par with Saudi Arabia's production levels). Russia also produces substantial volumes of natural gas, and serves as a conduit for transit of both goods to Europe. See the International Energy Agency, *World Energy Outlook* (2009) <http://www.worldenergyoutlook.org/docs/weo2009/WEO2009_es_english.pdf> accessed 27 August 2013.

8 Both Georgia (acceded in 2000) and Ukraine (which joined in 2008) control critical pipeline infrastructure used for the transit of natural gas. Accession negotiations are ongoing for Belarus, another important transit State.

9 WTO Panel Report, *Colombia—Indicative Prices and Restrictions on Ports of Entry (Colombia—Panamá)* *wt*/DS366/R (27 April 2009).

10 Disputes between Russia and Ukraine, which occurred in 2006 and 2009, led to major interruptions in the supply of natural gas to multiple countries in Europe. These disputes erupted, in part, over the calculation of Ukrainian transit tariffs. A similar dispute between Russia and Belarus, which occurred in in 2010, threatened to affect 6.2% of gas

while negotiations in other forums such as the Energy Charter Treaty (ECT) have failed to produce a set of comprehensive and detailed rules that respond to the most pressing political and technical challenges posed by the international transit in energy goods.[11] Ongoing WTO Doha Round negotiations in the area of trade facilitation could resolve some of the most critical areas of uncertainty,[12] however these talks remain beset by their own delays, reducing the likelihood that the WTO will deliver a new set of rules on energy transit in the near-term.[13] In the absence of a tailored set of rules developed either within the WTO or an alternative forum, it appears increasingly likely that the

---

flows to the European Union. See <http://www.bbc.co.uk/news/10375853> accessed 10 August 2013.

11 It should be noted that the Energy Charter Treaty, in its art. 7, already directly addresses the issue of energy transit by fixed infrastructure, requiring contracting parties to facilitate transit, obliging them to refrain from discriminating, or from interrupting transit flows. For a detailed discussion of ECT art. 7, see, *inter alia*: Danae Azaria, 'Energy Transit under the Energy Charter Treaty and the General Agreement on Tariffs and Trade' (2009) 27(4) Journal of Energy and Natural Resources Law 559; Lothar Ehring and Yulia Selivanova, 'Energy Transit' in Y. Selivanova (Ed.) *Regulation of Energy in International Trade Law* (Kluwer 2011). ECT members sought to elaborate upon the principles of art. 7 within a Transit Protocol that promised to further reduce restrictions on access and expand available infrastructure. However, as of November 2011, the Charter Conference opted to repeal the negotiating mandate for the draft Transit Protocol. The collapse of negotiations is at least partially attributable to the European Union's insistence that the EU be treated as a single unit under the Protocol, with the practical implication that Protocol obligations would not apply to inter-EU member transport of energy (art. 20—the so-called 'Regional Economic Integration Organization clause'). See <http://www.encharter.org/index.php?id=37> accessed 27 August 2013. The most recent version of the non-adopted Transit Protocol is available at: <http://www.encharter.org/fileadmin/user_upload/document/TTG_87_ENG.pdf> accessed 27 August 2013.

12 The current draft Trade Facilitation Agreement (TFA) expressly applies to fixed infrastructure for the transport of hydrocarbons, and seeks to address uncertainties associated with access and capacity constraints, public vs. private infrastructure, imposition of transit fees, and other issues. See WTO Doc. TN/TF/W/165/Rev14, p. 22. See also Azaria (n. 11) 562.

13 By the end of 2011, the WTO reported that Doha negotiations had stalled, and that Members were exploring alternatives to negotiations based upon the 'single undertaking' principle, by which 'nothing is agreed until everything is agreed' See World Trade Organization, *2012 World Trade Report* (2012) 22 <http://www.wto.org/english/res_e/publications_e/anrep12_e.htm> accessed 10 August 2013.

current WTO Agreement may be put to the test in a future dispute over access to, and management of pipeline infrastructure.[14]

Article V of the GATT obliges WTO Members to extend the objective right of freedom of transit to all goods from other Members, regardless of the origin or final destination of the goods.[15] Article V also sets out further disciplines on fees, formalities, and non-discriminatory treatment of goods in transit.[16] Although Article V makes no mention of fixed infrastructure such as pipelines, there is nothing in the text to suggest that pipeline transit is excluded from its scope, a matter that is discussed in further detail, below. Unlike traditional modes of transit such as rail lines, roads, and waterways, oil and gas pipelines impose fixed capacity constraints on the products that they convey, rendering them less capable of accommodating variable flows. Short of undertaking costly infrastructure expansion projects, an oil or gas transit State may not be able to accommodate all existing demand, and may be faced with the task of allocating access rights to only a limited set of users. The potential difficulties are not restricted to the issue of pipeline access and capacity constraints. Pipeline transit tariffs are frequently negotiated, and may differ, depending on the operator and the user.[17] Cross-comparison between pipelines—even those that exist under similar regulatory regimes and within the same jurisdiction—

14 Such disputes are not new to the WTO, although the WTO's Dispute Settlement Body has not been called upon to formally resolve Member disagreements over the transit of energy goods. In 2002, Members Slovenia and Croatia reported a dispute over the transit of hydrocarbons by road, with Croatia claiming that Slovenian measures constituted a violation of GATT art. V This disagreement was subsequently resolved through bilateral consultations. See WTO Doc G/C/W/360 (18 March 2002); WTO Doc TN/TF/W/2 (12 January 2005).

15 See GATT art. V, as discussed further in Section 2.

16 See GATT art. V, as discussed further in Section 2.

17 For a technical information on the modalities used and the complexities involved in establishing pipeline transit tariffs, see Energy Charter Secretariat, *Bringing Gas to the Market: Gas Transit and Transmission Tariffs in Energy Charter Treaty Countries—Regulatory Aspects and Tariff Methodologies* (2012) <http://www.encharter.org/index.php?id=584&L=0>; Energy Charter Secretariat, *Bringing Oil to the Market: Transport Tariffs and Underlying Methodologies for Cross-Border Crude Oil and Products Pipelines* <http://www.encharter.org/index.php?id=568&L=0>; see *also*: Energy Charter Secretariat, *Gas Transit Tariffs in Selected ECT Countries* (2006) <http://www.encharter.org/fileadmin/user_upload/document/Gas_Transit_Tariffs_-_2006_-_ENG.pdf> accessed 10 August 2013.

is often hindered by geographical, technological and other factors, all of which come to bear on the final operating cost and applicable user fees.[18]

The challenges of energy transit are often regional in nature. Transit States have significant incentives to grant their regional trading partners priority access to infrastructure, and perhaps more favorable terms of use, in a manner that fundamentally contradicts with the GATT Article V obligation of freedom of transit and the principle of Most Favored Nation (MFN) treatment. These tensions are perhaps best exemplified by the recent abandonment of ECT negotiations over the proposed Transit Protocol. Throughout Protocol negotiations, the European Union and Russia wrangled over the matter of regional integration, with the EU maintaining that the rules of the draft Transit Protocol should not be applied to energy flows originating and terminating within the EU as a unit.[19] The EU proposal, which was contained in Article 20 of the draft Protocol, would have resulted in a highly restrictive definition of 'transit' as applied to 'Regional Economic Integration Organizations' (REIOs), a species of regional trade agreement (RTA).[20] The EU stance on the transit of goods and regional integration long pre-dated Protocol negotiations, having first been formally articulated by the European Court of Justice (ECJ) in the *SIOT* case of 1983.[21] In *SIOT*, the ECJ considered the European Community's status as a Customs Union, as defined by GATT Article XXIV, and the implications for energy transit within the Community. The Court found that, as a consequence of this regional integration, 'the rules contained in [the] GATT govern only the Community's relations with other [GATT] Contracting Parties and cannot be applied within the Community itself.'[22] In other words, the Court interpreted the GATT Article XXIV exception as a blanket authorization

18 Transit States may apply different methodologies for calculation of tariffs, including distance-based 'capacity tariffs', distance-based 'commodity tariffs', 'entry/exit', and other methodologies. As one report notes: 'It may be impossible to compare entry/exit tariffs with distance-based tariffs as distance plays no part in entry/exit tariffs. Pipeline diameter and pressure are often important elements of tariff design', Energy Charter Secretariat, *Gas Transit Tariffs in Selected ECT Countries* (n. 17) 63–65. Many of the same considerations apply in the transit of oil.

19 See Draft Protocol art. 20. It should be noted that all the States within the EU have all ratified the Energy Charter Treaty in a dual capacity: both as individual States, as well as in their capacity as EU members.

20 Andrey Konoplyanik, 'Gas Transit in Eurasia: Transit Issues between Russia and the European Union and the Role of the Energy Charter' (2009) 27(3) J En & Nat Res L 445, 470.

21 *Case 266/81 SIOT v Ministero delle Finanze (1983) ECR 731.*

22 Ibid., 12.

for valid RTAs (or at least customs unions) to depart from GATT Article V rules for intra-RTA goods transit. While the ECJ maintained that 'the principles derived from Community law [on the transit of goods] substantially coincide with the rules derived from [the GATT] in that matter,'[23] the potential implications of the Court's broader logic are far-reaching. With over 511 known RTAs in existence as of the time of this writing,[24] the total derogation from Article V rules for RTAs could open the door to discrimination in the form of origin-based pipeline access rules, and differential approaches to pricing and charges, potentially further destabilizing the already fragile regime for international oil and gas transit via pipeline infrastructure.

The Russia-EU spat over regional integration and energy infrastructure may be a harbinger of disagreements to come, as energy transit States seek to allocate existing, limited pipeline capacity amongst prospective users. In the event that such a dispute is brought to the WTO, the WTO Dispute Settlement Body (DSB) will not only be obliged to clarify how the GATT's general rules on transit apply to the special category of energy goods. It may also be tasked with determining whether the view expressed in the *SIOT* case—namely, that Article V rules do not apply to transit amongst the members of properly formed RTAs—is valid, and thus permits WTO Members to accord energy transit preferences to their regional trading partners. While the scholarly community has already addressed many of the lingering questions as to Article V and its application to the transit of energy goods,[25] very little attention has been paid to the additional complications posed by regional integration.

1.1 *The Contribution of This Study*

This study is dedicated to an exploration of the relationship between GATT Article V rules on transit, and the Article XXIV conditional exception for RTAs. It attempts to shed some light on when a WTO Member, acting as a transit State for energy goods, may be authorized, or possibly even *required* by Article XXIV to accord its RTA trading partners priority access to energy transit infrastructure, as well as more favorable terms for this transit (e.g. the reduction or elimination of fees and other formalities). This study also seeks

23 Ibid., 22.

24 Per notifications to the WTO Secretariat as of 15 January 2012. For further information on these notified RTAs, readers may wish to refer to the WTO's comprehensive RTA database <http://www.wto.org/english/tratop_e/region_e/region_e.htm> accessed 10 August 2013.

25 See, *inter alia*, Ehring and Selivanova (n. 11); Martha Roggenkamp, 'Implications of GATT and EEC on Network-bound Energy Trade in Europe' (1994) 12 J. Energy & Nat Resources L 59; Azaria (n. 11).

to determine whether there are any types of preferential transit measures that Article XXIV will not authorize, even where they have been introduced as part of a valid RTA.

GATT Article XXIV provides a conditional exception for Members to depart from certain WTO rules, particularly the core principle of MFN treatment, which is reflected in the transit provisions GATT Article V. In brief, Article XXIV of the GATT authorizes Members to reduce and eliminate tariffs and other types of barriers for the trade occurring within an RTA, while leaving these measures in place for the bulk non-RTA trade. However, it is not clear whether the scope of the Article XXIV exception extends to Members' obligations under GATT Article V. Neither Article V nor Article XXIV contains any clear language to suggest that GATT obligations on transit are beyond the reach of the exception for RTAS.

Oil and gas transit States may find themselves under pressure to offer preferential access to their pipeline infrastructure for their regional trading partners,[26] to the possible detriment of other pipeline users. It is equally conceivable that a transit State may wish to reduce or eliminate the fees and formalities applied to oil or gas that originates in, or is destined for, one of its RTA partners. Such preferential treatment could result in the violation of multiple elements of GATT Article V, particularly if the action translates into reduced transit capacity for users that do not form part of an RTA. The violating Member would need to turn to Article XXIV in order to justify such treatment.

This does not exhaust the potential for interaction between GATT Articles XXIV and V. While the availability of the RTA exception, like the majority of the other exceptions within the WTO Agreement, depends on a Member's ability to demonstrate that certain stringent conditions have been met, Article XXIV

26 Indeed, this tension may arise in the case of Russia and its recently formed customs union with Belarus and Kazakhstan, a matter that is discussed at length within Russia's Working Party Report. Transit of energy goods is also flagged as an issue as indicated by art. 1152, which notes certain Members' 'concerns with regard to certain transit arrangements for energy products such as oil and gas.' art. 1161 of Russia's Working Party Report states that: 'the Russian Federation would apply all its laws, regulations and other measures governing transit of goods (including energy), such as those governing charges for transportation of goods in transit by road, rail and air, as well as other charges and customs fees imposed in connection with transit... in conformity with the provisions of art. V of the GATT 1994 *and other relevant provisions of the WTO Agreement.*' (Emphasis added). This final provision seems to signal Russia's intention to leave the door open for relevant exceptions provisions (e.g. art. XXIV) to apply to further obligations undertaken in the area of transit. See WT/ACC/RUS/70 and WT/MIN(11)/2 (17 November 2011) <http://www.wto.org/english/thewto_e/acc_e/a1_russie_e.htm> accessed 10 August 2013.

also exhibits an unusual feature not seen elsewhere. As will be discussed in further detail below,[27] it is not enough for a Member to merely eliminate a single tariff or restriction on trade coming from its RTA partners, and justify this action with reference to Article XXIV. In order to invoke Article XXIV for *any* prohibited form of preferential treatment, the Member must extend enough trade preferences to its RTA partners in order to cover 'substantially all' of the trade occurring within the RTA.[28] Put differently, the availability of Article XXIV as a defense for the violation of MFN (and arguably other core GATT rules) essentially depends upon an RTA's ability to achieve a critical mass of MFN violations. Thus, depending upon where transit measures fit within the overall scope of Article XXIV, it is conceivable that a Member could find itself under a *requirement* to offer its RTA partners priority access to its transit infrastructure, as well as more favorable terms of use, in order to satisfy the conditions of Article XXIV.

1.2 *Overview of This Study and Questions to be Addressed*

While this study primarily focuses on regional integration and the treatment of energy goods in transit, its findings are designed to be generalizable to the relationship between GATT Articles V and XXIV as a whole. This chapter proceeds as follows: Section 2 provides a brief refresher on the most important provisions of GATT Article V, with specific focus on areas of importance for the transit of energy goods over fixed infrastructure. Section 3 offers a detailed analysis of key elements of the GATT Article XXIV exception, with emphasis on the 'internal trade requirement' of the Article XXIV. Section 3 also sets out a proposed analytical framework to address the relationship between WTO rules on transit and regional integration. Section 4 applies this framework to two likely two energy transit scenarios.

In the first scenario, we assume that a WTO Member seeks to provide its RTA partners with preferential access to its energy transit infrastructure. We further assume that any increases in the capacity accorded to users from RTA partners will result in the consequent *reduction* of transit capacity available for other non-RTA users of the infrastructure. Users that do not come from RTA partners will experience an overall diminishment in the amount of oil or gas that they are able to channel through the transit State's territory. In the second scenario, we shall assume that the Member seeks to eliminate transit fees and

27 See Section 3.2 below.

28 See art. XXIV:8. The 'substantially all' requirement for a valid RTA is discussed in greater detail, in section 3.2 below.

charges for users from its RTA partners, while keeping these charges in place for all other users. As will be discussed below, either scenario would undoubtedly result in the violation of core elements of GATT Article V.

For both of the above scenarios, this study attempts to determine whether Article XXIV may permit, and indeed may even mandate such preferential treatment, or to the contrary, whether Article XXIV will not authorize either measure. The findings are based upon a close textual analysis of the relevant elements of Article XXIV of the GATT, as well as other pertinent WTO provisions, as interpreted by panels and the Appellate Body. Particular attention will be accorded to the impact of the 'internal trade requirement' found in GATT Article XXIV:8. In summary, this study responds to three key questions: First, it seeks to determine whether a WTO Member may be *required* to provide its RTA partners with preferential access to its energy transit infrastructure, or to exempt them from the application of legitimate transit charges for the use of its pipelines, in order to meet the conditions of GATT Article XXIV, even if such action violates GATT Article V. Second, even if a Member is not required to accord preferential terms of energy transit to its RTA partners, this study asks whether a Member may nevertheless be *permitted* to do so under Article XXIV. Finally, this study examines whether there are any types of preferential transit measures that Article XXIV cannot justify, and that GATT Article V will *prohibit* without exception.[29]

The answers to these questions will depend upon an assessment of where transit measures fit within the overall framework created by Article XXIV. As already noted, due to Article XXIV's conditions, which are predicated on achieving a critical level of derogation from core GATT principles and rules, the Article XXIV exception may do more than merely authorize a Member to extend preferential access and terms of transit to its RTA partners. Indeed, depending upon the circumstances, Article XXIV may *compel* a Member to do so.

2 GATT Article V and the Transit of Energy Goods—Context and Key Rules

Article V of the GATT contains a long-standing, yet little interpreted series of rules applicable to the transit of goods through the territories of WTO

29 It should be noted that this study does not consider the implications of private ownership of transit infrastructure, a matter sufficiently complex to justify separate analysis.

Members.[30] It establishes general obligations of transit State Members, as well as the corresponding rights of user Members, governing such matters as access, routes to be used, as well as any fees, formalities, charges and regulations applied in the process of transit. Although Article V does not mention energy goods by name—or any other category of goods for that matter—it is nevertheless likely to have very tangible implications for oil and gas transit States in the administration of their pipeline infrastructure. This section will explore some of these implications, drawing upon existing scholarly analysis, and will provide essential context for the study's later examination of the relationship between GATT Article V and the Article XXIV exception for RTAs as applied to energy transit. We begin by offering a review of certain key concepts and terms, reaffirming the argument, already put forward by other scholars, that the movement of oil and gas over fixed pipeline infrastructure meets the definitional requirements of transit of goods, thus falling within the scope of the rights and obligations of GATT Article V.[31] We will then explore several key rules within Article V, with a view to clarifying how they may interact with the RTA exception found in Article XXIV.

2.1 *Applicability—Does Energy Transit Fall within the Scope of* GATT *Article V?*

GATT Article V:1 provides that:

> Goods (including baggage), and also vessels and other means of transport, shall be deemed to be in transit across the territory of a contracting party when the passage across such territory, with or without transshipment, warehousing, breaking bulk, or change in the mode of transport, is only a portion of a complete journey beginning and terminating beyond the frontier of the contracting party across whose territory the traffic passes …

In order to determine whether products such as oil and gas, which travel via fixed infrastructure such as pipelines, fall within the scope of Article V, one must examine two key definitional terms, namely 'goods' and 'transit'.

---

30 For a concise history of the negotiation and codification of GATT art. V, from its origins as part of the Barcelona Convention to its present form, see 'Note by the Secretariat: art. V of the GATT 1994—Scope and Application', WTO Doc TN/TF/W/2 (12 January 2005).

31 This study does not address the transit of electricity over grid infrastructure, however this issue has been addressed by other works, notably, Ehring and Selivanova (n. 10).

Neither Article V, nor any other provision of the GATT provides a concrete definition of the term 'goods,' and some scholars have maintained that the drafters of the WTO Agreement intended to exclude energy goods from the Agreement's scope.[32] However, as Beatriz Huarte Melgar notes in her valuable commentary on the subject of energy transit, which is also found in this volume, there is little reason to question whether energy products such as oil and gas should qualify as 'goods' under the scope of the WTO Agreement.[33] In past disputes, the WTO Appellate Body has construed the term 'goods' broadly, even going so far as to find that it could encompass raw materials such as uncut timber, which have not yet entered the stream of commerce.[34] One of the earliest cases to find its way to the WTO dispute resolution system concerned the US regulatory regime for certain types of petroleum products,[35] a dispute that was resolved without any question as to whether the rules of the Agreement's 'goods pillar' were applicable. Whatever the potential arguments to the contrary, it would seem that the types of energy products that are transited over fixed infrastructure logically must be treated as 'goods' for the purposes of GATT Article V. These products are traded and sold, and have been classified in accordance with the World Customs Organization Harmonized Commodity Description and Coding System, which is used by the WTO in all tariff negotiations,[36] and can also serve as a valuable interpretive tool in understanding Members' commitments under the WTO Agreement.[37] Accordingly, this study proceeds upon the assumption that 'to the extent that energy... is

32 Azaria (n. 10) 565.

33 Beatriz Huarte Melgar, 'Energy Transit in International Law: Concept and Challenges' in F. Baetens and J. Caiado (Eds) *Frontiers of International Economic Law: Legal Tools to Confront Interdisciplinary Challenges* (BRILL 2014) 183.

34 Appellate Body Report, *United States—Final Countervailing Duty Determination with Respect to Certain Softwood Lumber from Canada,* DS257 (17 February 2004) para. 67.

35 *United States—Standards for Reformulated and Conventional Gasoline* WT/DS2/AB/R (20 May 1996).

36 For information on the WTO's use of the WCO Harmonized Commodity Description and Coding System (the 'Harmonized System'). Chapter 27 of the Harmonized System sets out the headings for energy goods such as petroleum and natural gas see the WTO website <http://www.wto.org/english/tratop_e/schedules_e/goods_schedules_e.htm> accessed 10 August 2013.

37 For an example of a case in which the Appellate Body endorsed the use of the Harmonized System as a tool to interpret the scope of a Member's tariff commitments, see Appellate Body Report, *European Communities—Customs Classification of Frozen Boneless Chicken Cuts* WT/DS269/AB/R (12 September 2005) para. 262.

a product, then all WTO provisions that contain disciplines on trade in goods are applicable.'[38]

Assuming that energy products such as oil and natural gas constitute 'goods' to which all GATT rules apply, a further definitional requirement must be met, namely that the movement of oil and gas via pipeline infrastructure constitutes 'transit' for purposes Article V.[39] To paraphrase the definition offered in Article V:1, goods, vessels, and 'other means of transport' will qualify as 'traffic in transit' when they pass through a Member's territory, but neither originate from nor are destined for final sale in that territory. The provision does not place any explicit restrictions on the mode or form of that transit (e.g. road or railway, versus pipeline). Some scholars have speculated that pipelines might be deemed to be 'other means of transport' as described in Article V:1,[40] leading to the possible conclusion that Article V would provide Members the right to construct new pipeline infrastructure in the territories of others. However, as elements of the drafting history suggest, 'other means of transport' was likely meant to include only mobile means, and not fixed infrastructure.[41] For the purposes of this study, it will be of little consequence whether pipeline infrastructure might be treated as a 'means of transport' for purposes of Article V. Given that Article V:1 does not restrict the definition of transit to certain types of products or modes of transport, as long as oil and gas qualify as 'goods,'[42] this should be enough to ensure that these products are covered by the disciplines of Article V.[43] The ongoing negotiations of the draft Trade Facilitation Agreement support this perspective, explicitly referring to transit via pipeline infrastructure as a mode of transit covered by GATT Article V.[44]

38 Gabrielle Marceau, 'The WTO in the emerging energy governance debate' (Draft for the Global Challenges at the Intersection of Trade, Energy and the Environment Conference, Graduate Institute, 14 October 2009) 1.

39 See GATT art. V:1.

40 See Huarte Melgar (n. 33), 199.

41 The records of committee meetings primarily discuss the term 'other means of transport' within the context of the debate over aircraft, and their treatment within art. V. See, *inter alia*, the Report of the Preparatory Committee of the International Conference on Trade and Employment, Committee II: Technical Sub-Committee, Economic and Social Council Doc. E/PC/T/C.II/42 (6 November 1946) 9.

42 See discussion of the term 'goods' (n. 33).

43 Ehring and Selivanova (n. 11) 57.

44 WTO, Negotiating Group on Trade Facilitation, TN/TF/W/165/Rev11 (7 October 2011).

2.2 *Transit in Energy Goods and the Article V Principle of Most-Favored Nation Treatment*

Article V:5 of the GATT elaborates upon a familiar principle that first appears in GATT Article I:1, namely the principle of MFN treatment. Article V:5 provides that:

> With respect to all charges, regulations and formalities in connection with transit, each contracting party shall accord to traffic in transit to or from the territory of any other contracting party treatment no less favourable than the treatment accorded to traffic in transit to or from any third country.

Article V prohibits the differential treatment of goods in transit when distinctions are made on the basis of origin or destination, something with obvious implications for a transit State that offers its regional trading partners preferential access and more favorable terms of use for pipeline infrastructure. An *Ad Article* to Article V affirms that transportation charges are covered within the scope of this provision,[45] and perhaps more critically, clarifies that MFN treatment for such charges will only extend to 'like products being transported on the same route under like conditions.'[46] This ostensibly offers Members the ability to peg transportation charges to the particularities of individual goods and routes, some of which may imply greater costs for the transiting jurisdiction. The operating costs associated with using pipeline infrastructure will vary widely depending on the type of system used, among many other important factors.[47] As a practical matter, it may prove difficult to compare these fees and distinguish legitimate variations from those driven by regional preferences.

Rules on access to pipeline infrastructure, which arguably fall under the heading of 'formalities,' are not granted similar flexibility, and arguably must be administered without regard to the route used or type product.[48] As a consequence, if a Member chooses to offer priority access to pipeline users from its regional trading partners, such action will likely constitute a violation of Article V as it applies to transit formalities, and will need to be justified by

45 Ad art. V (paragraph 5) clarifies: 'With regard to transportation charges, the principle laid down in paragraph 5 refers to like products being transported on the same route under like conditions.'

46 Ibid.

47 See Energy Charter Secretariat, *Bringing Gas to the Market* (n. 18).

48 Ehring and Selivanova (n. 11) 61–62.

the Article XXIV rules on preferential trade agreements, to the extent that this exception applies to Article V rules on transit.

2.3 *Transit in Energy Goods and the Article V Principle of Freedom of Transit*

Article V:2 contains the second provision that is likely to prove particularly relevant when considering preferential terms of access to pipeline infrastructure. This provision establishes a 'substantive right to freedom of transit' whereby a Member 'must not prevent transit' via its existing infrastructure.[49] Article V:2, first sentence provides that:

> There shall be freedom of transit through the territory of each contracting party, via the routes most convenient for international transit, for traffic in transit to or from the territory of other contracting parties. No distinction shall be made which is based on the flag of vessels, the place of origin, departure, entry, exit or destination, or on any circumstances relating to the ownership of goods, of vessels or of other means of transport.

In the sole WTO dispute to address the application of this provision, the Panel found that that Article V:2 'requires that goods from all Members must be ensured an identical level of access and equal conditions when proceeding in international transit.'[50] For transit via fixed infrastructure, an obvious difficulty might arise. As noted above, pipeline infrastructure, unlike roads or rail lines, imposes rigid capacity constraints and there will be little that a transit State can do to accommodate excess demand, at least in the near-term. A transit State that grants priority access to pipeline users from its regional trading partners, to the detriment of non-RTA users, may find itself in violation of Article V:2, which requires Members to provide 'identical possibilities of access to infrastructure,'[51] and expressly prohibits origin-based distinctions.

2.4 *The Concept of 'Reasonable' Transit Charges*

The final component of GATT Article V that is likely to prove highly relevant for our purposes is found in Article V:4, which provides: 'All charges and regulations imposed by contracting parties on traffic in transit to or from the territories of other contracting parties shall be reasonable, having regard to the

49 Ibid., 67. See also, Note By the Secretariat, 'Art V of GATT 1994—Scope and Application', TN/TF/W/2 (January 12 2005).

50 Panel Report, *Colombia Ports of Entry* (n. 9) para. 7.402.

51 Huarte Melgar (n. 33) 199.

conditions of the traffic.' This provision is given further texture and meaning by the preceding paragraph, Article V:3, which provides that no charges or duties shall be levied for transit 'except *charges for transportation* or those *commensurate with administrative expenses* entailed by transit or with the *cost of services rendered*.'[52] This provision merits brief mention here as it may offer a helpful interpretative tool in our subsequent analysis of the GATT Article XXIV:8 'internal trade requirement.'[53]

It would appear that the purpose of these two complementary provisions is to prevent Members from 'extracting a rent' from the transit of goods through their territories,[54] while nevertheless allowing Members to defray legitimate costs associated with the use of their infrastructure, and of course, those costs incurred in the administration of transit.[55] As shall be discussed below, when concluding a new RTA, a Member will need to look carefully at its existing restrictions on commerce, and determine whether certain measures need to be eliminated in order to meet the rigorous requirements of Article XXIV. Whether or not a transit regulation or charge is 'reasonable' under the standards set by Articles V:3 and V:4 will likely have some bearing on whether it must be eliminated for a Member's regional trading partners in order to meet the conditions imposed by Article XXIV. As we shall see, while Article XXIV requires Members to eliminate certain measures that unduly restrict trade flows, the GATT exception for RTAs does not oblige Members to subsidize the costs of trade for their RTA partners, and would not likely require the elimination of transit fees geared to recoup operating costs and render services.

3 The Article XXIV Exception—A Review of Key Requirements Relevant for Transit of Goods

GATT Article XXIV is an exception provision that offers parties to valid RTAs a defense for WTO inconsistent behavior,[56] particularly derogation from the

52 Emphasis added.

53 See section 3.2 below.

54 Ehring and Selivanova (n. 11) p. 74.

55 It should be noted that this study specifically does not focus on scenarios in which transit infrastructure is owned and administered by private corporate entities, without oversight by Member governments. Under such circumstances, the application of the various rules of GATT art. V is likely to be significantly attenuated. This is an area in which further scholarly would be valuable.

56 See Appellate Body Report, *Turkey-Restrictions on Imports of Textile and Clothing Products* WT/DS34/AB/R (19 November 1999) para. 45.

cardinal principles of MFN treatment and non-discrimination.[57] However, this defense is only available on *a conditional basis*. In order to qualify for the exception, an RTA must first meet a series of definitional requirements, and must fulfill the so-called 'external' and 'internal' trade requirements of Article XXIV. As compared with other GATT exception provisions, Article XXIV presents some highly unusual features.

Unlike classic regulatory exception provisions, which can only be invoked when Members demonstrate the presence of a genuine policy concern or risk,[58] the availability of Article XXIV is predicated upon a Member's ability to reach a certain threshold of trade liberalization within its RTA. WTO Members that form an RTA are thus required to extend trade preferences to one another on the basis of national origin, something that the GATT normally prohibits.[59] Put differently, in order for RTA Members to use Article XXIV to justify the violation of the MFN principle and other GATT rules, they must ensure that within the RTA as a whole, preferential treatment in violation of the MFN exceeds a certain threshold.[60]

The discriminatory liberalization authorized by Article XXIV is not without limits. In the formation of an RTA, Members must strike a balance that avoids actively prejudicing the rights of their non-RTA trading partners. Accordingly,

57 James Mathis, 'Regional Trade Agreements and Domestic Regulation: What Reach for "Other Restrictive Regulations of Commerce"? in L. Bartels and F. Ortino (eds), *Regional Trade Agreements and the WTO System*, (OUP 2006) 79; see *also*: James Mathis, *Regional Trade Agreements in the GATT/WTO: Article XXIV and the Internal Trade Requirement* (T.M.C. Asser Press, 2002).

58 As a practical example, GATT art. XX (a) provides a limited exception for measures 'necessary to protect public morals.' This provision allows Members to restrict trade, provided that they demonstrate that their measures meet a suite of conditions, including the requirement of a legitimate public moral ('public morals' are 'standards of right and wrong conduct'. See Panel Report, *United States—Measure Affecting the Cross-Border Supply of Gambling and Betting Services* WT/DS285/R (10 November 2004) para. 6.645), as well as a demonstration of the disputed measure's contribution to protecting that moral (a measure is 'necessary' when it is 'apt to make a material contribution to contribution' or 'be likely to make a material contribution' to the measure's achievement. See Appellate Body Report, *Brazil—Measures Affecting Imports of Retreaded Tyres* WT/DS332/AB/R (17 December 2007) paras 150 & 155.)

59 See, e.g., GATT arts I and III.

60 As is explained in further detail below, RTA partners must eliminate 'duties and other restrictive regulations of commerce' on 'substantially all' of the intra-RTA trade, per Arts XXIV:8(a)(i) and XXIV:8(b). This condition has come to be referred to as the 'internal trade requirement' of art. XXIV See Section 3.2 below.

a valid RTA must not *increase* the general level of restrictions applicable to non-RTA trade.[61] In the specific case of transit, this balancing between liberalization on the one hand, and the protection of third party rights on the other, presents a fair degree of legal uncertainty. It remains unclear whether access rights to transit infrastructure, along with fees and formalities, are to be classed within the group of measures that an RTA must eliminate in order to be validly formed under Article XXIV. If the answer is yes, an oil or gas transit State may be obliged to extend preferential access and terms of transit to its RTA partners.

On the flip side of the coin, increased access for one Member may lead to a proportionate decrease in access for another, particularly where fixed infrastructure is involved. Given the rigid capacity constraints imposed by pipelines, preferential treatment in pipeline access for RTA trading partners may serve to *restrict* the transit of energy goods coming from non-RTA parties, and thus lead to an increase in the overall restrictiveness on trade from Members outside of the RTA. The analysis offered below seeks to offer a better understanding of several elements of Article XXIV, as this will prove essential to our later examination of these potential tensions and problems.

3.1 *The 'External Trade Requirements' of Article XXIV*

GATT Articles XXIV:5 and XXIV:8(a)(ii) establish several conditions that a valid RTA must meet in terms of its trade with Members that do not form part of the RTA. While they are perhaps less important to our analysis than the 'internal trade requirement' of Article XXIV, they are nevertheless critical to the balancing to be achieved between RTA liberalization, on one hand, and the avoidance of increases to non-RTA Member trade restrictions, on the other.

Articles XXIV:5(a) and (b) limit the extent to which RTA members can *increase* their duties and 'other regulations of commerce' (ORC) on trade for non-RTA parties when forming new customs unions or free trade areas. While the rule for free trade areas (FTAs), as expressed in Article XXIV:5(b), sets out a zero-tolerance policy for increases in such duties and regulations (they '*shall not* be higher or more restrictive'), customs unions benefit from a greater degree of flexibility. Accordingly, Article XXIV:5(a) stipulates that increases in 'duties and other regulations of commerce' should not be 'on the whole higher

61 This condition has come to be called the 'external trade requirement' of art. XXIV It is discussed in greater detail, below. See Section 3.1 below.

or more restrictive than the general incidence of the duties and regulations of commerce applicable in the constituent territories prior' to formation.[62]

This provision may prove important when considering whether Article XXIV authorizes Members to provide their RTA trading partners with priority access to pipeline infrastructure. If access rights to pipelines fit the definition of 'other regulations of commerce' (ORC), it would seem that enhanced access for RTA partners, which incidentally serves to lessen the capacity available for others, could be viewed as an increase in restrictions on trade from Members that are not part of the RTA.

GATT Article XXIV:8(a)(ii) stipulates that a customs union must apply 'substantially the same duties and other regulations of commerce' to third countries.[63] The Appellate Body briefly addressed this provision in the *Turkey-Textiles* case, stating that 'substantially' implies 'something closely approximating 'sameness',' although parties to a customs union still enjoy 'a certain degree of flexibility' in terms of their individual external trade policies.[64] As it pertains to transit in goods, this provision may impose a requirement on customs union parties to harmonize their policies on transit charges, regulations and formalities. Of course, such harmonization would remain subject to the limits imposed by Article XXIV:5(a), and should not result in an overall increase in restrictions on external trading partners. Parties to FTAs, which generally do not establish a common commercial policy, are not allowed to raise their respective levels of duties and restrictions on third parties, per Article XXIV:5(b).[65]

3.2 *The 'Internal Trade Requirement' of Article XXIV*

This requirement is the most important for the purposes of this study and requires careful consideration. Particular focus is accorded to the terms of

---

62 The *Understanding on Article XXIV* clarifies that for duties, any evaluation shall 'be based upon an overall assessment of weighted average tariff rates and of customs duties collected (See Understanding on art. XXIV, art. 2). The *Understanding* does not offer a formula to assess the relative restrictiveness of ORC, and instead recommends a case-by-case examination of 'individual measures, regulations, products covered and trade flows affected'.

63 There is no such similar requirement for free trade areas.

64 Appellate Body Report, *Turkey-Restrictions on Imports of Textile and Clothing Products* WT/DS34/AB/R (19 November 1999) paras 49–50.

65 Art V:5(b) states that 'with respect to a free-trade area, the duties and other regulations of commerce maintained in each of the constituent territories... shall not be higher or more restrictive than the corresponding duties and other regulations of commerce existing in the same constituent territories prior to the formation of the free-trade area...'.

Article XXIV:8(a)(i), which apply to customs unions. However, due to a high degree of consistency in the language, analysis drawn from this provision is largely transferable to Article XXIV:8(b), which addresses FTAs. Article XXIV:8(a)(i) establishes requirements for the liberalization of trade within a qualifying customs union, such that:

> duties and other restrictive regulations of commerce (except, where necessary, those permitted under Articles XI, XII, XIII, XIV, XV and XX) are eliminated with respect to substantially all trade between the constituent territories of the union or at least with respect to substantially all the trade in products originating in such territories...

It is submitted that the term 'duties' should be interpreted to refer only to ordinary customs duties, and not other types of duties or charges (such as taxes and fees) that may be imposed at the border. Although the English version of the text does not refer explicitly to 'customs duties,' the French and Spanish versions are clear on this point, employing the terms *droits de douane* and *derechas de aduana*, respectively, and suggesting a narrow reading of the term 'duties' in the English version.[66]

According to GATT Article V:3, Members are not allowed to levy customs duties on goods in transit. It thus stands to reason that all legitimate charges, fees and formalities associated with transit in goods would be excluded from the scope of the term 'duties' in Article XXIV:8(a)(i). Thus, if transit access rules, charges and other formalities are to be covered by the internal trade requirement of Article XXIV, they must fit within the definition of 'other restrictive regulations of commerce,' a term that is explored below.

The second category, namely: 'other restrictive regulations of commerce' (ORRC), defines the types of measures, aside from customs duties, that must be eliminated for substantially all trade per the internal trade requirement of Article XXIV:8(a)(i). To date, the scope of ORRC has not been analyzed by the Appellate Body, and some disagreement remains among WTO Members as to its meaning.[67] However, comparison to other provisions within Article XXIV assists in placing the category of ORRC in context and defining its reach. It is particularly notable that Article XXIV:5(a) employs the term 'other regulations

---

66 All three versions of the text are treated as equally authoritative for purposes of interpretation.

67 Andrew Mitchell and Nicholas Lockhart, 'Legal requirements for PTAs under the WTO' in Lester and Mercurio (eds), *Bilateral and Regional Trade Agreements: Commentary and Analysis* (CUP 2009) 97; Mathis (n. 57) 82.

of commerce' (ORC) in its discussion of the 'external trade requirement.'[68] The word 'restrictive' is conspicuously absent from Article XXIV:5(a). Although it could be argued that any and all regulations of commerce could have a 'chilling effect' on trade and thus be considered restrictive,[69] Article XXIV appears to distinguish two distinct categories: ORC and ORRC. It thus seems to follow that the category of ORRC is comprised of a specific subset of regulations of commerce that can be identified by their relative restrictiveness.

Several other contextual elements provide further guidance. Both Article XXIV:8(a)(i) and the *Understanding on Article XXIV* refer to the elimination of restrictions on trade '*between* the constituent territories,'[70] indicating 'that the regulations to be eliminated under Article XXIV:8 are those that restrict the cross-border movement of goods between RTA parties.'[71] If this interpretation is accurate, ORRC would comprise those measures aimed specifically at imports, rather than measures that are applied to all goods in the normal course of trade. This is further reinforced by the types of measures listed as exceptions to XXIV:8(a)(i).[72] These provisions generally address border measures that place quantitative restrictions on imports (GATT Articles XI–XV), or that could lead to *de facto* quantitative restrictions on products by requiring that the products possess certain characteristics, or comply with certain standards (GATT Article XX). On this basis, it is submitted that the term ORRC generally encompasses 'border measures ... and importation/exportation restrictions,' as well as 'domestic regulations (fiscal or non-fiscal) that accord less favorable treatment to like imported products.'[73] This definition would include all 'protectionist trade measures ... and contingency trade defense measures such as anti-dumping and safeguard actions.'[74] It is further submitted that measures that are applied to goods in the normal course of trade, which do not

68 Art XXIV:5(a) states: 'with respect to a customs union, or an interim agreement leading to a formation of a customs union, the duties *and other regulations of commerce* imposed at the institution of any such union or interim agreement in respect of trade with contracting parties not parties to such union or agreement shall not on the whole be higher or more restrictive than the general incidence of the duties and regulations of commerce applicable in the constituent territories prior to the formation of such union or the adoption of such interim agreement, as the case may be;' (emphasis added).

69 Mitchell and Lockhart (n. 67) 97.

70 Emphasis added.

71 Mitchell and Lockhart (n. 67) 97.

72 '... except, where necessary, those permitted under Arts XI, XII, XIII, XIV, XV and XX ...'.

73 Mathis (n. 57) 91.

74 Ibid., 87.

specifically target imports, should be excluded from this category. If accurate, this finding would suggest that *legitimate* transit fees and formalities—namely those applied for the purpose of recouping operating expenses or for furnishing services—would not fall within the category of ORRC, and would thus not need to be eliminated as between RTA partners, something that is discussed in greater detail below in the context of our transit scenarios.

Another element within the Article XXIV:8(a)(i) internal trade requirement that requires definition is the term 'substantially all trade.' Neither the text of Article XXIV, nor the jurisprudence that have analyzed it offers a quantitative formula for the measurement of the 'substantially all' threshold. However, the Appellate Body has stated that this term connotes 'considerably more than merely *some* of the trade' flows within an RTA.[75] Furthermore, the Appellate Body has noted that the provision offers 'some flexibility' to Members in picking and choosing which measures and tariffs to eliminate, within limitations that remain undefined.[76] If raised in future disputes before the WTO DSB, it is likely that panels and the Appellate Body will approach the definition of 'substantially all trade' in a flexible manner, taking a case-by-case approach that examines both qualitative factors (e.g. the number of sectors covered by internal RTA liberalization) and quantitative factors (e.g. the overall percentage of trade of trade flows covered).[77]

The final element of Article XXIV:8(a)(i) that remains to be considered is the phrase: 'trade between the constituent territories … or at least with respect to substantially all the trade in products originating in such territories.' This portion of Article XXIV:8(a)(i) places concrete limits on precisely *what trade flows* fall within the bounds of the internal trade requirement. Given that this study addresses Article XXIV in the context of transit, including the movement of goods that may be destined for trade *outside* a given RTA, this final element is likely to prove decisive. The phrase 'trade between the constituent territories' appears to set the maximum scope of application of the internal trade requirement, to include goods originating in third countries. The subsequent phrase 'or at least' seems to introduce a minimum threshold for the types of goods considered under the internal trade requirement, namely those

75 Appellate Body Report, *Turkey-Textiles* (n. 64) para. 48 (emphasis original).

76 Ibid. The Appellate Body stated: 'Yet we caution that the degree of 'flexibility' that the sub-paragraph 8(a)(i) allows is limited by the requirement that 'duties and other restrictive regulations of commerce' be 'eliminated with respect to substantially all' internal trade.'

77 See Mitchell and Lockhart (n. 67) 96.

originating within RTA territories. In other words, at the very minimum, parties must eliminate restrictions on intra-RTA trade for substantially all goods 'originating' within the territories of the constituent members of the RTA. However, this provision does not appear to require the elimination of restrictions when the trade in question *does not occur* between RTA parties. Under this interpretation, restrictions on goods in transit that either originate from, or are bound for final sale in territories *outside* of the RTA would not be covered, as they would not impact 'trade between the constituent territories' of the RTA.

If we briefly return to the scenarios posed above,[78] we can already begin to appreciate how the Article XXIV internal trade requirement may come to bear on the particular question of energy transit. If, per our scenarios, the oil or gas that transits through a Member's territory originates in the territory of one of its RTA trading partners and is bound for final sale in another, this arguably would constitute 'trade between the constituent territories' of the RTA, in the meaning of GATT Article XXIV:8(a)(i). The transiting Member might thus need to consider whether the particular measures in question, whether they relate to access to transit infrastructure, or the fees and formalities associated with transit, constitute ORRC. However, if the oil or gas originates from, or is ultimately destined for another Member that is not associated with the RTA, this would no longer constitute 'trade between the constituent territories' of the RTA. As a practical result, the transiting Member would not need to determine whether its transit measures constitute ORRC; the Member will not be obligated to eliminate them in any case.[79]

3.3 *Additional Requirements to Employ Art XXIV as a Defense—the Turkey-Textiles Tests*

Beyond meeting the so-called 'internal' and 'external' trade requirements, the Appellate Body has determined that Article XXIV imposes two further conditions that must be met before RTA parties can use the exception as a defense for inconsistent behavior. Both of these conditions are found in the *chapeau* of Article XXIV:5, which states:

78 See section 1.2 above.

79 It should be noted that, even if the Member is not required to eliminate transit measures because they do not apply to trade as between constituent territories of its RTA, it might nevertheless wish to do so. In this case, the Member will need to determine whether art. XXIV will authorize this action, even if it does not require elimination of the measures.

> the provisions of this Agreement shall not prevent, as between the territories of contracting parties, the formation of a customs union or of a free-trade area or the adoption of an interim agreement necessary for the formation of a customs union or of a free-trade area...

The phrase 'shall not prevent' operates to introduce the Article XXIV defense.[80] According to the Appellate Body, this defense is only available if the WTO-inconsistent measure was 'introduced *upon the formation*' of the RTA.[81] Additionally, the defense is only available if, in the absence of the measure in question, the formation of the RTA would have been prevented.[82] Put differently, this requirement will only be met if there is no other 'reasonable alternative' measure that would have been less trade restrictive, yet allowed the RTA to be established.[83]

It is submitted that these two additional requirements should be seen to apply *only* to WTO-inconsistent measures that result in an *increase* in external trade restrictions for non-RTA parties, and not for measures that merely result in a *decrease* in trade restrictions amongst RTA parties. The Appellate Body made its findings on the *chapeau* of Article XXIV:5 in the context of a dispute over increases to quantitative restrictions on non-RTA trade, and did not apply these additional conditions to other measures.[84] Given that Article XXIV:5 aims to limit Members' ability to use their RTAs as an excuse to raise their restrictions on external trading partners,[85] the additional conditions of the *chapeau* make most sense when read specifically in this light. If RTA parties were required to prove that every decrease in trade restrictiveness was necessary to the formation of an RTA, this would undermine the very purpose of Article XXIV itself. Furthermore, since Article XXIV gives RTA parties 'discretion as to which internal trade restriction to eliminate and in which circumstances, provided that restrictions are eliminated on substantial all trade... it would go beyond the role of panels and the Appellate Body to second-guess

80 Appellate Body Report, *Turkey-Textiles* (n. 64) para. 45.

81 Ibid., 58 (emphasis added).

82 Ibid., 58.

83 Ibid., 62.

84 Ibid. The *Turkey-Textiles* dispute concerned the imposition of quantitative restrictions on textile imports, imposed by Turkey as part of its efforts to conclude a customs union with the EU.

85 Mitchell and Lockhart (n. 67) 88.

such decisions.'[86] For these reasons, this study proceeds upon the assumption that the two tests set out in the *Turkey Textiles* case apply exclusively to RTA-related measures that serve to increase restrictions on trade flows from outside of the RTA, and not to those measures that merely decrease restrictions on intra-RTA trade. As shall be discussed in further detail below, the *Turkey Textiles* requirements may be relevant when a transit State seeks to provide priority access to its pipeline infrastructure for regional trading partners. By contrast, the requirements are less likely to apply to the elimination of user fees for RTA trading partners.

4 Transit of Energy Goods and the Internal Trade Requirement of Art XXIV

Now that we have set out the key requirements of Article V as it applies to transit of energy goods, and have established the elements of Article XXIV that are most likely to have an impact on energy transit, we shall turn to an analysis of the relationship between Articles V and XXIV in the context of our two energy transit scenarios. This study seeks to address the extent to which the Article XXIV exception for RTAs may permit, and indeed even require, a Member to derogate from certain Article V rules.[87] It will also explore instances where

86 Ibid., 89. This perspective is supported by the findings of the Panel in the *Line-pipe Safeguards* case, in which it determined that the *Turkey-Textiles* (n. 64) tests should not be required for the elimination of barriers within an RTA. See Panel Report, United States—Definitive Safeguard Measures on Imports of Circular Welded Carbon Quality Line Pipe from Korea WT/DS202/R (8 March 2002) para. 7.148. Here, the Panel stated in part: If the alleged violation of GATT 1994 forms part of the elimination of 'duties and other restrictive regulations of commerce', there can be no question of whether it is necessary for the elimination of 'duties and other restrictive regulations of commerce'. While this finding was not reviewed by the Appellate Body on appeal and was deemed to be of no formal legal relevance for future disputes, see Appellate Body Report, United States—Definitive Safeguard Measures on Imports of Circular Welded Carbon Quality Line Pipe from Korea WT/DS202/AB/R (8 March 2002) paras 198–199, it serves as strong indication of how this provision might be addressed in the future.

87 By very definition, art. XXIV will not be applicable to certain obligations within art. V, and will only be relevant when preferential treatment accorded to an RTA party triggers a violation. For example, a Member would not logically be able to apply art. XXIV to justify a transit charge or regulation that is not 'reasonable', contrary to the requirements of art. V:4.

Article XXIV will not provide a serviceable defense for violations of Article V rules on transit.

In our first scenario, we assume that a transit State is considering whether it might rely on Article XXIV to offer its RTA partners preferential access to its energy transit infrastructure, thereby implicitly limiting the capacity available for other users. As noted above, this action is likely to constitute a violation of GATT Article V:5 because such action would depart from the requirement that Members accord MFN treatment to all goods in transit, regardless of origin.[88] It is also likely to violate Article V:2, which establishes an objective right of freedom of transit, and prohibits Members from making any distinctions based upon the origin or destination of goods.[89]

In the second scenario, we assume that the transit State already applies certain charges, regulations and formalities to energy goods in transit, and is considering whether it might rely on Article XXIV to eliminate these measures for its RTA partners. Such action is also likely to constitute origin or destination-based discrimination, leading to a violation of GATT Article V:5.

Before we determine whether Article XXIV will either compel or authorize a Member to take either of these courses of action, it is first necessary to consider whether and how the internal trade requirement of Article XXIV:8 applies to the measures that are described in our two scenarios.

4.1 *Pipeline Access Rules and the 'Internal Trade Requirement' of GATT Article XXIV:8(a)(i)*

Fixed pipeline infrastructure may not always offer the requisite capacity to meet total exporter demand, and thus rules on access, even if applied in a fair and non-discriminatory fashion, could always result in some restriction of the total volume of energy goods in transit at a given time. However, this does not automatically mean that such rules constitute ORRC and are otherwise subject to the internal trade requirement of Article XXIV. Our analysis requires a response to a two-part question, namely: Do rules on access to energy transit infrastructure constitute 'other restrictive regulations of commerce,' and are they applied to 'trade between the constituent territories,' in the meaning of GATT Article XXIV:8(a)(i)?

As discussed above, this study defines the category of ORRC as encompassing protectionist border measures, restrictions on importation and exportation restrictions, as well as domestic regulations that accord less favorable treatment to like imported products. In order to comply with the requirements

88 See section 2.2 above.

89 See section 2.2 above.

of Article V, rules on access to fixed infrastructure cannot be administered in a discriminatory fashion.[90] Members must not enact transit measures that distinguish between products on the basis of origin, destination or ownership. Also, by very definition, transit involves entry into and exit from the territory of the transiting Member,[91] rather than importation. For these reasons, this study submits that a transit State's rules on access to finite pipeline infrastructure would not fall under the definition of ORRC, unless they are based upon considerations such as the origin or the destination of the products in transit.

To answer the second part of our question, we must determine whether rules on access to fixed energy transit infrastructure are 'applied to trade between the constituent territories' of an RTA. Logically, the response will be context-dependent. One will only arrive at an affirmative answer to this question when exportation, transit, and importation all occur within the territories of an RTA. The new customs union formed between Russia, Kazakhstan and Belarus provides an apt example of where such a situation might occur. Natural gas extracted in Kazakhstan, transited through Russia, and destined for final sale in Belarus would constitute 'trade between the constituent territories,' and in the unlikely event that legitimate access rules on transit are deemed to constitute ORRC, Russia might be under a requirement to eliminate them. However, if the natural gas in transit continues through Belarus with a final destination of Germany, it is argued that such measures would no longer fall within the scope of the Article XXIV:8(a)(i) internal trade requirement, regardless as to whether they constitute ORRC, because the transit would no longer involve trade between RTA partners.

90 See art. V:2. In addition, the standard of 'reasonableness' imposed on all transit regulations and formalities by art. V:4 sets a relatively high standard against discrimination. In *Colombia-Ports of Entry* (n. 9) para. 7.148, the Panel pointed out that GATT art. V functions to protect Members 'from *unnecessary restrictions*, such as limitations on freedom of transit, or unreasonable charges or delays ...' thus equating a 'reasonable' transit measure with on that which is 'necessary'.

91 Art. V:1 states: 'Goods (including baggage), and also vessels and other means of transport, shall be deemed to be in transit across the territory of a contracting party when the passage across such territory, with or without trans-shipment, warehousing, breaking bulk, or change in the mode of transport, is only a portion of a complete journey beginning and terminating beyond the frontier of the contracting party across whose territory the traffic passes.'

4.2 *Transit Charges and Fees in the Context of the 'Internal Trade Requirement' of* GATT *Article XXIV:8(a)(i)*

The analysis for transit charges and fees is broadly similar to that for access rules, and also proceeds in two parts. First, we must determine whether transit charges and fees constitute 'other restrictive regulations of commerce' in the meaning of Article XXIV:8(a)(i). We must then determine whether they are applied to 'trade between the constituent territories' of the RTA in question. If both of these conditions are met, the transit charges and fees are likely to fall within the scope of the internal trade requirement of Article XXIV, and *may* need to be eliminated, provided that they apply to enough of the intra-RTA trade so as to reach the 'substantially all' threshold.[92]

Recalling our proposed definition of ORRC as encompassing protectionist measures and restrictions on the flow of goods, it is submitted that those charges and fees that Article V deems *legitimate* and authorizes Members to impose on goods in transit would not fall within this category. Charges levied to defray the costs associated with maintenance and the ordinary functioning of a pipeline would arguably be applied to the transport of all energy goods, whether in international transit or not. Such legitimate charges would not serve to restrict the flow of goods, and would thus not constitute ORRC. However, in the case that a Member applies a transit charge that does not comply with the requirements of GATT Article V because it is excessive, discriminatory, or otherwise geared to restrict the flow of energy goods, the charge would constitute an ORRC under our proposed definition. It should be recalled that GATT Article V permits members to impose 'reasonable' transit charges and fees,[93] which are defined to include 'charges for transportation', as well as other charges that are 'commensurate with administrative expenses entailed by transit of with the cost of services rendered.'[94] Charges that are applied for other purposes, particularly that of discrimination, are patently 'unreasonable' and are likely to violate Article V, paragraphs 3 and 4. Thus, by coming into full compliance with the terms of GATT Article V, the Member could simultaneously 'eliminate' transit charges and fees that constitute ORRC, thereby enhancing its adherence with the internal trade requirement of Article XXIV.

Similarly to our analysis for access rules, transit charges will only apply to 'trade between the constituent territories' of the RTA if the energy goods in question originate from, and are bound for, the territories of RTA trading partners. For example, energy goods that are produced, transited, and sold

92 The 'substantially all' threshold is discussed in Section 3.2 above.

93 GATT art. V:4.

94 Ibid., V:3.

exclusively within the jurisdictions of the constituent members of the EU will constitute 'trade between the constituent territories' of the EU customs union. However, if the energy goods are destined for another jurisdiction outside of the EU, the internal trade requirement of Article XXIV:8(a)(i) will no longer apply.

4.3 *Summary of Findings—What Impact Does Article XXIV Have on Energy Transit Measures?*

Based upon the analysis set out above, we can now turn to the key questions presented in Section 1.2, above, with a view to better understanding the relationship between Articles V and XXIV as they apply to energy transit. At the outset, this study noted that there might be three possible outcomes when the Article XXIV exception for RTAs is applied to transit measures maintained under Article V. First, it is conceivable that there are some transit measures that *must be eliminated* as between RTA parties in order to comply with the internal trade requirement of Article XXIV:8, particularly when these measures constitute ORRC and impact 'substantially all' of the trade between RTA members. Second, there may be certain transit measures that *may be eliminated* by virtue of the Article XXIV exception, even when they need not be eliminated as a strict condition of compliance with the internal trade requirement. Finally, there may be some transit measures *that cannot be eliminated* as between RTA members, even when the RTA in question has been validly formed and fully satisfies the internal trade requirement.

As noted above, access to Article XXIV as a defense for WTO inconsistent behavior is partially conditioned upon a given RTA's ability to achieve a certain level of internal trade liberalization. Measures that must be eliminated for 'substantially all trade' between RTA members are those that possess two characteristics. First, they must constitute either customs duties or ORRC. Secondly, they must be applied to goods traded *between* RTA partners, not just those that happen to pass through RTA territories while in transit. On this basis, it is submitted the internal trade requirement of Article XXIV is unlikely to *oblige* a transit State to provide its RTA partners with preferential access to its energy transit infrastructure, or to eliminate legitimate charges imposed to recoup costs associated with transit, as neither measure is likely to fall within the category of ORRC. Furthermore, even if such measures could be considered ORRC, they would only need to be eliminated where applied to 'substantially all trade between the constituent territories' of the RTA. Energy goods bound for sale outside of the RTA would not qualify. In the unlikely event that a particular transit measure engages the terms of the Article XXIV internal trade requirement, this would not necessarily mean that the transit State maintaining the measure would be obliged to eliminate it for its RTA trading partners. It should be recalled that the threshold of the internal trade requirement has been set at 'substantially all,' which leaves a margin of flexibility for a Member to pick and choose which of its ORRC to eliminate.[95]

We turn now to our second question, namely whether Article XXIV *may permit* the elimination of certain transit measures as between RTA partners, even when such elimination is not required as a condition of access to Article XXIV. One of the most challenging interpretive features of the Article XXIV exception is that its text does not expressly establish its limits as a defense. It remains unclear whether Article XXIV can hypothetically be used to justify all forms of GATT-inconsistent preferential treatment, or merely some. Guidance may be forthcoming from the object and purpose of Article XXIV, which, according to the Appellate Body is to 'facilitate trade *between* the constituent territories' of an RTA.[96] From this perspective, one might reason that if a charge on energy transit is applied to goods being traded between RTA parties, and the elimination of this charge would further facilitate trade between them, Article XXIV might very well justify such preferential treatment. This is less certain for transit charges that are applied to energy goods originating from, or destined for sale in territories outside of the RTA. As for access to transit infrastructure, the same logic would apply, subject to one very important caveat, which is discussed in our response to the third key question posed in this study.

Finally, this study asks whether there are any situations in which a transit State Member of the WTO *must refrain* from offering its RTA partners preferential access for energy transit, or from exempting its RTA partners from charges that are applied to non-RTA trading partners. Put slightly differently, we consider whether there are measures for which the requirements of GATT Article V prevail over the Article XXIV exception. This question is most relevant in a case where a Member seeks to accord greater access for RTA partners to its transit infrastructure. If in so doing, the Member directly reduces capacity available for other WTO Members by restricting the actual flows of non-RTA oil or gas through transit pipelines, such a measure might not only violate Article V, but could also disqualify the RTA under the external trade requirement of

95 See section 3.2 above.

96 The Appellate Body has noted that although this art does not contain any legal tests, it sets purposive language on RTA formation. See Appellate Body Report, *Turkey-Textiles* (n. 56) para. 57 (emphasis added).

Article XXIV:5.[97] Such treatment would likely only benefit from the Article XXIV exception if it was granted upon the formation of the RTA, and was necessary to the very formation of RTA, in line with the rigorous tests set out in the *Turkey-Textiles* case.[98]

5 Concluding Remarks

While this short study by no means exhausts all uncertainties that pervade the relationship between GATT Articles V and XXIV in the context of the very special category of energy goods,[99] it is hoped that it offers a useful framework for analysis on the issue, as well as some initial insights for future consideration and discussion. As demonstrated by the high-profile natural gas transit disputes between Russia and Ukraine,[100] as well as the abandonment of negotiations of the ECT Transit Protocol,[101] energy transit is a matter of strategic importance with implications well beyond the halls of the WTO. As the WTO expands to include more Members that are vital to the production and supply of energy goods, it is of critical importance that the existing areas of legal uncertainty be addressed. As has been shown above, it is unlikely that valid regional trade agreements under GATT Article XXIV will be required to establish preferential treatment in the area of energy transit. However, some

97 As discussed in section 2.1 above.

98 As discussed in section 2.3 above.

99 Several very important issues could not be addressed in this short document, including the question as to whether a fully integrated customs union might create a situation where transit ceases to exist, and all movement of goods between constituent territories is deemed to be transport. Another issue not discussed here pertains to the impact of art. XXIV:3, which provides special disciplines for 'frontier traffic'. In practice, this provision likely should not be viewed as applying to RTA transit in goods. A cursory review of the drafting history indicates that this provision established a savings clause that was meant to allow communities situated astride frontiers to exchange certain goods on the basis of local arrangements. See, *inter alia*: Verbatim Report from the Second Session of the Preparatory Committee of the United Nations Conference on Trade and Employment, Doc E/PC/T/A/PV/42 (18 August 1947) 18–20; Draft Report of the GATT Working Party II on Tariffs, Schedules and Customs Administration, Doc W9/20 (16 Feb. 1955); GATT Analytical Index, Spec (85) 60 (18 December 1985) Part III.

100 These disputes, which occurred in 2006 and 2009, and led to major interruptions in the supply of natural gas to multiple countries, centered on disagreements over energy prices, as well as transit tariffs.

101 Discussed in Section 1 above.

doubt remains as to what Article XXIV may nevertheless permit, provided that restrictions do not increase for non-RTA parties. This legal uncertainty may be a valuable incentive for WTO Members to push ahead in Doha Round negotiations and establish a tailored set of rules on the trade in energy goods. But until this happens, we will have to make due with the rulebook as it is.

CHAPTER 11

Internet Service Providers' Secondary Liability for Trademarks Violations in the EU and the US

Anna Giulia Micara[1]

1 Introduction

Today's electronic marketplaces and new business models offer unprecedented business opportunities and, at the same time, new ways to sell counterfeit goods. Recent case law on trademark counterfeiting concerning eBay, the online auction website, and the AdWords service of Google shows the need to balance between the legitimate activity and development of internet service providers (ISPs), or intermediaries, and the enforceability of intellectual property rights, especially trademarks, in the digital environment.

There have been attempts to regulate the liability of ISPs in several international forums but no multilateral binding agreements are dealing with those aspects as of yet. Within the WTO, the Council for Trade-Related Aspects of Intellectual Property Rights has had a mandate to examine the intellectual property issues arising in connection with e-commerce since 1998, but its work is still in progress. In this regard, the 2011 WTO Ministerial Conference decided to continue the reinvigoration of the work program.[2] Furthermore, certain countries, mainly developed ones, negotiated a multilateral agreement on intellectual property enforcement called the Anti-Counterfeiting Trade Agreement: the initial draft introduced provisions on ISPs liability, concerning copyright, but these were cut in the final version.[3] Besides, the entry into force of the Agreement is now uncertain as the EU Parliament

1 E-mail: anna.micara@unimi.it.

2 WTO Ministerial Conference, Work Programme on Electronic Commerce WT/L/843 (19 December 2011).

3 European Commission, Proposal for a Council Decision on the conclusion of the Anti-Counterfeiting Trade Agreement between the European Union and its Member States, Australia, Canada, Japan, the Republic of Korea, the United Mexican States, the Kingdom of Morocco, New Zealand, the Republic of Singapore, the Swiss Confederation and the United States of America, COM(2011)380 <http://ec.europa.eu/trade/tackling-unfair-trade/acta/> accessed 27 August 2013.

 | DOI 10.1163/9789004270190_012

rejected the treaty in June 2012. The issue has also been discussed in the World Intellectual Property Organization (WIPO) which in 2001 adopted a *Joint Recommendation Concerning Provisions on the Protection of Marks, and Other Industrial Property Rights in Signs, on the Internet* that provides for general rules on liability and infringement, although they are not binding.[4] Only at the bilateral level, within the context of the TRIPS-plus 'world',[5] binding provisions on ISP liability exist in trade agreements concluded by the US and the EU. An example is the agreement between the EU and South Korea, which contains provisions equivalent to those of the e-commerce Directive (ECD)[6] in order 'to ensure the free movement of information services and at the same time enforce intellectual property rights in the digital environment'.[7]

Considering the lack of regulation at an international level, this Chapter will analyse the liability of ISPs in the EU and the US, focusing on how courts are shaping the conditions and the extent of secondary liability of service providers.[8] The aim is to assess to what extent the EU and US approaches differ, thereby affecting the free movement of information services and hampering the development of these services, and to what extent these countries have managed to establish legal certainty on liability necessary for ISP activity. The main underlying question is who should bear the burden of policing the use of trademarks on the site: the right holders or the intermediaries? In general, the primary responsibility of enforcing private rights falls on their holders, the brand owners. At the same time, intermediaries' secondary responsibility

4 In this regard see also WIPO Standing Committee on the Law of Trademarks, Industrial Designs and Geographical Indications, 'Trademarks and the Internet', SCT/24/4 (31 August 2010) 2ff.

5 Nowadays intellectual property provisions which go beyond the TRIPS' minimum standards are mainly provided for by bilateral agreements while the WTO Doha round is progressing slowly. On this see, among others, Meir Perez Pugatch 'The international regulation of IPRS in a TRIPS and TRIPS-plus world' in S. Woolcock (ed.), *Trade and Investment Rule-making, The Role of Regional and Bilateral Agreements* (UN University 2006).

6 Directive (EC) 2000/31 of the European Parliament and of the Council on certain legal aspects of information society services, in particular electronic commerce, in the Internal Market ('Directive on electronic commerce') (2000) OJ L 178, arts 12–15.

7 Free Trade Agreement between the European Union and its Member States, of the one part, and the Republic of Korea, of the other part (2011) OJ L 127/6, art. 10.62.

8 A detailed assessment of direct infringement by ISPs is beyond the scope of this Chapter; see, among others, Nicole Van der Laan, The Use of Trade Marks in Keyword Advertising—Developments in ECJ and National Jurisprudence (2012) Max Planck Institute for Intellectual Property & Competition Law Research Paper No 12–06 <http://ssrn.com/abstract=2041936> accessed 27 August 2013.

is frequently debated: even when they are not direct infringers they could still exercise a more active role than, for example, postal services, and they have tools to take remedial actions against sellers. Furthermore, for rights holders, ISPs are easier to police compared to real infringers and usually solvent.[9] A balance should be found in order to enable holders to fight counterfeiting while giving intermediaries the ability to exercise their legitimate activity and develop their business models, without being subjected to unjustified economic and legal burdens.

2 The EU Approach

Within the EU, the ECD aims to 'contribute to the proper functioning of the internal market by ensuring the free movement of information society services between the member states' through the harmonisation of several aspects of e-commerce.[10] It has harmonised certain ISP liability's exemptions (so-called 'safe harbours') while, in general, the conditions under which ISPs liability arise must be sought in the context of national law. The harmonisation is also relevant because prior to the entry into force of the Directive, a number of members had no clear legislation in this area.[11] The harmonised exemptions concerned mere conduit (Article 12), caching (Article 13) and hosting (Article 14),[12] on which the cases analysed below are focused. The exemptions

---

9 In this regard see, for example, Joined Cases C-236/08 to C-238/08, *Google France SARL and Google Inc. v Louis Vuitton Malletier SA* (C-236/08), *Google France SARL v Viaticum SA and Luteciel SARL* (C-237/08) *and Google France SARL v Centre national de recherche en relations humaines (CNRRH) SARL and Others* (C-238/08) (2010) ECR I-2417, Opinion AG Poiares Maduro, para. 115: 'Trade mark proprietors have no legal problem in tackling counterfeit sites, as such sites are clearly involved in trade mark infringements; however, the practical difficulties of doing so should not be ignored. It is often difficult to determine the ownership of the sites, the applicable legislation and jurisdictional forum, and to pursue the respective procedures. Moreover, it is apparent that trade mark proprietors believe that other sites can swiftly replace those that are found to be in infringement'.

10 See Directive on electronic commerce (n. 6) art. 1.

11 See Copenhagen economics, 'Study on the economic impact of the e-commerce directive' (September 2007) <http://ec.europa.eu/internal_market/e-commerce/directive_en.htm> accessed 27 August 2013.

12 Art. 14 establishes a liability exemption for hosting activities, providing that: 1. Where an information society service is provided that consists of the storage of information provided by a recipient of the service, Member States shall ensure that the service provider is not liable for the information stored at the request of a recipient of the service, on condition that: (a) the provider does not have actual knowledge of illegal activity or infor-

are established in a horizontal manner, meaning that they cover liability, both civil and criminal, for all types of illegal activities initiated by third parties. Moreover, Article 15.1 prevents member states from imposing a general obligation on providers to monitor the information that they transmit or store, or a general obligation to actively seek facts or circumstances indicating illegal activity.

This Chapter will focus on safe harbours as interpreted by the ECJ in recent cases. The application of safe harbours depends on national courts and different approaches to the issue exist, despite the fact that many member states have transposed Articles 12–14 ECD into their legal systems.[13] This results from the significant discrepancies between the legal cultures in each EU member state due to the different sources of civil and criminal law. The Commission recognized that clarification of certain aspects is needed in order to ensure legal certainty, especially concerning the definition of intermediary activities and of actual knowledge, notice and take down procedures and Article 15.[14]

---

mation and, as regards claims for damages, is not aware of facts or circumstances from which the illegal activity or information is apparent; or (b) the provider, upon obtaining such knowledge or awareness, acts expeditiously to remove or to disable access to the information. (…) 3. This Article shall not affect the possibility for a court or administrative authority, in accordance with Member States' legal systems, of requiring the service provider to terminate or prevent an infringement, nor does it affect the possibility for Member States of establishing procedures governing the removal or disabling of access to information.

13 On French and German case law see Kurt M. Saunders, Gerlinde Berger-Walliser, 'The Liability of Online Markets for Counterfeit Goods: A Comparative Analysis of Secondary Trademark Infringement in the United States and Europe' (2011) 32 Nw J Int'l L & Bus 37; Katja Weckström, 'Liability for Trademark Infringement for Internet Service Providers' (2010) <http://ssrn.com/abstract=1633389> accessed 27 August 2013, 33–38.

14 Commission communication to the European Parliament, the Council, the Economic and Social Committee and the Committee of the Regions, 'A coherent framework for building trust in the Digital Single Market for e-commerce and online services', COM(2011)942, 5. Among the five priorities there is 'Develop the legal and cross-border offer of online products and services' and in particular take measures necessary to improve the implementation of the ECD (in particular through better administrative cooperation with the Member States and an in-depth evaluation of the implementation of the Directive), provide clarification, for example concerning the liability of intermediary internet providers. See also: Summary of results of the public consultation on the future of electronic commerce in the internal market and the implementation of the directive on electronic commerce <http://ec.europa.eu/internal_market/consultations/docs/2010/e-commerce/summary_report_en.pdf> accessed 27 August 2013.

2.1 *The Internet Service Providers' 'Active Role'*

This section analyses recent case law concerning online auction sites, particularly cases concerning the sale of counterfeit goods through eBay, as well as cases concerning keyword advertising, especially those involving the AdWords service. AdWords is an advertisement system operated by Google through which advertisers can select keywords in order for their ads to be displayed under the specific heading 'sponsored link', alongside natural results.[15] Usually legal actions arise from the fact that a trademark owner, *e.g.*, Louis Vuitton in a French case or Rosetta Stone in a US case below, sues Google for trademark infringement because Google gave advertisers (competitors but also counterfeiters of the owner) the possibility of selecting keywords which correspond to, *e.g.*, Vuitton or Rosetta Stone trademarks in order to display the ad of their goods and services.

In *Google v Louis Vuitton*, the Court affirmed that the AdWords is an information society service, since it is a service 'provided at a distance by means of electronic equipment for the processing and storage of data, at the individual request of a recipient of services and, normally, for remuneration'.[16] It therefore fits the definition of information society service of Directive 98/34/EC,[17] which the ECD refers to in its Article 2. Moreover, the ECJ confirmed that Google performs a hosting activity since the

15 It is interesting to note that Google supports its search engine, as well as a range of free applications, with its income from AdWords. Every time an internet user subsequently clicks on the ad's link, Google is remunerated in accordance with a price agreed beforehand ('price per click'). There is no limit to the number of advertisers that can select a keyword, and if all the ads relating to that keyword cannot be displayed at the same time they will be ranked according to the price per click and by the number of times that internet users have previously clicked on the ad's link. To get more insight on sponsored links see, among others, Stephen Kulk, 'Search Engines Searching for Trouble? Comparing Search Engine Operator Responsibility for Competitive Keyword Advertising Under EU and US Trademark Law' (July 2011) <http://ssrn.com/abstract=1911038> accessed 27 August 2013, 7ff.

16 Joined Cases C-236/08 to C-238/08, *Google France SARL and Google Inc. v Louis Vuitton Malletier SA* (C-236/08), *Google France SARL v Viaticum SA and Luteciel SARL* (C-237/08) *and Google France SARL v Centre national de recherche en relations humaines (CNRRH) SARL and Others* (C-238/08) (2010) ECR I-2417, para. 110.

17 Directive (EC) 98/34 of the European Parliament and of the Council laying down a procedure for the provision of information in the field of technical standards and regulations (1998) OJ L 204.

> referencing service provider transmits information from the recipient of that service, namely the advertiser, over a communications network accessible to internet users and stores, that is to say, holds in memory on its server, certain data, such as the keywords selected by the advertiser, the advertising link and the accompanying commercial message, as well as the address of the advertiser's site.[18]

Therefore, Google can benefit in principle from the liability exemption provided for in Article 14 ECD. However, referring to recital 42 ECD,[19] the ECJ stated that another condition is necessary in order to profit from this exemption: the service provider has to be neutral, 'in the sense that its conduct is merely technical, automatic and passive, pointing to a lack of knowledge or control of the data which it stores' whereas this is not the case if it plays an active role of such a kind as to give it knowledge of, or control over, those data.[20] In this regard, the ECJ affirmed that 'the mere facts that the referencing service is subject to payment, that Google sets the payment terms or that it provides general information to its clients cannot have the effect of depriving Google of the exemptions from liability provided for in Directive 2000/31'.[21] Nonetheless, the role played by an ISP 'in the drafting of the commercial message which accompanies the advertising link or in the establishment or selection of keywords is relevant'.[22]

---

18 *Google France and Google* (n. 16) para. 111.

19 According to recital 42 ECD 'The exemptions from liability established in this Directive cover only cases where the activity of the information society service provider is limited to the technical process of operating and giving access to a communication network over which information made available by third parties is transmitted or temporarily stored, for the sole purpose of making the transmission more efficient; this activity is of a mere technical, automatic and passive nature, which implies that the information society service provider has neither knowledge of nor control over the information which is transmitted or stored'. According to recital 43 ECD 'A service provider can benefit from the exemptions for 'mere conduit' and for 'caching' when he is in no way involved with the information transmitted; this requires among other things that he does not modify the information that he transmits; this requirement does not cover manipulations of a technical nature which take place in the course of the transmission as they do not alter the integrity of the information contained in the transmission'.

20 *Google France and Google* (n. 16) paras 113–14.

21 Ibid., 116.

22 Ibid., 118.

In the following case, *L'Oréal v eBay*,[23] concerning the sale of counterfeit L'Oréal goods on the online auction website eBay, the ECJ confirmed the notion of 'active role' as set out in *Google v Louis Vuitton*. Indeed the Court did not follow Advocate General (AG) Jääskinen's position on the interpretation of the ECD and on the substance of such an 'active role' requirement.[24] Arguably, the AG's position would have better reflected the fact that eBay or Google's involvement in marketing does not necessarily mean they would have knowledge or control of specific legal questions about whether a good is counterfeit. According to AG Jääskinen:

> 'neutrality' does not appear to be quite the right test under the directive for this question. Indeed, I would find it surreal that if eBay intervenes and guides the contents of listings in its system with various technical means, it would by that fact be deprived of the protection of Article 14 regarding storage of information uploaded by the users.[25]

Nevertheless, the ECJ followed the line of proponents of stricter online trademark enforcement,[26] stating that the operator who has provided assistance

23 Case C- 324/09, *L'Oréal SA and others v eBay International AG and others* (2011) ECR I-6011.

24 See Case C- 324/09, *L'Oréal SA and others v eBay International AG and others*, (2011) ECR I-6011 Opinion AG Jääskinen, paras 141–42: Indeed according to the AG, '(e)ven if recital 42 of the directive speaks of 'exemptions' in plural, it would seem to refer to the exemptions discussed in the following recital 43. The exemptions mentioned there concern—expressly—'mere conduit' and 'caching'. When read this way, recital 42 becomes clearer: it speaks of the 'technical process of operating and giving access to a communication *network* over which information made available by third parties is *transmitted* or *temporarily stored*, for the sole purpose of making the *transmission more efficient*' (my emphasis). To my mind, this refers precisely to 'mere conduit' and 'caching', mentioned in Articles 12 and 13 of Directive 2000/31'. 'Rather, in my view, it is recital 46 which concerns hosting providers mentioned in Article 14 of Directive 2000/31, as that recital refers expressly to the storage of information (…)'. (According to recital 46: In order to benefit from a limitation of liability, the provider of an information society service, consisting of the storage of information, upon obtaining actual knowledge or awareness of illegal activities has to act expeditiously to remove or to disable access to the information concerned; the removal or disabling of access has to be undertaken in the observance of the principle of freedom of expression and of procedures established for this purpose at national level; this Directive does not affect Member States' possibility of establishing specific requirements which must be fulfilled expeditiously prior to the removal or disabling of information).

25 Ibid., 146.

26 Legal victory for trademark litigants over intermediary liability, (13 July, 2011), <http://edri.org/edrigram/number9.14/ebay-loreal-case-ecj> accessed 27 August 2013.

which entails, in particular, optimising the presentation of the offers for sale in question or promoting those offers, must be considered not to have taken a neutral position.[27]

This case law contributes to an EU-wide uniform interpretation of relevant notions relating to the exemptions, although several definitions, such as 'search engine' or 'hyperlink', are still not uniform across the EU. However, this jurisprudence is still developing and the application of safe harbours is decided upon by national courts, taking into account the ECJ judgment. Unfortunately interpretations are diverging: some French courts found the electronic marketplace liable whereas other French courts as well as Belgian and German courts reached the opposite conclusion.[28] More specifically, certain courts, especially French ones, considered that eBay activities could not be limited to hosting since they also included brokerage.[29] Indeed the definition of the activity performed by ISPs is relevant because under Article 14 ECD, the safe harbour provision is applicable to hosting providers while courts deeming providers as brokers could apply national civil liability rules.[30] Hence, clarifications are needed concerning the application of the ECD to providers involved in multiple activities. At the same time, considering that a French court recently recognized that the hosting activity of Google cannot be excluded by brokering, and therefore applied the ECD,[31] it appears that the level of control and knowledge determining the active role of providers and the consequent possibility for ISPs to benefit from safe harbours, also needs to be clarified. This implies, for example, shedding light on whether neutrality should be excluded because Google controls at its discretion the order of display of the ads,[32]

27 *L'Oréal v eBay* (n. 23) para. 116.

28 Opinion AG Jääskinen (n. 24) para. 58. See, among others, *Lancôme v eBay* (31 July 2008) Tribunal de commerce de Bruxelles, and see n. 13 for German and French case law.

29 See, among others, *eBay Inc, eBay International v Christian Dior Couture* (2010) Cour d'appel de Paris; see, however, *eBay Inc., eBay International v Louis Vuitton Malletier* (3 May 2012) Cour de cassation. For EU member states case law see also Thibault Verbiest, Gerald Spindler, Giovanni Maria Riccio, Aurélie Van der Pierre, 'Study on the liability of internet intermediaries', (12 November 2007) <http://ec.europa.eu/internal_market/e-commerce/docs/study/liability/final_report_en.pdf> accessed 27 August 2013, 84–85.

30 In this regard see Patrick Van Eecke 'Online service providers and liability: a plea for a balanced approach' (2011) CMLR 48, 1468ff for EU national case law; Opinion AG Jääskinen (n. 24) paras 148–49.

31 *EBay Inc., eBay International v Louis Vuitton Malletier* (3 May 2012) Cour de cassation.

32 In this regard see *Olivier M. v Prisma Presse, Google*, (14 November 2011) Tribunal de Grande Instance de Paris.

or because it suggests alternative trademarks as keywords,[33] or even because providers explain and help users to get to know their tools, which is a basic need for ISPs. In this regard, although the ECJ excluded the active role in the event of 'general information', French courts considered that even the FAQs and '*consigne de rédaction*' of Google were not 'general information' because of their contractual nature.[34] In conclusion, hopefully the ECJ will rule again on neutrality in future cases in order to avoid ambiguities on these crucial issues.

2.2 *On 'Actual Knowledge' and 'Awareness'*

To benefit, in principle, from the safe harbour established by Article 14 ECD, the service provider should offer an information society service consisting of the storage of information provided by a recipient of the service. Then, even if it plays a passive role, and therefore does not have knowledge or control of relevant data, liability is excluded in certain cases, in particular if, according to Article 14.1 ECD,

> (a) the provider does not have actual knowledge of illegal activity or information and, as regards claims for damages, is not aware of facts or circumstances from which the illegal activity or information is apparent (therefore different knowledge requirements for criminal liability and claims for damages are set forth); or (b) the provider, upon obtaining such knowledge or awareness, acts expeditiously to remove or to disable access to the information.

The notion of knowledge is decisive in determining the extent of liability to which intermediaries are exposed. However, it is still not precisely defined.[35] According to the Commission, 'most Member States have literally transposed the condition of not having actual knowledge but some member states deviated from the explicit text of the ECD', and 'even when the term

33 Charles Gielen, 'Keyword advertising and European trademark law' (2010) <http://charlesgielen.com/2.html> accessed 27 August 2013, para. 20.

34 *Olivier M. v Prisma Presse, Google* (n. 32).

35 In this regard see Commission Staff Working Document, 'Online services including e-commerce in the single market', SEC(2011)1641, Accompanying the document Communication from the Commission to the European Parliament, the Council, the European Economic and Social Committee and the Committee of the Regions, 'A coherent framework to boost confidence in the Digital Single Market of e-commerce and other online services', COM(2011)942 final, 32ff; Summary of results of the public consultation on the future of electronic commerce in the internal market and the implementation of the directive on electronic commerce (n. 14), 10–11.

"actual knowledge" has been literally transposed it has given rise to diverging interpretations'.[36] Some member states, like Spain, consider only notifications by competent authorities as sufficient to assume actual knowledge, while Germany and Austria refer to general legal standards of obtaining knowledge of illicit content;[37] and some members do not provide for any distinction between actual knowledge and awareness.[38] Therefore, an intermediary can usually obtain actual knowledge through a court order or administrative authority notification, or through a notice (ranging from an informal notice by the right holder to a court order) or, in absence of a notice, if it has 'general awareness' that its site hosts illegal information.[39]

Right holders mainly support this last option, but if actual knowledge becomes 'general knowledge' then this would in practice lead to a general monitoring obligation, which is prohibited by Article 15 ECD. This should be avoided on account of being too burdensome for ISPs since they have to deal with such a large amount of data and therefore they cannot monitor everything. The first option is supported mainly by civil organizations in defence of the freedom of speech since it ensures that it is not up to private parties to define what is legal and illegal while taking into account that *de facto* private parties tend to take down the materials after any notice to avoid liability.[40] Furthermore, according to several organizations, entrusting ISPs with the role of assessing what is legal or illegal would create an excessive economic burden for them and the assessment could also require a significant amount of legal knowledge, for example, to distinguish between counterfeiting and parallel trade of trademarks.[41]

The second option, supported by many ISPs and right holders, is perhaps the more balanced and the one which will prevail. Indeed a notice and takedown (NTD) procedure could allocate the primary policing obligation on enforcement on right owners. At the same time, adequate safeguards have to

36 SEC(2011)1641 (n. 35) 33.

37 Verbiest, Spindler, Riccio, Van der Pierre (n. 29) 28; Opinion AG Jääskinen (n. 24) paras 160–62.

38 Verbiest, Spindler, Riccio, Van der Pierre (n. 29) 34.

39 SEC(2011)1641 (n. 35) 33.

40 Joe McNamee, 'The slide from 'self-regulation' to corporate censorship, the scale and significance of moves to entrust internet intermediaries with a cornerstone of democracy—open electronic communication networks' (2011) EDRI <www.edri.org> accessed 27 August 2013; Lecture by Sjoera Nas, Bits of Freedom, SANE, The Multatuli Project ISP Notice & take down (1 October 2004) <http://www.bof.nl/docs/researchpaperSANE.pdf> accessed 27 August 2013.

41 On the difficulties in assessing illegal materials see also Van Eecke (n. 30) 1465ff.

be put in place so as to balance intellectual property enforcement and legitimate content, also considering that ISPs could be held liable both for having omitted to act after receiving a notice or for having removed contents on the basis of an erroneous notice.[42] Unfortunately, at present at the EU level there are voluntary non-binding tools[43] and a multitude of different procedures[44] but the Commission planned to adopt a horizontal initiative on notice and action procedures[45] and, the ECJ gave some guidance in *L'Oréal v eBay*.[46]

Concerning the notion of awareness, in *L'Oréal v eBay* the ECJ had the opportunity to clarify that the referring court should evaluate the 'awareness of facts or circumstances from which the illegal activity or information is apparent', considering that a provider is not entitled to benefit from the Article 14 ECD exemption if it is 'aware of facts or circumstances on the basis of which a diligent economic operator should have identified the illegality in question and acted in accordance with Article 14(1)(b)'.[47] The Court refers here to the situation 'in which the operator of an online marketplace uncovers, as the result of an investigation undertaken on its own initiative, an illegal activity or illegal information', and 'the situation in which the operator is notified of the existence of such an activity or such information'.[48] In the latter case, the ECJ recognizes that a notification of allegedly illegal activities or information

42 SEC(2011)1641 (n. 35) 44.

43 For example, on May 2011 a representative group of right holders and internet platforms signed, under the auspices of the Commission, a Memorandum of Understanding (Brussels, 4 May 2011) aimed at reducing the sale of counterfeits via e-commerce platforms and to enhance collaboration on NTDs. Among the main provisions: 'The signatories agree that the primary responsibility for the protection and enforcement of IPR remains with the respective Right Owners and that it is the primary responsibility of Internet Platforms to enable a safe online environment for consumers. Hence, it is the parties' goal to collaborate in the fight against the sale of Counterfeit Goods over the Internet', Internet platform commit to offer 'efficient and effective', 'accessible' NTD while right owners commit to 'use NTD offered by Internet Platforms', to 'join respective rights protection programs of Internet Platforms' (in cases where it is obvious that notifications are made without exercising appropriate care, right owners may be denied or may have only restricted access to NTD) and 'to take commercially reasonable and available steps to effectively fight counterfeiting at its source'.

44 On national NTD procedures see SEC(2011)1641 (n. 35) 42ff; Verbiest Spindler Riccio Van der Pierre (n. 29) 106–15.

45 COM(2011)942 (n. 14) 15.

46 Indeed the ECD refer to NTD procedures in art. 14.1.b.

47 *L'Oréal v eBay* (n. 23) para. 120.

48 *L'Oréal v eBay* (n. 23) para. 122.

cannot automatically preclude the safe harbour of Article 14, since it may turn out to be insufficiently precise or inadequately substantiated. Nonetheless, the notification still represents

> as a general rule, a factor of which the national court must take account when determining, in the light of the information so transmitted to the operator, whether the latter was actually aware of facts or circumstances on the basis of which a diligent economic operator should have identified the illegality.[49]

In this regard, there is a common trend across member states toward a concept of knowledge or awareness being deemed to exist in cases of manifestly or obvious unlawful content: for example in Austria one refers to 'obvious to any non-lawyer without further investigation', therefore trademark infringement is not considered manifestly illegal, while in Germany the Federal Court considered that trademark infringements formed a 'clear infringement'.[50] However, this remains a highly controversial issue and the ECJ, referring to the illegal information for 'which a diligent economic operator should have identified the illegality in question', has established a more restrictive criterion than the notion of 'manifestly illegal content' of Article 14(1)(a).[51]

3 The US Approach

In the US, provisions on secondary liability for providers are established in the 1998 Digital Millennium Copyright Act (DMCA)[52] but this concerns only copyright, it does not have a horizontal approach as the ECD has. The DMCA provides a number of safe harbours from liability from specific intermediary activities (transitory communication, system caching, storage of information

49 Ibid., 122.

50 See Verbiest, Spindler, Riccio, Van der Pierre (n. 29) 38–9; SEC(2011) 1641 (n. 35) 35.

51 On this aspect see also Van Eecke (n. 30) 1467.

52 The Digital Millennium Copyright Act (1998). It has to be noted that, in practice, according to Weckström 'internet intermediaries have interpreted the safe harbour of the DMCA to extend to trademark law as well and made available procedures to rights holders for expedited processing of infringement claims', Weckström (n. 13) 39.

on systems or networks at direction of users and information location tools).[53] The ECD, which entered into force two years later, was modelled after the DMCA and therefore many elements present similarities, such as the notions of 'actual knowledge', 'awareness' or 'storage'.[54]

Concerning trademarks, the Lanham Act,[55] which contains the federal statutes governing trademark law in the US, is silent on secondary trademark liability. Indeed this type of liability for trademark infringement is a judicially created doctrine that has been imported from the common law of torts.[56] There are two possibilities to prove secondary liability: first, vicarious liability for trademark infringement refers to the responsibility of a defendant who has a partnership, such as agency or similar type or relationship, with the direct infringer. It also encompasses cases in which the defendant has the authority to bind the direct infringer in transactions with third parties or in which the defendant and the direct infringer jointly own or control the means of infringement. Second, contributory liability has been shaped in the Supreme Court case *Inwood* and it is applicable:

> if a manufacturer or distributor intentionally induces another to infringe a trademark, or if it continues to supply its product to one whom it knows or has reason to know is engaging in trademark infringement, the

53 Section 512(c) limits the liability of service providers for infringing material on websites (or other information repositories) hosted on their systems. It applies to storage at the direction of a user. In order to be eligible for the limitation, the following conditions must be met:—The provider must not have the requisite level of knowledge of the infringing activity, as described below.—If the provider has the right and ability to control the infringing activity, it must not receive a financial benefit directly attributable to the infringing activity. -Upon receiving proper notification of claimed infringement, the provider must expeditiously take down or block access to the material. See 'The Digital Millennium Copyright Act of 1998', US Copyright Office Summary (December 1998) 11.

54 In this regard see Miquel Peguera, 'The DMCA Safe Harbors and Their European Counterparts: A Comparative Analysis of Some Common Problems' (2009) Colum J L & Arts, 32 <http://papers.ssrn.com/sol3/papers.cfm?abstract_id=1468433> accessed 27 August 2013, 487–90 and 494–98.

55 Lanham (Trademark) Act (1946). However, it has to be noted that it includes a specific safe harbour (section 32(2)(A) and (B)) which had little practical significance, on this see Kulk (n. 15) 42–50.

56 See *Hard Rock Café licensing Corp v Concession Servs Inc*, 955 F.2d 1143, 1148 (7th Cir. 1992); *Metro-Goldwin Mayer Studios Inc. v Grokster Ltd.* 545 US 913–930 (2005); *Inwood Laboratories Inc. v Ives Laboratories Inc.* 456 US 844 (1982).

> manufacturer or distributor is contributorially responsible for any harm done as a result of the deceit.[57]

The case law analysed below mainly refers to *Inwood* so it is evident that in the US the notion of knowledge is crucial, as it is in the EU, and there are many other similar notions such as 'control' or 'promptly remove'.

3.1 *On 'Specific Knowledge'*

In *Tiffany v eBay*, Tiffany, the world-famous purveyor of jewellery, sued eBay alleging that 'eBay's conduct—facilitating and advertising the sale of Tiffany goods that turned out to be counterfeit—constituted direct and contributory trademark infringement, trademark dilution and false advertising'.[58] Indeed the amount of counterfeit Tiffany goods sold through eBay was consistent and Tiffany considered the eBay systems insufficient to address the problem of counterfeiting.[59]

The plaintiff argued that eBay was liable since it continued 'to supply its service to one whom it knows or has reason to know is engaging in trademark infringement', according to the *Inwood* second prong. The District Court previously declined to hold eBay contributorially liable for the infringing conduct of sellers when Tiffany submitted a Notice of Claimed Infringement (NOCI) form, which is a possibility of the right holder who discovered a potential infringement to report the listing to eBay. If the NOCI contained all required information, eBay removed the listings 'promptly' (usually within 24 hours or less, 70–80% of them were removed within 12 hours from notification).[60] This was not challenged by Tiffany on appeal. Moreover, the Court did not consider NOCI sufficient for the ISP to have to automatically or permanently suspend a seller (one strike rule) since, among other reasons, the NOCI 'did not constitute a definitive finding that the listed item was counterfeit' (therefore declining eBay liability in this case).[61] This judgment is relevant because it endorsed the tools established by eBay to reduce the sale of counterfeit goods, clarifying that

57 *Inwood* (n. 56) 853–54.

58 *Tiffany (NJ) Inc. and Tiffany and Company v eBay Inc.* 600 F.3d 93 (2nd Cir. 2010) 101.

59 eBay has shaped several programs aiming at fighting counterfeiting such as an eBay fraud engine which monitors the website and automatically search for activity violating eBay policies or the Verified Rights Owner (VeRO) Program, which is a notice and take-down system.

60 *Tiffany (NJ) Inc. and Tiffany and Company v eBay Inc.*, 576 F. Supp 2d 463 (S.D.N.Y. 2008) 516–8.

61 *Tiffany v eBay* (n. 60) 487 and 517.

NTD procedures prepared by service providers can be sufficient to avoid their liability (also considering that the DMCA set forth an NTD procedure concerning copyright cases while it contains no specific provisions on trademarks). Moreover, the Court gave some guidance on the definition of 'promptly', while at the EU level 'expeditiously' still lacks full clarification.[62] At the same time, the case is specific to eBay's tools and it should not be taken for granted that it could be extended to other cases.

Secondly, Tiffany disagreed with the District Court statement 'that eBay lacked sufficient knowledge of trademark infringement by sellers behind other non terminated listings to provide a basis for *Inwood* liability'.[63] Tiffany provided evidence that eBay knew of the sale of counterfeit Tiffany products on its website but the District Court noted that 'courts have been reluctant to extend contributory trademark liability to defendants where there is some uncertainty as to the extent or the nature of the infringement'.[64] The Court of Appeal agreed with the District Court, stating that a service provider must have more than a general knowledge or reason to know that its service is being used to sell counterfeit goods: 'some contemporary knowledge of which particular listings are infringing or will infringe in the future is necessary'.[65] Therefore, the Court affirmed a restrictive interpretation of the notion of 'knowledge' and of the *Inwood* test, as expressed in the earlier *Sony* case. In the latter case from 1984, Universal Studios and Walt Disney held copyright on various television programs that individual television-viewers had taped using Sony's recorders.[66] Relying on the notion of contemporary knowledge seems to confirm that right holders have to bear the primary burden of policing the use of trademarks on the site[67] as providers have no obligation of general monitoring (indeed, eBay refused to monitor its website and pre-emptively remove listings of Tiffany jewellery before they were made public). A different judgement would have jeopardized the business model itself and could have favoured monitoring and censorship of users' information by eBay and Google. Article 14 ECD seems to be interpreted in a similar manner although the matter has not been clarified

62 SEC(2011)1641 (n. 35) 37–8.

63 *Tiffany v eBay* (n. 60), 106.

64 Ibid., 508.

65 *Tiffany v eBay* (n. 58), 107. See also 108: 'Insofar as it speaks to the issue, though, the particular phrasing that the Court used—that a defendant will be liable if it 'continues to supply its product to *one* whom it knows or has reason to know is engaging in trademark infringement' id at 854 (emphasis added)—supports the district court's interpretation of *Inwood*, not Tiffany's'.

66 *Sony Corp of America v Universal City Studios Inc.* 464 US 417 (1984).

67 Saunders, Berger-Walliser (n. 13) 9.

by the ECJ yet.[68] Moreover, it would be interesting if the Court were to consider whether actual knowledge may refer to future infringements.[69]

The Court of Appeal also agreed with the District Court, affirming that

> if eBay had reason to suspect that counterfeit Tiffany goods were being sold through its website, and intentionally shielded itself from discovering the offending listings or the identity of the sellers behind them, eBay might very well have been charged with knowledge of those sales sufficient to satisfy *Inwood*'s 'know or has reason to know' prong.[70]

Indeed 'wilful blindness is equivalent to actual knowledge for purposes of the Lanham Act'.[71] According to Tiffany the general antifraud measures taken by eBay were inadequate and eBay could have done more to prevent the listing of counterfeit goods through the use of filters, data mining and other tools. However, the District Court, as followed by the Court of Appeal, did not consider eBay wilfully blind. Otherwise the *Inwood* 'reason to know' standard would be 'inflated into an affirmative duty to take precautions against potential counterfeiters even when eBay had no specific knowledge of the individual counterfeiters'.[72]

3.2 *On Rosetta Stone v Google*

In *Tiffany* the District Court (and subsequently the Court of Appeal) confirmed *Inwood* which applied to manufacturers and distributors of goods, and extended it to providers of services. The Ninth Circuit affirmed that the *Inwood*

---

68 However, for a critic of the 'specific knowledge' standard see Dennis Lievens, 'eBay Accessory Liability for Counterfeiting—Why Joint Tort Liability Just Doesn't Cut the Mustard' (2011) IIC, vol. 42/5, 521–25. The Author also consider unsatisfying that in *Tiffany v eBay* the court rejected the notion of 'reasonable anticipation' (*Tiffany v eBay* (n. 60) 501–3) according to which a second defendant can be held jointly liable if the actor fails to take reasonable precautions against the occurrence of the third person's infringing conduct in circumstances in which the infringing conduct can be reasonably anticipated.

69 See, among others, Emilio Tosi, 'Le responsabilità civili', in Emilio Tosi (ed.), *I problemi giuridici di internet, dall'e-commerce all'e-business*, (Giuffré 2003), 545ff; Marcello De Cata, *La responsabilità civile dell'Internet service provider*, (Giuffrè 2010) 293, Opinion AG Jääskinen (n. 24) para. 162, Van Eecke (n. 30) 1476ff.

70 *Tiffany v eBay* (n. 58) 109.

71 *Hard Rock Café Licensing Corp v Concession Services Inc* (n. 56) 1149.

72 *Tiffany v eBay* (n. 60) 515. In this regard see also *Hard Rock Café v Concession Services* (n. 56) 1149.

test for contributory trademark infringement applies to a service provider if it exercises sufficient control over the infringing conduct.[73] Although in a previous case the District Court of the Central District of California stated that eBay had no control over the allegedly infringing items,[74] the District Court in *Tiffany* considered that eBay exercised sufficient control. EBay argued that its service 'is more like an online classified ads service than an online flea market' and argued that 'it lacked such control', since it 'never took possession of the items sold via its website', 'it could not physically inspect, examine, or authenticate such items' and it 'has limited control over the listings and advertisements on its website'.[75] However, the District Court noted that eBay retains significant control over the transactions conducted through its website: 'by providing the software to set up the listings and store listing information on its servers, eBay supplies the necessary marketplace for the sale of counterfeit goods' and 'eBay takes an active role in supplying customers—namely registered buyers—to registered sellers, and actively facilitates transactions between them'.[76] Furthermore, 'eBay has actively promoted the sale of Tiffany jewellery items', moreover, 'eBay profits from the listing of items and successful completion of sales', and 'eBay maintains significant control over the listings on its website'.[77] These considerations were not disputed by eBay on appeal but the Court of Appeal recognized that the 'limited case law leaves the law of contributory trademark infringement ill-defined' and *Tiffany* was the first application of it to an online marketplace.[78]

However, these arguments do not imply equivalent effects on liability as the EU's 'active role' standard has. In this regard, it is also interesting to analyse *Rosetta Stone v Google*, a US case similar to *Google v Louis Vuitton*. In this case, Rosetta Stone, a corporation providing language learning products, sued Google for contributory infringement relying as evidence upon Google's 'Query Suggestion Tool', the trademark-specific version launched after Google changed its trademark policy in 2009, and 'its purported allowance of known infringers to bid on the Rosetta Stone marks'.[79] Rosetta Stone put forward that 'the Query Suggestion Tool's function of generating suggested keywords

73 *Lookheed Martin Corp v Network Solutions Inc.*, 194 F.3d 980, 984 (9th Circuit, 1999).

74 *Hendrickson v eBay, Inc.*, 165 F. Supp 2d 1082—Dist. Court, CD California 2001.

75 *Tiffany v eBay* (n. 60) 506.

76 Ibid., 506–7.

77 Ibid., 506–7.

78 *Tiffany v eBay* (n. 58) 105.

79 *Rosetta Stone Ltd. v Google Inc.*, 730 F. Supp 2d 531 District Court for the Eastern District of Virginia, Memorandum opinion (2010) 547.

for advertisers encouraged them to bid on brand names, which directly induced advertisers to infringe the Rosetta Stone Marks'.[80] Second, Rosetta Stone argued that 'by allowing counterfeiters to open AdWords accounts and to bid on the Rosetta Stone marks, despite receiving notice of their counterfeit status, Google was supplying a service to those it knew or had reason to know was engaging in trademark infringement'.[81] As documented, from September 2009 through March 2010, Rosetta Stone notified Google of approximately 200 instances of Sponsored Links advertising counterfeit Rosetta Stone products. The Court, however, stated first that

> the mere existence of a tool that assists advertisers in optimizing their advertisements does not, in itself, indicate intent to induce infringement. The Google's Query Suggestion Tool operates by searching or indexing the particular website identified by an advertiser and returning a limited number of keyword ideas for websites not affiliated with the URL.[82]

Secondly, the Court rejected the application of *Inwood* by affirming that Google was not continuing to 'supply a service to those it knew or had reason to know was engaging in trademark infringement', recalling *Tiffany*. Indeed in *Tiffany* the Court had stated that despite eBay's promotion of certain vendors of premium branded jewellery and its encouragement to those vendors to take advantage of the demand for Tiffany merchandise, its relationship with third parties' advertisements was insufficient to warrant a finding of contributory trademark infringement. Some contemporary knowledge was deemed needed. Like Tiffany, according to the Court, Rosetta Stone failed to show that Google knew of the alleged infringing activity by its AdWords advertisers and the Court added that 'there is little Google can do beyond expressly prohibiting advertisements for counterfeit goods, taking down those advertisements when it learns of their existence, and creating a team dedicated to fighting

80 Ibid., 547.

81 Ibid.

82 Ibid. Rosetta Stone is a Virginia-based corporation that provides technology-based language learning products and services and that registered the trademark Rosetta Stone; the company brought action against Google alleging that Google was helping third parties to mislead consumers and misappropriate the Rosetta Stone Marks by using them as keyword triggers for Sponsored Links and using them within the text or title of the Sponsored Links. Google was helping these advertisers misdirect web users to websites of companies that (i) compete with Rosetta Stone, (ii) sell language education programs from Rosetta Stone's competitors, (iii) sell counterfeit Rosetta Stone products, or (iv) are entirely unrelated to language education.

advertisements for counterfeit goods'.[83] In other words Google did not turn a blind eye to Rosetta Stone complaints. Moreover, as Rosetta Stone admits, it cannot determine whether a Rosetta Stone product is a counterfeit without physically inspecting it.[84]

In conclusion, US courts do not have an approach similar to that of the EU concerning the 'active role' requirement, therefore directing more attention towards the relevant business tools. However, the *Rosetta Stone* dispute has yet to be settled since the Court of Appeal recently vacated the District Court's order to the extent that it granted summary judgement in favour of Google regarding Rosetta Stone's contributory infringement claim.[85] Therefore, some conclusions could change and certain issues could be further clarified in the future.

4 Conclusions

Case law on secondary liability in the US is still not fully settled, and even less so in the EU. Nonetheless, applications of such liability are developing, which poses a challenge for courts and legislators alike.[86]

Judicial outcomes have diverged in different jurisdictions. Secondary liability has been the subject of contrasting legal rulings on whether the providers are liable for trademark infringement committed by users of their services. In particular, the case law analysed shows that the US has an approach more favourable for intermediaries than its EU equivalents, especially France, which is home to many luxury brands. As a result, the practices and procedures of service providers, such as auction sites, and the enforcement strategies of brand owners must be tailored according to jurisdiction and legislation, which are

83 Ibid., 548.

84 Ibid.

85 *Rosetta Stone v Google* 676 F.3d 144 (4th Circuit 2012) 163–65. See also considerations on the judgment of the district court concerning contributory infringement in Brief of Amici Curiae eBay Inc. and Yahoo! Inc. in support of Google Inc., 12/6/2010, 11–20; Brief for Amici Curiae Carfax Inc., Ford Motor Company, Harmon International Industries Inc., the Media Institute, Viacom Inc and Blues Destiny records LLC in support of plaintiff-appellant Rosetta Stone Ltd., 11/1/2010, 4–22.

86 For example, in the late 90s in the US there were cases where the use of a trademark in a meta-tag, which brought to the display of a competitor company in the search engine (Alta Vista), had to be subject to owner consent according to US courts, see *Oppedhal & Larson v Advanced Concepts* D. Colorado 97–Z-1592 (1997). For US case law in the late 90s and the beginnings of 2000 see Tosi (n. 69) 106ff.

in turn determined by different national interests.[87] This is an obstacle to free movement of information society services and a barrier to international trade. However, civil and criminal law fall mainly under the regulatory sovereignty of states, since they are sensitive issues relating to different legal systems, so harmonised international rules are developing very slowly.

Moreover, different approaches in legislation and case law affect legal certainty concerning cross-border activities, amounting to another obstacle to the free provision of cross-border services. Service providers and brand owners have to face legal uncertainty, as many aspects have not been settled by courts or legislators: the crucial notions of information society service, actual knowledge, awareness or requirements for notifications have still not been entirely clarified. This ambiguity represents a serious drawback for providers and holders' activities.[88]

The balance between trademark holders and intermediaries, which reflects the importance of fighting counterfeiting while ensuring access of internet services to consumers,[89] is slowly being found. While in the US more attention seems to be paid to new business models tools, the more restrictive EU approach, concerning for example neutrality of information society services, could represent a limit to intermediaries' activity and development. In the end, considering that eBay and Google share an interest in stopping counterfeiting in order to maintain the trust of consumers, collaboration between holders and intermediaries is crucial in order to combat widespread counterfeiting.[90]

---

87 See WIPO SCT/24/4 (n. 4) Annex 1, 1.

88 For example, the ambiguity of many ECD provisions is pointed out as a problem by intermediaries and holders several times in the Summary of results of the public consultation on the future of electronic commerce in the internal market and the implementation of the directive on electronic commerce (n. 14) 10ff.

89 Weckström (n. 13) 42.

90 *Tiffany v eBay* (n. 60) 469: eBay has 'an interest in eliminating counterfeit Tiffany merchandise from eBay (...) to preserve the reputation of its website as a safe place to do business'. The same can be said for Google: it would run counter to good business practice for Google to encourage and provide advertising space to those it knows are infringing on the Rosetta Stone Marks (*Rosetta Stone v Google* (n. 79) 548).

Index